Praise for *The Book You Need to Read to Write the Book You Want to Write:*

'Absolutely spot on. I can't imagine there are any better books on the subject than this one.'
Louis de Bernières

'Reading *The Book You Need* is like getting useful advice from your own personal mentor, one who is wise, experienced, encouraging, and delighted to share their encyclopedic knowledge of literary craft. For anyone who wants to be a better writer - listen carefully. The authors know what they're talking about.'
Tara Ison, novelist; Professor of Fiction, Arizona State University

'Whether you are a beginner or an advanced fiction writer, this book is an essential companion. From getting started to navigating the publishing industry and all that falls between, *The Book You Need* examines the key concepts necessary to write your novel, offering practical, insightful and expert advice.'
Tiffany Atkinson, poet; Professor of Poetry, University of East Anglia

'Years of teaching expertise condensed into one of the most comprehensive journeys through the craft that I've seen. This book teaches in the most natural way, guiding you under the surface of a wide range of good writing, deep into the practical processes that bring it to life.'
Philip Gross, poet, winner of the T. S. Eliot Prize; Emeritus Professor of Creative Writing, University of South Wales

THE BOOK YOU NEED TO READ TO WRITE THE BOOK YOU WANT TO WRITE

Have you ever wanted to write a novel or short story but didn't know where to start? If so, this is the book for you. It's the book for anyone, in fact, who wants to write to their full potential. Practical and jargon-free, rejecting prescriptive templates and formulae, it's a storehouse of ideas and advice on a range of relevant subjects, from boosting self-motivation and confidence to approaching agents and publishers. Drawing on the authors' extensive experience as successful writers and inspiring teachers, it will guide you through such essentials as the interplay of memory and imagination; plotting your story; the creation of convincing characters; the uses of description; the pleasures and pitfalls of research; and the editing process. The book's primary aim is simple: to help its readers to become better writers.

Teachers of the *Guardian*'s creative writing Masterclasses, and co-founders of the University of Cambridge's Master's programme in creative writing, Sarah Burton and Jem Poster draw on a wealth of teaching experience in a variety of contexts, from informal community education to PhD supervision. Sarah Burton is a novelist (*The Strange Adventures of H*, 2020), biographer (*A Double Life: A Biography of Charles and Mary Lamb*, 2003, shortlisted for the Mind Book of the Year Award) and social historian (*Impostors: Six Kinds of Liar*, 2000). Jem Poster is a novelist (*Courting Shadows*, 2002; *Rifling Paradise*, 2006), poet (*Brought to Light*, 2001), literary editor (*Edward Thomas: Prose Writings Vol. III*, 2018) and Emeritus Professor of creative writing, Aberystwyth University. Together Sarah and Jem run *Between the Lines*, an online mentoring programme for writers.

THE BOOK YOU NEED TO READ TO WRITE THE BOOK YOU WANT TO WRITE

A HANDBOOK FOR FICTION WRITERS

SARAH BURTON
AND JEM POSTER

CAMBRIDGE
UNIVERSITY PRESS

CAMBRIDGE
UNIVERSITY PRESS

University Printing House, Cambridge CB2 8BS, United Kingdom

One Liberty Plaza, 20th Floor, New York, NY 10006, USA

477 Williamstown Road, Port Melbourne, VIC 3207, Australia

314–321, 3rd Floor, Plot 3, Splendor Forum, Jasola District Centre,
New Delhi – 110025, India

103 Penang Road, #05–06/07, Visioncrest Commercial, Singapore 238467

Cambridge University Press is part of the University of Cambridge.

It furthers the University's mission by disseminating knowledge in the pursuit of
education, learning, and research at the highest international levels of excellence.

www.cambridge.org
Information on this title: www.cambridge.org/9781316513446
DOI: 10.1017/9781009072571

First published 2022

A catalogue record for this publication is available from the British Library.

Library of Congress Cataloging-in-Publication Data
NAMES: Burton, Sarah, 1963– author. | Poster, Jem, author.
TITLE: The book you need to read to write the book you want to write : a
handbook for fiction writers / Sarah Burton, Jem Poster.
DESCRIPTION: Cambridge ; New York, NY : Cambridge University Press, 2022. |
Includes bibliographical references and index.
IDENTIFIERS: LCCN 2021048673 (print) | LCCN 2021048674 (ebook) | ISBN
9781316513446 (hardback) | ISBN 9781009072571 (ebook)
SUBJECTS: LCSH: Fiction – Authorship. | Fiction – Technique. | LCGFT:
Handbooks and manuals.
CLASSIFICATION: LCC PN3355 .B84 2022 (print) | LCC PN3355 (ebook) | DDC
808.3–dc23/eng/20211103
LC record available at https://lccn.loc.gov/2021048673
LC ebook record available at https://lccn.loc.gov/2021048674

ISBN 978-1-316-51344-6 Hardback
ISBN 978-1-009-07373-8 Paperback

For our students,
past, present and future

CONTENTS

Contents

PREFACE

Welcome to this book. Perhaps you've already begun your journey as a writer, or perhaps you're about to take your first exploratory steps. In either case you'll find in these pages a comprehensive guide, supportive yet relaxed, illustrative rather than dogmatic, and allowing space for the development of your own particular talent.

This book doesn't claim to turn you into a best-selling author. It doesn't even promise to give you a fast-track to getting an agent or the inside knowledge on getting published. It doesn't because there's actually no secret to how these things happen. The surest way of becoming a published writer is to become a better writer.

That's the focus of this book. We don't have a formula (because there isn't one) and although we'll be offering plenty of advice, we won't be giving you rules, because unless we want all writers to be writing in the same way rules are not going to be helpful. And although this book is written by writers, we don't aim to make you write the way we write. We want to help you write the way *you* write, to develop your own unique voice.

ACKNOWLEDGEMENTS

The authors would like to thank Adrian Barlow, Jenny Bavidge, Kathleen Beckett, Linda Fisher, Midge Gillies, Stephanie Hale, Lisa Hitch, Richard Johnstone, John Lennard, Julia Prendergast, Katherine Roddwell and Stuart Sillars.

Our particular thanks to our agent, Eli Keren, and our editor Emily Hockley.

Thanks, too, to Simon Armitage and Faber and Faber for permission to quote in full 'I'll Be There to Love and Comfort You', and to all the writers whose work is quoted here.

– I –

Getting started

~

Writing is hard enough yet there are many ways in which we add to our own difficulties. Perhaps most significant is our tendency to ask: 'Am I good enough?' Maureen Duffy speaks for many of us when she says that being a writer feels like 'a terrible impertinence', explaining that 'the people I admire, my particular saints, are dead writers and being a writer is somehow daring to measure yourself against them'.[1] Our literary heroes can seem to loom over us, impossible to match, mocking our efforts. But it's important to remember that all the writers you've ever admired had their own particular heroes – that this is just part of the condition of being a writer.

So for the moment, let your heroes recede into the background. Think of their work as part of the richness of your experience, not as a barrier to any achievement of your own. If everyone was daunted by what had gone before, there would be no record-breaking sprints, no life-saving vaccines, no new technology, no innovation of any kind. And anyway, you're not setting out to write the way others write. You're setting out to write the way *you* write.

So how do you find your own voice? You may already have hit on a style that works well and if so, that's excellent. Or you may find that your voice – or the various voices you're trying out – sounds inauthentic. Perhaps you think your voice lacks individuality – you don't even think you have a style at all. Or perhaps your writing is perfectly fine; the problem is that it doesn't excite you.

The only way you're going to discover what you can do is by trying things out. If you're going to make progress you're going to have to be prepared to experiment. You might already not be liking the sound of this, as experiments can end in failure – indeed, they are often expected to. A scientist may carry out hundreds of experiments before she can discover the combination that works. All those failures are needful; none of them is absolute. Every success stands on the shoulders of multiple failures. So if you're going to progress you need to be prepared to experiment, and if you're prepared to experiment, you must expect, accept and even embrace failure – learning to put the term, conceptually, in inverted commas – as a necessary function of the writing process. Even the humblest writing implement implicitly defends the inevitability of making mistakes: you can write with one end and erase with the other precisely because a pencil is deliberately designed to accommodate your right to change your mind.

Think of it this way: a novel which wins a prestigious literary prize will have been through numerous drafts. Yet the writer would not, in retrospect, consider any of those drafts as failures; she will have seen them as necessary steps on the path to success. It might be that only a quarter of her first draft has survived into the final product, yet the book would not exist unless she had allowed herself to write that first unsatisfactory draft. And this holds true right down to the level of the sentence. You may decide to cross out a phrase you have written, but if you then discover a better one, you'll find this is often precisely because you have allowed yourself to write that not-quite-satisfactory phrase in the first place. If you won't allow yourself a mistake – a misstep – you'll be looking at a blank page for a very long time, and it will still be blank when you return to it the next day and the day after that. A page with writing on it, on the other hand, holds the potential to multiply into more pages.

So the willingness to experiment – and to fail – is absolutely key if you want to develop your writing skills. James Baldwin believed that writing was simply 'a polite term' for experimenting.[2] Experimentation can feel scary, but that's no reason to avoid it. When Margaret Atwood was writing *The Handmaid's Tale* (1985) she had never attempted anything like it before – all her previous fiction had been realistic. She describes the unsettling nature of the experiment: it gave her 'a strange feeling, like skating on river ice – exhilarating but unbalancing. How thin is this ice? How far can I go? How much trouble am I in? What's down there if I fall?'[3] In fact, most landmark fiction has done something which hasn't been tried before. What you are attempting is comparatively modest: being prepared to try something *you* haven't tried before. Actors rehearse, dancers and musicians practise, artists do preliminary sketches and so on – and writers, too, are allowed to take faltering first steps which may be only a pale foreshadowing of their mature work. It's not just permissible; it's essential.

Before we leave the f-word, it's worth paying attention to the courageous sector of writers whose failures happen in full view of the audience. While a play will go through several drafts, it's not until it's performed that a playwright can see what might still be wrong with it. Yet they have to be prepared for that to happen. Samuel Beckett's lines from his novella *Worstward Ho* (1983) are often quoted: 'Ever tried. Ever failed. No matter. Try again. Fail again. Fail better.'[4] He believed that 'to be an artist is to fail, as no other dare fail, that failure is his world and the shrink from it desertion'.[5] More prosaically, Edward Albee said of fellow playwright, Pulitzer Prize-winning Sam Shepard: 'Sam was always taking chances, always being original. ... Somebody who was willing to fail and fail interestingly. And if you're willing to fail interestingly, you tend to succeed interestingly.'[6] If these great playwrights were willing to fail in front of an audience, you can certainly afford to fail in private.

In order to write effectively we need to remember that our literary heroes, however talented, were or are mere mortals, who had to work through their mis-steps too. But who else might be sitting on your shoulder, emanating negative vibrations? Well, your nearest and dearest for a start, and perhaps your parents in particular. If you're going to write to please your parents, it's extremely optimistic to expect your writing to please anyone else. No writer was ever well served by the voice of an imagined other saying 'You can't write that.' Such censorship stifles creativity, closing down avenues of exploration.

This isn't a bridge you have to cross yet, anyway. Your parents, partner, children or friends won't be reading what you've written until you're ready to show it to them. By that time you will have a different relationship with what you have written and a more confident sense of who you are as a writer. And it is *fiction*, after all. You are entitled to make full use of any of your experiences – to record them or to reconfigure them in new forms: they belong to you. Don't write to be liked and don't write to impress – not every reader will like you and not every reader will be impressed, and you will end up with something dishonest anyway. Ernest Hemingway had the right idea when he wrote to F. Scott Fitzgerald: 'For Christ sake write and don't worry about what the boys will say nor whether it will be a masterpiece … I write one page of masterpiece to ninety-one pages of shit. I try to put the shit in the wastebasket.'[7]

Hemingway was famous for his practical views on writing, although there's no evidence that one of the most widely quoted pieces of advice was actually his at all: 'write drunk; edit sober'. The most likely source appears to be Peter De Vries who in his novel *Reuben, Reuben* (1964) has a character say: 'Sometimes I write drunk and revise sober … and sometimes I write sober and revise drunk. But you have to have both elements in creation – the Apollonian and the Dionysian, or spontaneity and restraint, emotion and discipline.'[8] Somewhat more elaborate than the advice to 'write drunk; edit sober', the insistence on the necessity for both 'spontaneity and restraint, emotion and discipline' in the creative process is extremely useful. While we wouldn't recommend writing under the influence (no one mentions editing with a hangover) the inexperienced writer will certainly benefit from taking a relaxed and uninhibited approach to the first draft. Indeed, a number of very experienced writers are perfectly comfortable with a distinctly underwhelming first draft. Frank O'Connor said: 'I don't give a hoot what the writing's like, I write any sort of rubbish which will cover the main outlines of the story, then I begin to see it',[9] while James Thurber reported that his wife 'took a look at the first version of something I was doing not long ago and said, "Goddamn it, Thurber, that's high-school stuff." I have to tell her to wait until the seventh draft, it'll work out all right.'[10]

Ray Bradbury (who had a sign over his desk stating: DON'T THINK) had a different version of 'write drunk; edit sober', but it confirms the idea that a certain sense of abandon is appropriate at the first creative stage and that more careful consideration can come later:

> The history of each story ... should read almost like a weather report: Hot today, cool tomorrow. This afternoon, burn down the house. Tomorrow, pour cold critical water upon the simmering coals. Time enough to think and cut and rewrite tomorrow. But *today – explode – fly apart – disintegrate!* The other six or seven drafts are going to be pure torture. So why not enjoy the first draft, in the hope that your joy will seek and find others in the world who, reading your story, will catch fire too?[11]

(Subsequent drafts will not *necessarily* be 'pure torture' but it's fair to acknowledge there are usually some difficult moments.) So these writers, at least, lend their vote to the 'don't get it right; just get it down' school of first drafting. Only you will know just how well this will serve you, but you may well find that having started to write in a provisional and rough style, you hit your stride once you've warmed up and have a better sense of what you're writing. You can always go back and tidy up the early stuff later.

The early stages of this process often seem unsatisfactory and you may well feel dispirited at times, so it's important to remind yourself that you're not alone – far from it. Here's Virginia Woolf's account of her character Orlando's experience of writing

5

his novel – an account that clearly in some measure reflects her own experience:

> Anyone moderately familiar with the rigours of composition will not need to be told the story in detail; how he wrote and it seemed good; read and it seemed vile; corrected and tore up; cut out; put in; was in ecstasy; in despair; had his good nights and bad mornings; snatched at ideas and lost them; saw his book plain before him and it vanished; acted his people's parts as he ate; mouthed them as he walked; now cried; now laughed; vacillated between this style and that; now preferred the heroic and pompous; next the plain and simple; now the vales of Tempe; then the fields of Kent or Cornwall; and could not decide whether he was the divinest genius or the greatest fool in the world.[12]

So accept the difficulties, expect things to be initially unsatisfactory, and start putting the words on the page. And while we acknowledge the need for preparation, let's keep in mind E. L. Doctorow's wise observation on the subject: 'Planning to write is not writing. Outlining a book is not writing. Researching is not writing. Talking to people about what you're doing, none of that is writing. Writing is writing.'[13]

— 2 —

Memory and imagination

Aspiring writers are often told: 'Write what you know.' But what does this really mean? It doesn't mean that if you're a doctor in a paediatric unit you should write exclusively about a character who's a doctor in a paediatric unit (although your specialised knowledge in this area would doubtless be an advantage if you chose to do so). It's broader than that. But how do we know what we know? When Shakespeare created compelling characters such as Othello and Shylock, he didn't know what it was to be an African or Jewish inhabitant of a European city – but he did know what it was to be an outsider, and he found in his own remembered experience the basis for an understanding of his characters' imagined lives.

Both Othello's and Shylock's stories are set in a city Shakespeare never visited, and writers are often in the position of writing not only of a physical location they don't know, but of somewhere they can't even hope to visit: the past. As we shall see later, Henry James thought that attempting to write historical fiction was pointless, because although we might get the 'facts' right it's impossible to reconstruct the way people thought – and hence the way the world seemed – in the past.[14] Geraldine Brooks grappled with this problem when writing *Year of Wonders* (2001), a novel set in a real historical situation, when the small village of Eyam in Derbyshire became infected with plague and sealed itself off to avoid spreading the disease to neighbouring communities. She realised, however, that although the events she was trying to reconstruct occurred over three centuries earlier, there were many parallels between Eyam then and the small rural community in which she now lived; just as people are in many ways the same the world over, so people in the past are very like people now – their hopes, fears, griefs and joys are similar to ours. She reasoned that the bedrock of human experience is essentially the same in any age, and this is part of what, as writers and human beings, we know. 'It is human nature to imagine, to put yourself in another's shoes', she writes. 'The past may be another country. But the only passport required is empathy.'[15] Empathy is an act both of memory and of imagination, and our writing is enriched when we harness the two.

All writing has to be 'what you know'; it can reasonably be argued that you can't write what you don't know. Whatever we invent is based on something known to us – our own experience, to which we apply our imagination. And in those cases where we have to increase the stock of what we know – through research – our writing reflects our newly acquired knowledge.

We are already applying imagination to memory when we recall an event from the past. If you were to set yourself the ten-minute task of writing down a memory from your childhood and were then asked whether, in order to fill in any gaps in your memory, you had made anything up (why you were there, who else was there, what the occasion was, when it happened), you would be very likely to say that you had – in fact, that you had been obliged to, because otherwise the narrative would have had distracting gaps or uncertainties in it. However, you would probably maintain that the account was essentially true.

The truth of an event may not, in any case, be easy to establish. You will probably recognise this experience: you are among old friends or family members when one of them starts to recall an event at which others were present. Members of the group will disagree on the detail – perhaps even on bigger issues – because the fact is that each individual has their own version of what happened. This is partly because they were experiencing it from their own unique perspective (and we shall have more to say later about the individual point of view) and partly because memory doesn't unfold as a continuous spool of events and experiences. We don't preserve a frame-by-frame record of the past; what we retain is more like snapshots in an album, and we have not all taken the same snapshots; we have remembered what seemed to affect us as individuals most deeply at the time. We can't recall every incident which happened between the snapshots so we imaginatively reconstruct what *must* have happened between them. It is natural for humans to make connections in this way, to create narratives that suggest causes and effects. This is why dreams are at once so fascinating and so frustrating – they seem to be no respecters of cause and effect or of seamless narrative: we can step out of a restaurant and be on a ship, or turn out of a corridor and be in a forest. It's not a frame-by-frame narrative; connections seem to be missing. And our desire for connections – our desire to make sense – drives our automatic habit of filling in the gaps. When we remember, we are to a large extent reconstructing the past.

Everything you have lived through is material for your writing. (Hemingway maintained that the best early training for a writer is an unhappy childhood,[16] and while this can be taken as part joke, his point has substance.) However, we don't simply report our own lives. As Maureen Duffy puts it: 'the experience has to be worked on, wrought up and transformed, not simply regurgitated'.[17] The experiences may be whole episodes of our lives or the briefest moments: a look, a phrase, a smell. Terry Pratchett described writing as 'a process of breaking yourself and everything you've done into little bits and pasting them onto something else'.[18] The fact that fiction draws on the writer's own lived experience gives readers their most intimate connection with the writing; as Carol Shields observes: 'We love fiction because it possesses the texture of the real.'[19] But what makes a novel or a short story something both less and more than autobiography or memoir is its implicit acknowledgement of deviation from the facts in the service of a wider and deeper truth.

Professional writers are often exasperated by how often they are asked: 'Where do you get your ideas from?' The frequency with which the question is posed suggests that most people don't realise how close the writer's way of thinking is to the generality of the population. We all have ideas, we all exercise our imaginations. We all consider 'what if ... '. We all project and plan and guess and improvise. Writers are not the only ones who lie in the bath composing the perfect thing they *should* have said in response to a colleague's criticism earlier in the day, or rehearsing their response to an event which might never happen. Anyone can read something in the newspaper, or overhear a snippet of conversation and think: 'I wonder what story lies behind that', or 'I wonder what that was like.' With writers these speculations are peculiarly significant: they have a potential value, a possible purpose. We might be able to recycle, repurpose or repair and somehow re-use the stuff that surrounds us. Writers are not necessarily more observant than other people, but we pay attention to the value of what we observe, because that is the stock we draw on when we write.

William Faulkner had this to say on the subject:

> A writer needs three things, experience, observation, and imagination, any two of which, at times any one of which, can supply the lack of the others. With me a story usually begins with a single idea or memory or mental picture. The writing of the story is simply a matter of working up to that moment, to explain why it happened or what it caused to follow.[20]

What Faulkner appears to be describing in that 'single idea or memory or mental picture' is what others might call 'inspiration': a catalyst, a creative spur, an idea that stimulates further ideas. Inspiration comes both from outside and from within: often we observe an event, or are struck by an image, that illuminates and enables us to recognise something we already know deep down. As Ray Bradbury sees it: 'You are, in effect, dropping stones down a well. Every time you hear an echo from your Subconscious, you know yourself a little better. A small echo may start an idea. A big echo may result in a story.'[21]

The important thing to know as you start taking yourself seriously as a writer is that you already possess the stock you need. You have your own storehouse of experience and your own imaginative scope within you; you already have on board the necessary resources to create fiction. Bradbury expresses this well: 'When people ask me where I get my ideas, I laugh. How strange – we're so busy looking out, to find ways and means, we forget to look *in*. The Muse ... is there, a fantastic storehouse, our complete being. All that is most original lies waiting for us to summon it forth.'[22]

Sometimes inspiration has a social or moral dimension. Harriet Beecher Stowe was impelled to write *Uncle Tom's Cabin* (1852) by the plight of enslaved people. As she wrote to her editor in 1851:

> Up to this year I have always felt that I had no particular call to meddle with this subject, and I dreaded to expose even my own mind to the full force of its exciting power. But I feel now that the time has come when even a woman or a child who can speak a word for freedom and humanity is bound to speak. The Carthaginian women in the last peril of their state cut off their hair for bow strings to give to the defenders of their country, and such peril and shame as now hangs over this country is worse than Roman slavery, and I hope every woman who can write will not be silent.[23]

Stowe's writing was, of course, to help change the course of history. Anna Akhmatova felt duty-bound to bear witness to the effects of Stalin's Terror, describing herself (as author of the poem cycle *Requiem*, which details sufferings under Stalin's purges) as the 'mouth through which a hundred million scream'. Seeing migrant workers battling floodwaters in California in 1938 led John Steinbeck to write *The Grapes of Wrath* (1939). In each case the writer was moved to bear witness through the medium of fiction or poetry; the suffering of others (and in Akhmatova's case, also her own) was the spur – the inspiration – to write.

Even where the source of our inspiration may seem difficult to trace, it generally proceeds from our own experiences. These can be specific experiences (for example, professional work in a particular field) or emotional or psychological experiences (a significant relationship or life event – Hemingway advised Scott Fitzgerald: 'when you get the damned hurt, use it'[24]), or observations at the margins of our own lives – things we have seen or heard about.

If you look carefully at a piece of your own writing you will be able to identify one or more of these sources feeding it. And if you know enough about a favourite writer's life you will be able to detect these tributary streams running into the river of her written work. We can see how three streams of experience (professional, emotional and observational) operated within Charlotte Brontë when she wrote *Jane Eyre* (1847).

Charlotte Brontë's work as a governess was tedious and largely unrewarding, yet she was able to exploit this experience when creating her memorable heroine Jane Eyre. She also drew on her own experience of being in love with a married man – in real life a senior teacher, Constantin Heger – and transmuted it into Jane's relationship with Edward Rochester, the father of her pupil. Unrequited love, like the profession of governess, is hardly a rarity, but the third point of inspiration is extraordinary. In 1839 when she was visiting Norton Conyers, a house in North Yorkshire, her host told her the legend of a mad woman who had been confined in an attic room in the house, a room still known as 'Mad Mary's Room'. When Charlotte wrote *Jane Eyre* (published eight years later) she clearly drew on this story: the 'mad woman' in the attic becoming the model – or inspiration – for poor Bertha Mason, Rochester's violent and crazed wife. Charlotte took facets of her own unexceptional professional experience, a chapter of her own emotional history and a disturbing legend and wove them into a masterpiece: the story of a governess who falls in love with her employer who, unknown to her, already has a wife, insane but undivorceable, living in the same house.

Jane Eyre can be seen to have been inspired, then, by things Charlotte Brontë knew first-hand and heard about second-hand –

but they all formed part of her own experience. Seen in this light, all inspiration has its source within us. We may all carry the material for a great novel around inside our heads; the art lies in how we recognise those materials and the way we put them together.

J. R. R. Tolkien draws on images of natural growth to describe the development of a narrative: a story, he says, doesn't grow out of what is clearly seen in front of you, like 'the leaves of trees', nor by systematic study, 'by means of botany and soil-science'. Instead, 'it grows like a seed in the dark out of the leaf-mould of the mind: out of all that has been seen or thought or read, that has long ago been forgotten, descending into the deeps'. He adds that selection plays a part in the composition of these buried resources; what makes us all unique as writers depends on 'what one throws on one's personal compost heap'.[25]

We'll notice that Tolkien's compost-recipe includes the writer's reading among its ingredients, and it's worth emphasising that other works of art may be a potent and legitimate source of inspiration. We're not talking here about plagiarism – the deliberate theft of other people's words and ideas – but about the fact that our compost heap is likely to include novels, poems, plays, films, paintings, sculpture and music, and that it would be very odd indeed if none of these provided any sustenance for the growing seed. Kate Hamer's *The Girl in the Red Coat* (2015) began for her with an image:

> The starting point for *The Girl in the Red Coat* came from a very strong image I had of a young girl, standing against the background of a forest. She was wearing a red coat and I knew somehow that she was lost. Somehow the image just wouldn't go away and a couple of weeks later I sat up in bed and wrote the first chapter of the novel in one go.

The image didn't come simply from Hamer's personal experience or her own imagination. She goes on to relate it to her long-standing interest in film, and to two films in particular:

> I watch a lot of films and am influenced by film as much as books. I think the red coat has a wider resonance than my novel – it brings to mind films such as *Don't Look Now* and *Schindler's List* and that was quite deliberate.[26]

Leaving aside the often unanswerable question of just when, in the creative process, the source of an image or idea becomes known to the author, we nevertheless understand from the phrase 'quite deliberate' that in this case there was an early recognition of the connection to the red-coated girls in the two films mentioned; but there's a deeper source, which seems, from Hamer's account, to have been recognised at a much later stage. As she points out, the original red-coated child 'is of course Little Red Riding Hood. I loved fairy tales as a child and after I finished writing the novel it occurred to me that Carmel [the girl of the novel's title] is actually none other than Red Riding Hood.'

Conventional literary criticism spends a good deal of time mapping the sources of the texts it examines, and here Hamer pre-empts the critics, opening her hand to display some of the source material she had at her disposal when writing the novel. This kind of self-analysis is entirely appropriate, but we should beware of assuming that our sources of inspiration can always be located and explained. At different times and to different degrees, many writers will have a sense that their work is mysterious in its origins and inherently resistant to analysis.

Toni Morrison's account of the genesis of *Beloved* (1987) preserves a sense of mystery even as it locates the moment of inspiration among everyday matters – the writer's loss of her job, time spent sitting on the porch of her house overlooking the Hudson River, her reading of a newspaper clipping summarising the story of an escapee from slavery arrested for killing one of her children. That clipping was obviously an important part of the novel's inspiration, but it wasn't enough: the historical character, Morrison realised, was 'to a novelist, confining. Too little imaginative space there for my purposes.' The territory she needed to enter was formidable and pathless. To invite readers (and myself) into the repellant landscape (hidden, but not completely; deliberately buried but not forgotten) was to pitch a tent in a cemetery inhabited by highly vocal ghosts.

What she goes on to describe suggests the incursion of the other-worldly into the world of known things – into a world neatly marked out by paths and lawns:

> I sat on the porch, rocking in a swing, looking at giant stones piled up to take the river's occasional fist. Above the stones is a path through the lawn, but interrupted by an ironwork gazebo situated under a cluster of trees and in deep shade.
>
> She walked out of the water, climbed the rocks, and leaned against the gazebo. Nice hat.[27]

The tone is pointedly matter-of-fact, but the visitant is the ghost who will haunt the disturbing narrative that Morrison is about to write. This is the true moment of inspiration, the moment when, out of the incomprehensible agitation the writer has been feeling, something unforeseen and not entirely explicable begins to take shape.

Morrison is describing the inception of her novel, but we should remember that any moment in the writing of a work of fiction can produce something unforeseen, maybe even something that runs counter to the writer's original plans. A plot may suddenly develop in a way we hadn't anticipated; a character may surprise us by saying something that shows her in a new light. While not necessarily in the fullest sense mysterious, these disturbances in the planned trajectory of our narrative suggest the incompleteness of authorial control.

For the ancient Greeks inspiration had a source beyond the mind of the writer: the Muse, as invoked by Homer in the opening lines of the *Odyssey*, was a divine being who breathed into the poet the imaginative understanding and energies required for his task. We can't know how literally this idea was taken at the time, and we're unlikely to take it literally now, but it's useful to remind ourselves that the creative process isn't entirely governed by the conscious mind of the writer. As we step out from the known (perhaps our own experience, or a piece of evidence thrown up by our research) into the new and pathless territory of the imagination, we will be obliged to recognise the difficulty of the enterprise, but we may also discover the true centre of our narrative.

It's good for us as writers to move outside our comfort zones and into less predictable territory – this is when our imaginative powers flourish and grow, because they simply have to. This handbook will give you guidance to help you on your way, but the journey itself, with its risks, its discoveries and its satisfactions, will be your own. Keep trying things out, exploring new imaginative possibilities, hoping at some point to find you have created something fine and original – a sentence, a paragraph, a novel. Whatever the end result, the journey will expand your understanding of the world and heighten your ability to put your understanding into words.

− 3 −

Character

~

Character and plot are inextricably intertwined. You can't have a plot without characters because it's through the actions of the characters that plot is developed. Ask someone to summarise the plot of a film they've just seen or a book they've just read and they're very likely to begin: 'There's this guy who … ' or 'It's about a girl who … '. The trajectory of the story is the journey of its characters. There will be an external story (the events that occur) and an internal story (the effects these events have on the character and how they influence her actions). It's a two-way relationship: characters make things happen and the things that happen affect the development of the characters.

Introducing characters

There are two principal ways of introducing characters into fiction. One is to introduce them explicitly by painting a detailed portrait showing their appearance (and often personality) before allowing them to assume their role in the story. Here Charles Dickens introduces us to Jack Dawkins ('The Artful Dodger') in *Oliver Twist* (1838):

> The boy … was about his own age, but one of the queerest-looking boys that Oliver had even seen. He was a snub-nosed, flat-browed, common-faced boy enough, and as dirty a juvenile as one would wish to see; but he had got about him all the airs and manners of a man. He was short of his age, with rather bow-legs, and little, sharp, ugly eyes. His hat was stuck on the top of his head so slightly that it threatened to fall off every moment, and would have done so very often if the wearer had not had a knack of every now and then giving his head a

sudden twitch, which brought it back to its old place again. He wore a man's coat, which reached nearly to his heels. He had turned the cuffs back half-way up his arm to get his hands out of the sleeves, apparently with the ultimate view of thrusting them into the pockets of his corduroy trousers, for there he kept them. He was altogether as roystering and swaggering a young gentleman as ever stood three feet six, or something less, in his bluchers.[28]

Although there's a vibrant energy in this description, what we're shown is essentially a portrait: we might imagine an equivalent painting in oils, giving much the same information. Thomas Hardy's description of Elfride Swancourt in *A Pair of Blue Eyes* (1873), though less sharp in its delineation (and the lack of definition is part of the point of the description) is also a portrait, provided as a prelude to the action of the novel:

Personally she was the combination of very interesting particulars, whose rarity, however, lay in the combination itself rather than in the individual elements combined. As a matter of fact you did not see the form and substance of her features when conversing with her; and this charming power of preventing a material study of her lineaments by an interlocutor, originated not in the cloaking effect of a well-formed manner (for her manner was childish and scarcely formed) but in the attractive crudeness of the remarks themselves. She had lived all her life in retirement – the *monstrari digito* of idle men had not flattered her, and at the age of nineteen or twenty she was no further on in social consciousness than an urban young lady of fifteen.

One point in her, however, you did notice: that was her eyes. In them was seen a sublimation of all of her; it was not necessary to look further: there she lived.

These eyes were blue; blue as autumn distance – blue as the blue we see between the retreating mouldings of hills and woody slopes on a sunny September morning. A misty and shady blue, that had no beginning or surface, and was looked *into* rather than *at*.[29]

It's not, of course, that we won't learn more about these characters as the narrative progresses, but you'll see that we're being given a substantial amount of information about them early and directly, in capsule form – in a nutshell as the saying goes.

The other (and now more usual) way of introducing our characters is to set them loose in the story, allowing the reader to build up a picture principally by seeing them in action from the outset. The effect is more like that of film: we watch the characters in motion and pick up clues from their actions. Here's how William Trevor introduces his protagonist in 'The General's Day' (1967):

> General Suffolk pulled on two grey knitted socks and stood upright. Humming a marching air, he walked to the bathroom, intent upon his morning shave. The grey socks were his only apparel and he noticed as he passed the mirror of his wardrobe the white spare body of an elderly man reflected without flattery. He voiced no comment nor did he ponder, even in passing, upon this pictured nakedness. He was used to the sight; and had, over the years, accepted the changes as they came. Still humming, he half filled the wash-basin with water. It felt keenly warm on his fingers, a circumstance he inwardly congratulated himself on.
>
> With deft strokes the General cleared his face of lather and whisker, savouring the crisp rasp of razor upon flesh. He used a cut-throat article and when shorn to his satisfaction wiped it on a small absorbent pad, one of a series he had collected from the bedrooms of foreign hotels. He washed, dressed, set his moustache as he liked to sport it, and descended to his kitchen.
>
> The General's breakfast was simple: an egg poached lightly, two slices of toast and a pot of tea. It took him ten minutes to prepare and ten to consume. As he finished he heard the footsteps of the woman who daily came to work for him.

As readers, we have a pretty clear picture of the General, but it is based to a great extent on what we infer, as distinct from what we have been explicitly told. He hums a military tune; he passes his reflection without pondering the signs of ageing; he shaves deftly and 'sets' his moustache; there's a marked precision about the preparation and consumption of his breakfast. Here, each action is suggestive: our sense of the character depends on the way we are invited to improvise the rest of the picture, to deduce the meaning of his behaviour. Yet despite the amount of room left for the individual reader to participate imaginatively in the realisation of the General as a character, a writer as skilled as Trevor can nevertheless ensure that readers will share a broad understanding of who the General is.

You may well be familiar with the concepts of *showing* and *telling* – alternative methods of storytelling which are both at your disposal – and we will be paying attention to these throughout the book. The options available when you introduce your characters to your readers include *telling* (explicit characterisation – Dickens's Artful Dodger and Hardy's Elfride Swancourt) and *showing* (implicit characterisation – Trevor's General) and you could visualise these two methods by thinking of your reader as guest A at your dinner party. You have decided to seat her next to guest B. Do you tell A a lot about B before B arrives so that A is in some sense prepared for B when they meet, or do you just let them get to know each other with no introduction beyond their names?

A well-drawn character often accumulates in the reader's mind rather than springing fully fledged from the first page – she grows on us in a way that suggests her complexity. Allowing your reader to find out about the character little by little tends to feel more realistic simply because that's how we tend to get to know people in real life. When we meet a new person our first impression is often significant but inevitably incomplete. We'll quickly, even subconsciously, start making judgements about them. Their appearance and demeanour will suggest something of their essential nature to us. Each new thing we hear them say will add to the picture, sometimes building on what we've already decided about them, sometimes causing us to scrub out an earlier assumption and replace it with a new one. We meet Clive at a reception; he will say something which makes us think he is, perhaps, a bit arrogant, but soon afterwards he says something extremely generous about a rival which makes us take our scoring for 'arrogance' down a few notches. He may look as though he is scanning the room for someone more interesting or important to talk to (suggesting that he's rude), but then we learn he is seeking out someone to whom he has to convey an urgent message he has been entrusted with (suggesting that he's conscientious). Conversely, our assumptions may be confirmed by further evidence. Because we make assumptions and consolidate or revise those assumptions moment by moment, we develop a more personal knowledge of Clive than if the host had said: 'And Clive will be here – he can seem a bit full of himself but he'd do anything for you.'

Each of the two principal ways of introducing character has its own particular effect on the reader, but also very specific benefits to the writer. If we're going to tell the reader from the outset who this person is, we have, as writers, the advantage of going into the story with a very concrete sense of who we're dealing with: we've already done a good deal of work and are able to present a solid overview of them before the reader has even seen them in action. When, on the other hand, we write with a more fluid sense of who a character is, showing rather than telling, the options available to that character for action or transformation are greater, and this can be extremely helpful when we're finding our way into a story.

One great advantage to the writer in *showing* character is that you will almost always add value to the scene in the process. If we were *telling* we could write:

> Millie kept up a veneer of capable respectability but feared that at heart she was what her neighbours would consider a slattern.

This isn't wrong, but we might think of how to demonstrate or suggest this rather than baldly stating it. In the light of what we know, what sort of behaviour might exemplify Millie's character? Picture Millie in her domestic setting and we might find ourselves coming up with something like this:

> Millie was about to finish sweeping the floor when the doorbell went. Damn, she thought. The dustpan was still at the end of the alley by

the dustbin. What would Mrs Newbold think if she saw this mess of sweepings in the corner of the kitchen? This was not the detritus of one day. Or one week. And she shouldn't keep her visitor waiting. After a moment's deliberation Millie lifted up the corner of the back door mat and swept the pile of dirt under it, making a mental note to deal with it the moment Mrs Newbold left.

We've found a way of showing an aspect of Millie's personality, certainly, but we've found so much more. We've started to suggest *location* (there's an alley); *character* (the idea that keeping Mrs Newbold waiting is a worse sin than failing to finish her cleaning might tell us something about her, or about Mrs Newbold); and we've also, should we choose to exploit it, introduced an unexploded bomb – the pile of dust under the rug which has the potential to 'pay off' later. The reader will already be filling in the gaps (imaginatively participating), creating a picture of Millie's kitchen. We're also subtly encouraging the reader to ally herself with Millie – to see things her way – and to develop an interest in what happens to or around her. We wouldn't have got any of this added value by sticking with the version that *tells* us, in abstract terms, who Millie is.

So *showing* can often produce more interesting results than merely *telling*. It's not that you shouldn't ever tell – sometimes you have no alternative – but that the act of showing forces you, the writer, to envisage your characters more fully, to see them in their context and to think about how their personality informs their actions. It might be that you end up not even using the paragraph about Millie's dust dilemma, but working it through has helped you fill her out a little because you have inhabited her world. You are inside looking out, rather than outside looking in. As writers, we must be willing to immerse ourselves in the consciousness of our characters. Eudora Welty explained:

> What I do in writing of any character is to try to enter into the mind, heart and skin of a human being who is not myself. Whether this happens to be a man or a woman, old or young, with skin black or

white, the primary challenge lies in making the jump itself. It is the act of a writer's imagination that I set most high.[30]

Look at how Alice Munro opens her short story 'Royal Beatings' (1977). By starting with a threatened event she manages not only to give an impression of the character of Rose, but also to hint at the characters of her stepmother and father:

> *Royal Beating.* That was Flo's promise. You are going to get one Royal Beating.
>
> The word 'Royal' lolled on Flo's tongue, took on trappings. Rose had a need to picture things, to pursue absurdities, that was stronger than the need to stay out of trouble, and instead of taking this threat to heart she pondered: How is a beating royal? She came up with a tree-lined avenue, a crowd of formal spectators, some white horses and black slaves. Someone knelt, and then blood came leaping out like banners. An occasion both savage and splendid. In real life they didn't approach such dignity, and it was only Flo who tried to supply the event with some high air of necessity and regret. Rose and her father soon got beyond anything presentable.
>
> Her father was king of the royal beatings. Those Flo gave never amounted to much; they were quick cuffs and slaps dashed off while her attention remained elsewhere. You get out of my road, she would say. You mind your own business. You take that look off your face.

We're immediately recruited to Rose's perspective – in fact we're taken right into her imagination – and while Munro doesn't describe either her stepmother or father, we gain a strong impression of them. This kind of characterisation can often be more effective than explicit description; seeing characters in action enhances the illusion that we're dealing with living, breathing people.

Character and plot

We've noted that characters provide plot by their actions, but even when a character isn't directly shaping the story – when she is subject to external forces beyond her control – the way she responds to those forces informs the story's direction. A very clear example of this can be found in the Swedish film *Force Majeure* (Ruben Östlund, 2014). A family is on holiday at a ski resort, sitting at a table on a terrace overlooking the mountains when there's an avalanche: a mass of shifting snow is speeding down a slope directly towards them. We might expect the rest of the film to be about the family's survival and escape following the avalanche but in fact the whole of the rest of the film depends on the father's reaction in the moment of the avalanche. He picks up his gloves and phone and leaves his wife and two children at the table. The mother shelters the children under her arms and the avalanche passes leaving the people on the terrace lightly covered in fine snow but unhurt; the fallout from the husband's reaction becomes the drama – how will the family deal with his instinctive abandonment of them? The avalanche is the event that sets the action in motion, but it's the characters' attempts to come to terms with the father's response that is the film's real story.

Many stories have their avalanche equivalent: a situation arises which forces the protagonist to embark on a course of action – to make a choice. Conflicts of loyalty, characters forced to decide between two evils, characters whose motives are compromised – these are eternal themes, much exploited by Shakespeare and his contemporaries and still to be found at the core of many stories today, whether these are told in books or films, on radio or television. Characters are often put in positions of great stress, and the decisions they make tell us who they are, or who they have become in the course of the story. They are agents of the plot, which defines them at the same time as being defined by them.

Characters are individuals

You may feel that you are not all that interested in character – that you have things you want to say about the world and its injustices and that your characters are simply mouthpieces to help you to say those things. The problem with this is self-evident: your characters won't be characters but ciphers – opinions with names attached to them. If you want to write about issues and are not interested in characters you would serve your ends much better by writing non-fiction.

If we accept that characters must be something more than mouthpieces for the author, we'll also appreciate that simple generic indicators are unlikely to make for strong or convincing characterisation. An inner-city social worker isn't a character any more than an upland sheep farmer is a character: those features don't tell us anything about their personalities. You know you have a character when you begin to envisage them reacting in a particular way to a particular event.

Let's imagine three characters in an otherwise empty train late at night during a period of high anxiety about terrorist attacks. They suddenly realise that there's a rucksack on the seat that doesn't belong to any of them. How do they respond? If they all respond in the same way you don't have three characters, you just have three people with different names. If one of them wants to look inside the bag, another wants to pull the emergency cord and the third starts to have a panic attack, you have characters, because they are individuals, acting in accordance with who they are – and what is more, those individuals will generate a story, through their actions, interactions and reactions.

We often think generically when we begin to outline a character. That's natural and understandable, but good writers know that the broad-brush sketch needs to be developed into something more complex and less obvious. This was a vitally important consideration for Sara Collins when she began to write *The Confessions of Frannie Langton* (2019). The novel chronicles the life of a woman born into slavery, and Collins felt a need to challenge expectations set up by earlier slave narratives:

Slavery is one of those topics people expect to be written about in a certain way. Historically, slave narratives were written with an agenda: to inform white readers about the terrible suffering endured by slaves, and thereby persuade them to the abolitionist cause. It's the kind of writing that tells you what happened to a person, but not much about who they were. ... Unless we're careful in the way we write about slavery now, we risk getting stuck in the same mode as those early chroniclers, reducing our characters to stereotypes from whom no one expects anything other than suffering.[31]

The reader of the novel will understand that its protagonist and narrator, Frannie, lives under various forms of constraint, but she certainly isn't a passive sufferer. Her ability to read, acquired early in life, gives her a resource denied to most enslaved people, and is in part responsible for her refusal of victimhood and for the acts of self-determination the narrative hinges on. She explicitly acknowledges that her behaviour defies expectation, not least in her relationship with Langton, the brutal slave-owner with whom she travels to England:

> The anti-slavers are always asking me, what was done to you, Frances? How did you suffer? They don't believe any of it could have been done to you unless you were forced. ... What would they say if I told them I pinned my own self to Langton, even after we came here? That I was the one who followed him? Oh, how they'd leap away! Uncommon, unlikely. But true.[32]

It's not simply that actions and characteristics that appear uncommon or unlikely *may also* be true; we can go further, understanding that the uncommon or the unlikely is often precisely what makes our characters seem most authentic. We need to step clear of stereotypes, working with our characters to find the unexpected in them. In order to create (or discover) Frannie's complex character, Collins had to free her from the weight of expectation:

> I had to allow her to make the kinds of choices I hope I wouldn't have made, and that we aren't necessarily used to seeing from characters like her. Yet the more I did, the more complex and compelling she became, and the more she seemed to take on real flesh.[33]

Collins's idea that the writer might have to stand back, allowing the character to do things differently, is an important one. All fictional characters emerge from the consciousness of the writer, but if they merely reflect the thoughts, feelings and personality of their creator, they are unlikely to live on the page. If you find that your characters seem dull or inert it's worth asking yourself a few questions. Are you allowing them to say things you wouldn't say, do things you wouldn't do, think things you wouldn't think? Are they clearly differentiated from one another? Do they ever argue with each other? If they do, are you careful to avoid weighting the argument in favour of the character whose beliefs most resemble yours? If you answer any or all of these questions in the negative, consider the possibility that you need to step back and let your characters breathe.

Character and narrative voice

The close relationship between character and plot is of course only one of the ways in which character development is integrated with other aspects of writing. Your narrative voice also has a huge impact on how you write character. If your story is written in the first person, all characters, including the narrator himself, are described from his perspective, and in his voice. Consider the opening of J. D. Salinger's *The Catcher in the Rye* (1951):

> If you really want to hear about it, the first thing you'll probably want to know is where I was born, and what my lousy childhood was like, and how my parents were occupied and all before they had me, and all that David Copperfield kind of crap, but I don't feel like going into it, if you want to know the truth. In the first place, that stuff bores me, and in the second place, my parents would have about two haemorrhages apiece if I told anything pretty personal about them. They're quite touchy about anything like that, especially my father. They're *nice* and all – I'm not saying that – but they're also touchy as hell. Besides, I'm not going to tell you my whole goddam autobiography or

anything. I'll just tell you about this madman stuff that happened to me around last Christmas just before I got pretty run-down and had to come out here and take it easy.

While we are swept up into Holden Caulfield's worldview we're not blinded to the possibility that other people might not consider his parents 'touchy as hell', or that his revelations would be unlikely to induce haemorrhages. They may simply be private people who would feel uncomfortable at their teenage son broadcasting intimate family details. Also, despite his protest that he is not going to tell us his 'whole goddam autobiography or anything', he does actually let us know a lot about himself – so we are immediately alerted to the fact that we may get something other from him than what he says – or thinks – he's giving us in his telling of the story. We discuss unreliable narrators in Chapter 8, but it's worth just flagging up here that a first-person narrative is inevitably going to present all characters in the story through the lens of the narrating character and that is going to be a partial view, filtered through (and restricted by) the character's experience and agenda.

How many characters?

We can create problems for ourselves by having too many or too few characters. In a short story too many characters can quickly make the story unwieldy and risk distracting the reader from the narrative as they try to remember or work out who everyone is; in a novel we have more time and greater space, allowing for a larger canvas with more characters, yet we still have to be careful not to baffle the reader by introducing them to too many people at once. This has the same effect as being introduced to a number of new people in quick succession round a dinner table.

Conversely, an underpopulated novel puts the characters under a bright spotlight. Restricting a scene or a story to two characters makes for intensity but it also narrows the reader's knowledge of them, since they will tend to be seen only as they are *to each other*. We know that in our own lives we present different selves in different contexts and to different people: you are not exactly the same person to your colleagues as you are to your partner, to your child, or to your child's teacher; when helping someone across the road we're unlikely to present the same self as when stopped by the police. Showing a character engaging, in different combinations, with other individuals can provide narrative depth and complexity, and the possibilities of interaction increase exponentially with each added character. Of course this doesn't mean that the more characters you have the better your story will be, but it's worth bearing in mind that interaction is energy. If your characters feel tired and uninteresting, it may be helpful to experiment by introducing one or more new characters; as in life, the introduction of any new character inevitably alters the dynamic, and the effect may be to enliven the entire narrative.

Minor characters

Minor characters may not need to be drawn in as much detail as major characters, simply because they are not going to take up so much of the reader's interest and time. However, as Sarah Waters has pointed out, it is important to respect your minor characters and think about what the rest of their story might be.[34] Characters who have only a single function in a story can add value if you make them more than a name on the page.

Aunt Em in L. Frank Baum's *The Wizard of Oz* (1900) hardly appears in the book at all, and the author devotes only one paragraph to her, yet in that paragraph he tells us a great deal about her character and history:

> When Aunt Em came there to live she was a young, pretty wife. The sun and wind had changed her, too. They had taken the sparkle from her eyes and left them a sober grey; they had taken the red from her cheeks and lips, and they were grey also. She was thin and gaunt, and never smiled now. When Dorothy, who was an orphan, first came to her, Aunt Em had been so startled by the child's laughter that she

would scream and press her hand upon her heart whenever Dorothy's merry voice reached her ears; and she still looked at the little girl with wonder that she could find anything to laugh at.[35]

The description of Aunt Em also gives us a sense of the upbringing of our main character, adding to our understanding of the texture of Dorothy's world. We find a minor character with a similar function in O. Henry's 'The Furnished Room' (1904), in a scene set in a dismal cityscape, where a young man is working his way along a street of 'crumbling red mansions':

> To the door of this, the twelfth house whose door he had rung, came a housekeeper who made him think of an unwholesome, surfeited worm that had eaten its nut to a hollow shell and now sought to fill the vacancy with edible lodgers.
> He asked if there was a room to let.
> 'Come in,' said the housekeeper. Her voice came from her throat; her throat seemed lined with fur.

Again, we see a minor figure used not so much to contribute to the plot as to add to the texture of the story. Described in terms that border on the grotesque, the housekeeper helps to define this land of dank and greasy rented rooms.

The art is to find the fine line between adding interest or value with a minor character and distracting the reader from the story you want them to be following. But it may happen that you become so interested in a minor character you have created that you give them more to do and they become increasingly important to the main story. If that happens, don't automatically resist it: your character's development may help to generate a new and more rewarding narrative.

Character isn't fixed

As writers we usually aim for consistency in our characters, but we need to think carefully about what we mean by both consistency and inconsistency. When, in life, somebody acts, as we say, 'out of character', they are behaving (as we see it) unexpectedly; but every uncharacteristic act in life will have an explanation – something we didn't see, or failed to interpret correctly. A normally mild-mannered office worker punches his boss – nobody in the office expected it, but it's fair to assume that there's a story behind it: perhaps the employee has recently lost his father, perhaps his wife walked out on him that morning, perhaps he has been brooding on being passed over for promotion. In writing fiction we're perfectly entitled to create characters whose behaviour changes radically at one or more points in the narrative, but we'd normally do well to reveal some of the background to the change before we get to it. If we don't – if we let the change come, inexplicably, out of nowhere – that's when our readers are likely to complain of inconsistency.

But they might reasonably complain, too, if our characters show little or no change, if the trajectory of their experience is too flat and their natures too bland. When we think about it, we'll realise that most serious works of fiction show at least one character developing in some significant way, responding to the events in which they play a part; indeed, character development may be a novel's main story. You may have come across the term 'Bildungsroman', meaning literally 'education novel', 'education' in this context implying a young protagonist's discovery of the world and his own place in it. In D. H. Lawrence's *Sons and Lovers* (1913) we see Paul Morel exploring his own sexuality through relationships with women, in the long shadow of his mother's influence; in *A Portrait of the Artist as a Young Man* (1916) James Joyce shows his protagonist, Stephen Dedalus, gradually breaking free of the constraints of family, nation and religion to stand, at the novel's conclusion, on the brink of an artistic life; while Zora Neale Hurston's *Their Eyes Were Watching God* (1937) chronicles the journey of its protagonist, Janie Crawford, from girlhood to maturity, following her progress through three marriages as she searches for a reality corresponding to an intense early revelation of what love and marriage might ideally mean.

Hurston's novel works rather differently from the other two examples. While both Lawrence and Joyce deal chronologically with the lives of their protagonists, taking them through to the critical moment at which they launch themselves into the wider world, Hurston frames her narrative in such a way as to suggest, in its powerful conclusion, that Janie's quest has ended in a kind of satisfaction. Even if she hasn't found exactly what she was looking for, she has arrived at a resting place:

> Here was peace. She pulled in her horizon like a great fish-net. Pulled it from around the waist of the world and draped it over her shoulder. So much of life in its meshes! She called in her soul to come and see.[36]

In each of these three cases the psychological journey is transformative, but in no case would we describe the character's transformation as unexpected; on the contrary, the steps that lead to it are built into the fabric of the narrative. The change may ultimately be radical, but the character isn't inconsistent. As writers, we need to carry our readers through the various changes our characters undergo – not necessarily *explaining* every twist and turn in their shifting relationship with the world they inhabit, or analysing every thought and feeling, but *revealing*, through careful exposition, the nature and causes of change.

Planning characters

There's a widely promoted view that, before you start writing, you need to create a detailed dossier for each of your characters, covering every aspect of their lives, from where they went to school to their favourite food. By all means do this if you genuinely find it useful, but be aware that the approach can be problematic. Firstly, creating the dossier is one of those activities that feels like writing but can actually be a distraction from your real task; it can even be an excuse for not writing (as can, for example, the quest for the perfect notebook, excessively lengthy research, reorganising your bookshelves or sharpening every pencil in the house). Secondly, it can go on and on: there's potentially no limit to what might be listed, from a character's star sign to the contents of her wardrobe. Some of this may prove vital to your plot, but a great deal will prove irrelevant. Thirdly, and most importantly, the more detail you pin down before you start your story, the less likely you are to explore available possibilities in the process of writing. For example, it might solve a major problem for you at some point in your narrative to let your character have an older brother, but if you've decided beforehand that he's an only child, you may fail to see the possibility; the initial decision, firmly inscribed in your dossier, may set artificial limits to your explorations.

William Trevor has a very different approach:

> You invent the people and then you probe them as deeply as you can. First of all you've got a vague person, literally like a character coming into one of your own dreams, then you try to see how he or she works. You would then suggest this without pigeon-holing the thing. It's almost as if you invent somebody and then watch him with a camera.[37]

It's important to note that Trevor isn't suggesting that a writer should – or could – begin to write without any sense at all of who his characters are – that 'vague person' is there from the start – but he does suggest the value of allowing yourself to get to know your characters gradually in the process of working with them, rather than trying to see them in their entirety before starting to develop your narrative.

If Trevor's starting point strikes you as *too* vague, you might want to consider a middle way, the loose outline. This is a series of broad indicators you provide for yourself, signposts rather than route maps. A loose character outline for a teenage girl in a novel about family life might look something like this:

Katherine (Katie?)

In first term at college studying (?)art – anyway, something no one else in the family can relate to. Is she happy at college? Is home a respite or can't she wait to go back?

Friends? – maybe one close friend, someone she can reveal herself to. Friend not at university – a former schoolfriend on a different path in life?

Relationships with sibling/s – are these under pressure from some source beyond the family? One sibling in trouble of some kind? Involved in crime – drugs?

Relationship with father – perhaps she is very like him – is this a source of closeness or of discord?

Relationship with mother – mother irritates her – perhaps mother's concerns strike daughter as intrusive.

These questions and suggestions could well be enough to set things moving, without depriving your character of the space she needs to breathe and grow. Our characters are not, of course, real people, but we usually want to create the impression that they are. For this to happen the writer, as well as the reader, needs to be curious about them, and curiosity is most likely to arise when we give our characters a freedom that feels like autonomy; when we allow them to surprise us.

− 4 −

Plot and structure I

∼

Getting to grips with plot

This chapter will focus on the short story. There's a practical reason for this: to make our points we shall need to summarise plots, and it's obviously neater and easier to do so with a brief narrative than a long one; our focus will also allow us to examine the distinction between two main types of short story, the event-plot story and the Chekhovian or 'slice-of-life' story. Although the event-plot story is more or less restricted to shorter forms, much of what we have to say about plot in relation to the short story can also be applied to the novel.

We've seen that plot and character are indivisible because characters make (and are made by) plot. This is true even in very simple moral tales such as Aesop's fables and Jesus's parables: while the characters are not highly developed they have characteristics which differentiate them (the improvident grasshopper and the diligent ant of the fable; the uncaring priest and Levite and the compassionate Samaritan of the parable) and which affect the outcome of the story. Jokes – which are often very short stories with a twist – can also follow a simple character-based, or rather characteristic-based, pattern. Any joke the English might tell about an Irishman, a Welshman or a Scotsman, for example, locates its comedic element in these stereotypical figures acting in character: each is supposed, for the sake of the joke, to be a fool, a thief or a miser respectively, and the joke finds its meaning from these assumed characteristics being played out in a specific context. So even the most basic plots depend on some kind of character, however crude, being ascribed to the protagonist. They may behave in character (the industrious ant) or out of supposed character (the parables' first audience would have been prejudiced against Samaritans), but character remains a necessary element of the story.

Although we can't consider plot entirely separately from character, it might be useful to begin by looking at plots in which character appears to take a back seat and the value of the story is largely located in the (sometimes ingenious) plot itself. These are often called event-plot stories. One of the oldest event-plot stories in the English language is written in verse: 'The Pardoner's Tale' from Geoffrey Chaucer's *The Canterbury Tales* (c. 1387–1400). The story goes like this:

Three unruly young men (they are described as 'riotoures' – which doesn't have an exact modern equivalent – 'yobs' is probably the closest term) are drinking in a tavern when they hear a bell tolling, signifying a funeral. They learn that that the dead man is an old friend of theirs and that he was killed by a criminal called Death who has been murdering people in nearby villages. Emboldened by drink, they resolve to 'slay this false traitor, Death'; they swear an oath of allegiance to live and die for one another, and set off to find him. On the way they accost a poor old man, accuse him of being in league with Death and demand to know where Death can be found. The old man points out a path leading to a copse. There, he says, they will find Death under an oak tree.

The three run to the appointed place where they find a great pile of gold coins. They decide this great good fortune is destined for them. However, they reason that people seeing them transporting such a quantity of gold are bound to assume they have stolen it, so they will have to wait until nightfall before carrying it off. Deciding they need provisions while they wait, they draw lots: the youngest draws the short straw and is dispatched back to town to get food and drink while the other two guard the treasure.

As soon as he is gone the other two, reasoning that a third of the treasure is good, but half is even better, decide to take all the treasure for themselves. To prevent the youngest claiming his portion they will stab him to death when he returns. Meanwhile, the youngest has been plotting to keep all the treasure for himself. To this end he buys poison and pours it into two of the three bottles of wine he has bought. He returns to the copse with the provisions. As Chaucer suggests, the outcome is almost inevitable now:

> Why make a sermon of it? Why waste breath?
> Exactly in the way they'd planned his death
> They fell on him and slew him, two to one.
> Then said the first of them when this was done,
> 'Now for a drink. Sit down and let's be merry,
> For later on there'll be the corpse to bury.'
> And, as it happened, reaching for a sup,
> He took a bottle full of poison up
> And drank; and his companion, nothing loth,
> Drank from it also, and they perished both.[38]

It's a brilliant plot and a perfect example of an event-plot story. Such stories often have a 'twist' or 'trick' ending which, ideally, the reader hasn't anticipated. The ending might, as in this case, serve justice. A twist ending always depends on one or more characters not having the full picture – some important fact or action is not available to them. The reader may have the full picture before the climax (as in this case, where we know what both parties are plotting) or the full picture may not be revealed to the reader until it is revealed to the characters.

The story is unusual in that the three main characters are hardly differentiated at all – Chaucer doesn't give them names and refers only to 'the worst' of them and 'the youngest' of them – and in fact the reason this moral story has three protagonists instead of one is because the plot requires it. Nevertheless the characters direct the plot. They had several opportunities to make things turn out differently. If they hadn't decided to go looking for Death to punish him, if they hadn't intimidated the old man into telling them where Death could be found, if they'd stuck to their plan to share the gold – the ending would have been different. The ending is not inevitable at the outset; they make the ending inevitable by their decisions and actions. The characters shape the plot.

In Chaucer's tale the man sent for provisions doesn't know that the two men in the copse are planning to kill him, and the two men in the copse don't know that the man sent for provisions is planning to kill *them* – but the reader is in full possession of the facts. However, a common variant on the 'twist' story keeps certain vital information from the reader as well as the protagonists. A classic example of a synchronised 'reveal' (where the reader understands what has happened in the same moment as the main character understands) occurs in Guy de Maupassant's 1884 short story, 'The Necklace'. The plot goes like this:

Mathilde Loisel is pretty but poor. She lives in Paris, is married to a clerk in the Department of Education and is dissatisfied with her lot. She longs for the material things she can't have and wishes in vain for a different life – one where she has sumptuous furnishings, food and clothes; where she is fêted and flirted with. She has a wealthy friend, Mme Forestier, but rarely sees her as the contrast in their fortunes is too much for her to bear. When the couple receive an invitation to a ball, her husband thinks she will be delighted by the opportunity to mix with high society – but she weeps, for she has nothing appropriate to wear. She persuades him to buy her a new dress. The day approaches but still Mathilde is unhappy – she has no jewellery to wear to the ball. Her husband hits on the idea of asking Mme Forestier if Mathilde can borrow something. Mathilde duly goes to Mme Forestier who offers Mathilde the freedom of her jewellery case. Among the many lovely things there Mathilde sees a superb diamond necklace – the most striking item in the box. Mme Forestier agrees to lend it to her.

The big day arrives and Mathilde is indeed the belle of the ball – the Minister and other high officials pay her attention and queue up to dance with her – it is everything she has dreamed of. In the small hours she and her husband prepare to leave; they hurry, as Mathilde doesn't want anyone to see the shabby wraps she's brought for the journey home. They walk for a while before they find a rundown cab to take them the rest of the way. It's all over. Back to real life. At home Mathilde takes a final look at herself in all her glory before her mirror and finds that the diamond necklace is gone.

Horrified, they search the dress and the wraps; they retrace their footsteps, go to the cab offices and the police; they advertise, offering a reward – and they wait. After a week without news they decide, in desperation, that the only thing to do is to replace the necklace with one similar and they finally find one. They have half the necessary amount in savings and they scrape the rest together through a series of hastily arranged loans. They buy the necklace and Mathilde takes it to Mme Forestier, who suspects nothing.

Here Maupassant cuts a long story very short. Ten years pass, during which Mathilde, having dispensed with the maid and moved to cheap lodgings, does all her own housework and that of other people, and takes in laundry while her husband does extra book-keeping at night, all to pay off the loans. By the time the money is paid off Mathilde looks old and worn out. Occasionally she sits before her mirror and wonders how different everything could have been, had she not lost the necklace.

One day she bumps into Mme Forestier. Her friend, still youthful and pretty, does not recognise Mathilde at first. She asks how this change in appearance came about and Mathilde, now her debts are paid, tells her the whole story. Mme Forestier is greatly surprised; as she explains to Mathilde, the necklace she lent her was merely costume jewellery – paste diamonds – of little value.

Although this may be the best-known of Maupassant's short stories, it's far from typical of his work and indeed the showmanship of 'The Necklace' has been criticised because 'the final line ... arrives with the boom-tish of a club comedian's punchline'.[39] This is surely preferable, however, to Maupassant going on to point up the moral of the story: the abrupt ending strongly suggests he wishes us to find one for ourselves.

While on one level the story can be read as an account of a stroke of bad luck followed, ten years later, by a revelation which reveals Mathilde's sacrifice to have been unnecessary, Mathilde is in fact the author of her own misfortune. If we look carefully at the story we'll see that it's not just a single random event which ruins Mathilde – that event is an expression of her psyche, of an attitude which places undue value on how things *seem*. Right from the outset Mathilde is driven by appearance; the things she craves are all about image. She wishes to be celebrated, to be found attractive, to have all the accoutrements of success, and she believes that this will make her happy. This is why she fixes on the shiniest item in the jewellery box and assumes its value. Her preoccupation with appearance sends her into a sulk: if she can't have a new dress she refuses to go to the ball; if she can't have jewellery, she won't be seen there either. But the image she finally achieves can only last as long as the ball itself: when she leaves to go home she has to put on the shabby old wraps and take a street cab. Driven by pride, she hurries to avoid being seen, throwing on the wraps (is this when the necklace is lost?), rushing into the street (is it now?), then walking quickly away to avoid being seen waiting outside in her dowdiness (or now?). The fact that the necklace is never found means we can't know when she lost it, but Maupassant suggests that the loss has to do with her haste which, in turn, has to do with her obsession with her own image.

The story is designed so that (ideally) the reader learns the true value of the necklace at exactly the same moment as Mathilde, in the very last sentence of the story. When Mathilde chose the necklace, Maupassant could have had Mme Forestier say something like: 'Of course you may borrow that – and don't worry if anything happens to it as it's only paste.' Then, of course there would have been no story – and perhaps this is not only because there would have been no drama over its loss: we might wonder whether Mathilde would have wanted to borrow it once she knew the diamonds were fake. Alternatively, Maupassant could have had the true value of the necklace kept from Mathilde when she borrowed it, but (as in Chaucer's tale) could have let the reader in on the facts – with a sentence like this, for example: 'Little did Mathilde know the necklace was worthless.' While there could then still have been a story, we, as readers, would not have participated to the same extent in Mathilde's horror at the loss and the anxiety of the fruitless search, or her subsequent sacrifices. Much of the success of this kind of short story depends on withholding crucial information from the reader.

Such synchronised moments of discovery by reader and character are key to the pleasure of reading long fiction too, of course. As children, reading *The Wizard of Oz* we discover at the same moment as Dorothy that the wizard she and her friends have pinned their hopes and dreams on is not a wizard at all but 'a humbug';[40] readers of Daphne du Maurier's *Jamaica Inn* (1936) will remember the sickening twist, described by Julie Myerson as 'the cold-sweat moment when you realise that, just like Mary [the novel's protagonist], you've been so busy fighting off the visible baddies that you've let yourself be blind to the real evil, the most dangerous force of all, which has been waiting there quietly all along'.[41]

Inexperienced writers will often give the reader the whole picture, while withholding information only from the protagonist, not realising that they have effectively cut the strings which tie our sympathies to the protagonist's fortunes. (Chaucer gets away with it partly because the duplicity occurs late in the story, but primarily because the emotional value in the denouement doesn't depend on us caring about the robbers but on our appreciating the way their murderous plans backfire.)

We've seen from these examples that the plot of the story is linked to the nature of the protagonist, so that there is a kind of poetic justice in the outcome. Revisiting such stories you can see how thoughtfully they are put together and how early the writer lays the groundwork for the fall. Maupassant gives us a portrait of vain and superficial Mathilde right at the start of the story; Chaucer cleverly has the three men swear an oath early in the story 'to live and die each of them for another' – which, in a perverse way, is exactly what happens. The art is to feed the reader information which is digested without awareness, at that stage, of its full import.

In 'The Gift of the Magi' (1906) O. Henry serves us with a plot which might owe something both to 'The Pardoner's Tale' and 'The Necklace':

Della and Jim are poor and young and in love. It's Christmas and we are with Della in their shabby apartment as she weeps over the fact that she has no money to buy Jim a present. She owns only one thing of value and that is her beautiful hair. She sells it to a wigmaker for twenty dollars with which she buys a gold chain for Jim's gold watch – an heirloom which he is reluctant to use because it hasn't a chain. However, she's worried about what Jim's reaction to her haircut will be.

Jim comes home from work and, as she feared, seems unable to get over the fact that she has cut her beautiful hair. Still dazed, he nevertheless assures her that he doesn't love her any less. He gives her *her* Christmas present, which she opens. She shrieks with joy and then bursts into tears:

> For there lay The Combs – the set of combs, side and back, that Della had worshipped long in a Broadway window. Beautiful combs, pure tortoise shell, with jewelled rims – just the shade to wear in the beautiful vanished hair. They were expensive combs, she knew, and her heart had simply craved and yearned over them without the least hope of possession. And now, they were hers, but the tresses that should have adorned the coveted adornments were gone.

And that could be the ending. But there's more. Della gives Jim his present – the gold chain for his prized watch. He explains that he sold the watch in order to buy the combs.

Just as the robbers' greed and Mathilde's vanity drove their stories to their conclusions, so Della's and Jim's willingness to sacrifice their most prized possessions is paid back in the irony of a matching sacrifice which renders both gifts redundant. In this instance we see no poetic justice – on the contrary, we feel that the couple are the undeserving victims of the story's twist – but again we recognise that their natures have driven the plot.

Examining these plots, we'll develop a keener understanding of the intricacies of the well-written event-plot story: each story hinges on what is revealed, at what stage and to whom. In Chaucer's story the reader is explicitly told that the two men guarding the treasure plan to kill the youngest man, and that, at the same time, the youngest man plans to poison them; here the plot depends principally on what the characters know or don't know – on neither party knowing what the other is up to. In 'The Gift of the Magi' the reader is with Della as she sells her hair and buys the watch chain; we're only told later that, while we were watching her, Jim was somewhere else selling his watch and buying the combs; in this instance information is hidden from the reader as well as from both characters (Jim is, of course, ignorant of that part of the action which is known to Della and the reader). The equivalent in 'The Necklace' is not a parallel hidden event, but a hidden condition: the actual value of the necklace. These examples remind us that plot may be (and usually is) something far more complex than a straightforward sequence of events; the way in which those events are displayed and ordered may be crucial to a story's success.

The plots of these stories can be summarised fairly neatly, albeit with some loss of power and elegance. When, however, we turn to the other principal type of short story – known as the Chekhovian or 'slice-of-life' story – we discover that summarising the plot is largely unhelpful in trying to communicate what a story is actually about. 'Chekhovian' refers to the Russian writer, Anton Chekhov (1860–1904), and we might begin by considering

Chekhov's own contribution to the genre that bears his name. As William Boyd describes it:

> Chekhov … revolutionised the short story by transforming narrative. Chekhov saw and understood that life is godless, random and absurd, that all history is the history of unintended consequences. He knew, for instance, that being good will not spare you from awful suffering and injustice, that the slothful can flourish effortlessly and that mediocrity is the one great daemonic force. By abandoning the manipulated beginning-middle-and-end plot, by refusing to judge his characters, by not striving for a climax or seeking neat narrative resolution, Chekhov made his stories appear agonisingly, almost unbearably lifelike.[42]

Boyd's analysis neatly captures the essence of Chekhov's most characteristic stories. 'The Malefactor' (1885) is a story about a judgement but is not itself judgemental; its conclusion offers neither climax nor resolution; and the dialogue, between a petty thief and the magistrate who is trying him, is so lifelike that it might almost be a court transcript.

Chekhov begins by describing the malefactor of the title, Denis, a small, skinny fellow, pockmarked, unkempt and barefoot. What follows is a dialogue in which neither party seems able to grasp the other's point of view. The crime itself is ambiguous: on the one hand, Denis has simply pilfered a few iron nuts to weight his fishing line; on the other, these nuts were fixings for the railway lines, and their removal could have endangered lives. When the magistrate points this out, Denis is indignant:

> 'For how many years has the whole village been unscrewing nuts, and not an accident yet? If I were to carry a rail away, or even to put a log across the track, then, perhaps, the train might upset, but, Lord! a nut – pooh!'
> 'But can't you understand that the nuts fasten the rails to the ties?'
> 'Yes, we understand that, and so we don't unscrew them all; we always leave some; we do it carefully; we understand.'

It would appear that he doesn't really understand. He seems to miss the point repeatedly, not least when the magistrate tells him he will be sent to prison:

'How do you mean – to prison? Your honour, I haven't time! I have
to go to the fair to collect the three roubles that Gregory owes me
for tallow.'

Obtuse and inconsequential on Denis's side, frustrated and
impatient on the magistrate's, the dialogue leads nowhere, and
can't resolve anything – indeed, Denis is still talking as he is led
away: the story finishes on a dash, apparently in the middle of his
speech: 'Flog a man if he deserves it – '. The question of what Denis
deserves (how serious is his crime? how severely should he be pun-
ished?) lies at the heart of the story, but the text offers no answers.

Whatever we might say about the three event-plot stories we
have looked at, it wouldn't be that they're like life: their success
depends on extraordinary alignments of events, utterly uncharacteristic of day-to-day living. What Chekhov did was to give value
to ordinariness, to the everyday, to things we readily recognise.
He found human beings sufficiently interesting as his subject and
didn't see a need to manoeuvre them into unlikely situations. He
rejected plot as a primary focus in favour of narratives reflective
of the human condition.

Later short stories by writers such as James Joyce and Katherine
Mansfield seemed, like Chekhov's, to record rather than direct
the lives of their characters, and to resist evaluating their actions
and decisions. Liberated from a conventional idea of plot these
authors usually located their stories in the mundane lives of their
characters, in the small dramas of everyday life. If we think about
plot-driven stories as containing a sequence of pivotal events or
actions, the Chekhovian short story is more about lived moments:
moments in a relationship, for example, or moments of character
development occasioned by sudden understanding or acceptance.
Joyce described such moments as 'epiphanies'. It is revelation,
rather than event, that governs the plot here; and what is revealed
may still be obscure, and may offer no way forward for the protagonist. Joyce's 'Eveline' (1904) is about a girl *not* leaving home;
'Araby' (1914) is about a boy *not* finding what he seeks.

Such stories, characterised as they are by the untidiness and confusion of real life, can tap directly into the reader's own life experiences – experiences which, after all, rarely have much in common with the neat patterning of event-plot stories. 'Araby' epitomises the 'epiphany' story – the story of a moment of realisation in which the character is suddenly exposed to the truth of his existence. A summary of the plot gives you little of this: the narrator recalls being a boy with a crush on his friend's sister and a longing to go to the Araby bazaar to buy her something. He arrives late, as it is closing, and is disconcerted by overheard adult banter between the staff. He buys nothing and returns home. Almost nothing has happened and yet everything has changed. It's worth quoting from Chris Power's finely judged account of the story and its effects, an account that simultaneously provides insight into Joyce's dark, elusive narrative and illustrates the way in which a story of this kind may resonate with the reader's own experience:

> I was 16 when I first read Araby, and in the autumn of that year I got into what was, at that point, the worst trouble I'd ever been in. The police called my parents, and my parents, in a fury, tracked me down and ordered me home. I was a slow train and a long walk away, and over the course of that endless, anxious journey, night fell. Ever since, I always think of it when I read about the boy travelling to Araby in the 'deserted train' that 'crept onward among ruinous houses and over the twinkling river'. Both journeys led from a carefree childhood into a graver space: towards, in Hugh Kenner's description of Araby, 'an echoing and empty humiliation'. In symbolic terms, neither journey would have been well served by daylight.
>
> When the boy reaches his destination, most of the stalls are closed and 'the greater part of the hall was in darkness. I recognised a silence like that which pervades a church after a service.' Here, on the darkening floor of the shabby bazaar, Joyce's story becomes a requiem. The boy sees a young woman flirting with two men, and the sexual atmosphere of their exchange confuses him. When the woman grudgingly serves him he tells her he doesn't want anything. As he

leaves the bazaar, empty-handed but possessed of a new and bitter knowledge, he hears a voice 'call from one end of the gallery that the light was out. The upper part of the hall was now completely dark.'

We are present at the passing of the narrator's childhood, its lights dwindling around him. 'Gazing up into the darkness,' he tells us: 'I saw myself as a creature driven and derided by vanity; and my eyes burned with anguish and anger.' Here, at the story's end, we find ourselves thrown back to its beginning, which carries the presentiment of death in its 'dark dripping gardens where odours arose from the ashpits'.

In an evening the narrator has moved from an innocent boy playing in the last light of childhood, to an anguished young man who has come to realise that maturity is not the realisation of childhood's promise, but its loss.[43]

This is one reader's response, but Joyce's skill in communicating the universal through the specific means that most adult readers are likely to feel some kind of affinity with his protagonist: we've all felt humiliated by the vanity of our own expectations, or realised we've got it all wrong, or been oppressed by the frustration of being where we are or who we are. Such stories evoke situations and states of mind that we recognise and relate to; we bring an answering sympathy to the experience of the story. It's in no way dismissive of the skill with which O. Henry manipulates his material in 'The Gift of the Magi' to observe that Joyce's story of a gift unbought resonates at a deeper level than Henry's tale, and tells us more about our own lives.

As writers, we need to consider these matters – not because we have to decide on which side of the notional boundary we stand (it's not necessarily an either/or situation), but because we need to understand the likely effects of our writing on our readers.

In shifting the emphasis from plot to character, the Chekhovian story typically moves us away from clear and inevitable outcomes towards uncertainty and irresolution; from neatness and order into the more difficult terrain of alienation and disillusion. Throughout the twentieth century and up to the present day, most serious practitioners of the art of the short story have tended to follow and extend the Chekhovian model. Oblique and often enigmatic, their stories may not yield up their meaning at a single reading.

Take Ernest Hemingway's classic, 'Hills Like White Elephants' (1927), which starts and ends with a couple waiting for a train at a railway station and in which (on the surface at least) nothing much happens in between. In common with other Chekhovian stories, this is a piece which, for most readers, isn't fully accessible at the first encounter, but grows in depth on each successive reading.

We're not told the proper names of the characters (though the woman is addressed as 'Jig') or what they look like; the issue pre-occupying them is never named but we know what it is. We'll revisit this story later, but for present purposes it's exceptionally useful because its setting provides an apt imagistic representation of the slice-of-life short story. The station is in a desert: tracks extend into the distance on either side. We can figure the tracks which will carry the couple off into the future as the story after the written narrative has ended; the tracks leading to the station can be figured as the part of their journey that precedes the written narrative. The narrative itself occupies only the space taken up by the station. So these stories imply a past and a future but only occupy a slice out of the middle – a section of track, a junction perhaps. What precedes the narrative, and what follows it, are out of sight, but we are aware of their existence and their connection to the story we are being told.

Telling it slant

Poet Emily Dickinson's injunction to 'Tell all the truth but tell it slant' offers a concept useful to fiction-writers. Maupassant and O. Henry in their different ways tell their stories slant – deliberately not giving us all the facts in their chronological order – while Chekhov, Joyce and Hemingway may serve up significant moments which require the reader to help supply the meaning, to read between the lines. Telling a story slant can also be a way of delivering a meaning that might be less appealing to a reader (or more apparent to a censor) if it were told more conventionally or obviously. Allegory is an obvious example of telling a story slant to this end: we might think of George Orwell's *Animal Farm* (1945) where a simple story is played out as a kind of code, in this case to provide a political message.

When handled skilfully, fiction can be a beguiling and engaging way to carry or promote a moral or political message. While all fiction carries some kind of message, writing which contains social criticism presents an extra difficulty in that it often has to bring its readers to an understanding – if not endorsement – of the point of view of a character with whom they might not readily identify. Our demographic, our life experiences, our previous knowledge, have all contributed to our embracing certain values and narratives and resisting, suspecting or rejecting others. Some values are broadly endorsed by the majority and can, in a sense, be banked on, but these are not fixed: they change according to time and place. Attitudes to gender and sexual orientation, as well as race, caste and class continue to vary across the world. So even something approaching consensus about equality, or right and wrong, may be tricky. Writers who are moved by injustice are often engaging with a large constituency of readers who might disagree with their standpoint if it were set out issue by issue.

If you're hoping your writing might adjust the way people think about certain political, social or economic issues you will do well to avoid simplifying the moral situation into a battle between perceived good and perceived evil (whichever side wins). There's no reason to believe that watching a battle in which the reader has already staked his claim on the side of your perceived evil is going to change his mind merely because, in your story, his side lost. People are unlikely to relinquish their deeply held beliefs unless something underpinning their prejudices is disturbed by your story. So you first have to work on your reader, playing upon the values he might share with you before challenging those he doesn't.

One way of doing this is by approaching the story from an unconventional angle – approaching it slant – so that the reader is not already on the defensive, is not immediately seeing the conflict in bald partisan terms, but is arriving at a place where the issues you want to expose can be seen in a new light, and in a way that resists the narrow lens of prejudice. The way we plot our stories may be crucial to our success in winning our readers' sympathy.

Erskine Caldwell's short story, 'Daughter' (1935), begins with news circulating in a small town – news about a neighbour who has been arrested and put in the town jail. As a curious crowd gathers round the jail, it emerges that Jim Carlisle has shot dead his eight-year-old daughter because she kept saying she was hungry and he 'just couldn't stand to hear it'. It emerges that although Jim has worked hard all year round, he was wrongly blamed for the death of Colonel Maxwell's mule and Maxwell confiscated his crop as recompense, leaving him and his daughter destitute. The story ends with a man in the crowd fetching a crowbar and preparing to release Jim from jail.

The injustice of the situation that led to Jim's terrible act is clear and is what incenses the crowd and elicits pity from the reader. It is Caldwell's narrative skill that enables us to feel sorry for a man who has just killed his own daughter. How does he achieve this? It has a lot to do with where he chooses to start the story. A less imaginative writer might automatically begin with earlier events, with the little girl asking repeatedly for food, and Jim coming to his awful decision, or start the story even earlier, detailing the catalogue of bad luck and unjust treatment that has led Jim to a situation where he has no food for his daughter. But the way Caldwell tells it is much more like the way stories unfold in real communities. An appalling piece of news sends shockwaves rippling through the crowd but is then unpicked as the reader learns, alongside the townsfolk, what lies behind the incident. Events around the jail seem to unfold in real time and the talk of the neighbours furnishes us with the unseen, earlier events – the history that has led Jim to this point.

So the reader, who might have taken at face value a news headline such as 'SHARECROPPER SHOOTS DAUGHTER FOR ASKING FOR FOOD' or 'MOB SPRINGS CHILD-MURDERER FROM JAIL', is encouraged to see the event in human terms; he has been taken to a vantage-point where he understands that a truer story might be something like 'LANDLORD'S GREED LEADS TO CHILD'S DEATH', and he might well sympathise with, or at least understand, the crowd's desire to release Jim. And in considering the interplay between the perpetrator of the crime and the forces underlying the crime – the energy that drives the narrative – the reader might also be led to a more critical examination of his own social context.

Plotting is similarly important to another tale of social deprivation, Mary E. Mann's 'Little Brother' (c. 1890). The opening of the story sets up the location and situation with admirable economy as the narrator leads us to the home of the Hodds, an impoverished family in her parish:

> I met the parish nurse hurrying from the cottage in which a baby had, that morning, been born, towards a cottage at the other end of the village where a baby was due to be born, that night.
>
> 'All well over!' she said. 'Mrs Hodd going on nicely as can be expected.'
>
> 'She ought to be used to it by now, Nurse! The thirteenth!'
>
> 'Well, this one is dead, born dead.'
>
> 'What a mercy!'
>
> But our nurse does not like a case where the baby is born dead. 'Such a beautiful child too!'
>
> 'It's more than can be said of the other twelve.'
>
> 'How can you tell?' Nurse said. 'Look at their clothes; look at their hair, standing on end; look at the scenes they live in!'

The narrator stops to talk to Mr Hodd, who is cutting turnips in the yard. He is unsympathetic to his wife's experience. 'She's

51

borne you many children, Hodd,' the narrator remonstrates. 'The place is chuck full of 'em,' retorts Hodd. 'You stamp on 'em as you walk.' His callousness is shocking, but the narrator holds her tongue. The little boy helping Hodd says that his mother has instructed them 'to make a box to put little brother in' for burial.

The narrator enters the cottage:

> In the kitchen I passed through on my way upstairs, a pair of Hodds, of too tender an age to be at school, were seated on a sack – again, a sack! – spread before the fire, and were playing with a large battered doll. Mrs Hodd, above, lay in her big squalid bed, alone.

A conversation with Mrs Hodd leads naturally to discussion of the dead baby:

> 'I should like to see the poor baby, Mrs Hodd. I hear it was a very fine child.'
>
> 'Mine allers is!' Mrs Hodd testified. 'A crop o' heer he'd got all over his poll like golden suverins. My little uns, they're all that plased wi' their little brother! A fine hollerin' there'll be when he's took off to the buryin'.'
>
> 'Where is he? Look, I've brought a few flowers to lay upon his tiny coffin.'
>
> Mrs Hodd, without lifting her tousled head, cast a glance of enquiry round the almost bare room. Near the door a rude bed had been made by spreading a towel over a frowsy pillow laid on two chairs.
>
> 'Ain't he theer?' the woman asked, her eyes upon the chairs.
>
> 'Nothing's there, Mrs Hodd.'

When the visitor goes downstairs to investigate, she finds the children still at play:

> They were striving to draw over the rigid legs of the doll the grey calico nightgown of which they were stripping it when I saw them last. Their fat dirty little hands trembled with their eagerness to accomplish this feat. The mite who had the toy on her knees rocked herself maternally, and gave chirrups of encouragement as she worked.
>
> 'Theer! Put ickle arms in! Put in ickle arms!'

You may already have worked out for yourself the story's macabre conclusion. It's a story that leaves the reader reeling, partly from the realisation that the children are playing with their dead brother and partly from Mrs Hodd's defence of their behaviour: 'Other folkes' child'en have a toy, now and then, to kape 'em out of mischief. My little uns han't.' And while we find the thought of children playing with a dead baby appalling, Mann is asking us to look at the circumstances in which this can happen – in which this is the greatest tenderness shown towards a baby whom others consider to be nothing but an unnecessary extra expense. Mann has shocked us, but with serious purpose. If it's difficult to answer the question as to whether the baby is more appropriately honoured by being left upstairs on a dirty makeshift bed than by the children treating it like a doll, that's because the question is genuinely perplexing; and if we look beneath the surface of the narrative we shall find, as in 'Daughter', the larger social concern that informs it.

As in Caldwell's story, we see, if we examine the plotting, that it is the order in which information is released that gives 'Little Brother' its potency and allows us to be ambushed and moved by its message. The parish nurse may seem at first sight irrelevant to the story, but her words ('look at the scenes they live in!') suggest at the story's outset that social deprivation is the real explanation for the family's condition; the tableau of the children playing with their dead brother is seen early on, but understood only towards the story's conclusion, at which point Mrs Hodd's explanation of her children's behaviour returns, from another angle, to the matter raised by the nurse at the beginning – the inequality that, as Mrs Hodd sees it, deprives some children of the toys that others take for granted.

If we return to our two principal categories of short story, we'll see that 'Little Brother' has elements of both. In its focus on ordinary life in a small village, as well as in its withholding of explicit judgement by the narrator, it seems strongly Chekhovian (compare it with 'The Malefactor'), while its conclusion involves the kind of reveal typically associated with the event-plot story. Mann's story reminds us that genre-distinctions are useful only insofar as they serve our need for definition: as writers, we should understand that their purpose is not to constrain our writing but to give us ways of thinking about the broad and varied territory we occupy.

− 5 −

Plot and structure II

~

The patterns of plot

Let's look now at a story most readers will know – the story told by the film that made Steven Spielberg a household name. *Jaws* (1975, script: Carl Gottlieb and Peter Benchley, based on Peter Benchley's 1974 novel) had a simple but compelling plot, which Christopher Booker summarises as follows:

> [*Jaws*] told how the peace of a little Long Island seaside resort, Amity, was rudely shattered by the arrival offshore of a monstrous shark of almost supernatural power. For weeks on end the citizens are thrown into a stew of fear and confusion by the shark's savage attacks on one victim after another. Finally, when the sense of threat seems almost too much to bear, the hero of the story, the local police chief Brody, sets out with two companions to do battle with the monster. There is a tremendous climactic fight, with much severing of limbs and threshing about underwater, until at last the shark is slain. The community comes together in universal jubilation. The great threat has been lifted. Life in Amity can begin again.

Booker then goes on to summarise the plot of an Anglo-Saxon epic poem first written down a thousand years earlier:

> The first part of *Beowulf* tells of how the peace of the little seaside community of Heorot is rudely shattered by the arrival of Grendel, a monster of almost supernatural power, who lives in the depths of a nearby lake. The inhabitants of Heorot are thrown into a stew of fear and confusion as, night after night, Grendel makes his mysterious attacks on the hall in which they sleep, seizing one victim after another and tearing them to pieces. Finally, when the sense of threat seems almost too much to bear, the hero Beowulf sets out to do

battle, first with Grendel, then with his even more terrible monster mother. There is a tremendous climactic fight, with much severing of limbs and threshing about underwater, until at last both monsters are slain. The community comes together in jubilation. The great threat has been lifted. Life in Heorot can begin again.[44]

The comparison provides the starting point for *The Seven Basic Plots* (2004), in which Booker demonstrates that across the world and throughout history certain archetypal plots have been used over and over again: he identifies these plots as Overcoming the Monster, Rags to Riches, The Quest, Voyage and Return, Comedy, Tragedy and Rebirth. Booker was not, of course, the first person to notice the recurrence of story-patterns: the eighteenth-century critic, Samuel Johnson, told his biographer, James Boswell, of his intention to produce a work 'to show how small a quantity of *real fiction* there is in the world; and that the same images, with very little variation, have served all the authors who have ever written'.[45] Johnson's vast workload prevented him from finding the time to pursue the project, but there were other attempts before Booker's to pin down these ubiquitous story-shapes, and we might usefully survey some of the best-known.

In his study *Technique of the Drama* (1863), Gustav Freytag analysed a range of plays, showing that the five-act structure followed a common pattern which can be summarised as follows:

Exposition – the set-up (characters and context)
Rising action – the events which lead towards a crisis
Climax – the crisis/turning point
Falling action – the events which result from the crisis
Catastrophe/dénouement – everything is sorted out/resolved: the end.[46]

It's worth bearing in mind a couple of points. Firstly, as the title of his book suggests, Freytag was writing about stage plays, not prose fiction; secondly, he was writing before Chekhov and the rise of Modernism, drawing on the plays available to him at the time. This doesn't mean that his theory is completely irrelevant to our purposes, but it does suggest that we'd be unwise to appropriate it, wholesale, as a model for our own fiction.

Joseph Campbell's analysis of hero myth narratives, *The Hero with a Thousand Faces* (1949), puts the protagonist very much at the heart of story, identifying seventeen stages of 'the hero's journey', which fall within three main sections: *Departure, Initiation* and *Return*.[47] Campbell's writing has influenced works as diverse as George Lucas's *Star Wars* films and Richard Adams's rabbity quest-narrative *Watership Down* (1972).

Twenty years later Tzvetan Todorov examined the plots of four stories from Boccaccio's *Decameron*, extrapolating from them a more general theory of plot structure involving 'the shift from one equilibrium to another'.[48] The theory has been widely popularised, particularly in film studies, with the plot stages set out along the following lines:

Equilibrium
Disruption of equilibrium
Recognition of disruption
Attempts to restore equilibrium
Re-establishment of equilibrium

Theories such as these, while undoubtedly interesting, are usually of limited use to writers. It's perfectly possible to pick (let's say) one of Booker's seven classic plot shapes, mould your story closely to it and still have written a bad book. And plenty of great books don't readily or neatly fit the classic moulds (while *Lord of the Rings* arguably fits all seven of them). The theories offer us a useful way of understanding the various shapes stories may take, but if we take them as rules or templates for the creation of new stories we may hinder our own explorations.

At the most basic level, the shape of a story is pretty much inevitable. We start with a character, and that character must have a context. In order for there to be a story at all we need something to happen. So either the character makes something happen or something happens to him, to which he responds. That cannot resolve the situation completely, otherwise there is no more story, so there have to be further event steps or complications before the situation is resolved. If the character hits a problem that makes progress impossible, the story stops – so that can't happen; if the character can easily achieve a solution, the story ends prematurely – so that can't happen either. The character has to encounter a mixture of fortune – good and bad things, advances and reversals – and this necessarily means that he is on some kind of mission, on a path strewn with obstacles. Finally the situation is either resolved – whether in success or failure – or ends without resolution.

These are a story's bones, but they have accrued tissue which helps the necessary elements to work together to make the story feel more satisfying. One example concerns the relationships which inevitably develop between the main character and other characters. These will in turn develop a dynamic and interest of their own and play crucial roles in delivering the plot. Another is a variation in the scale of events. A series of small and irritating setbacks is not as interesting as a situation which grows in complexity or difficulty. To maintain interest your story is likely to have one (or more) real crises in it, where all the manifestations of the problem so far are concentrated in a decisive event, usually a clash or collision. This clash can be between competing individuals or forces or the protagonist's own competing needs (does she marry for love or for security? does he betray his brother or his country?) and they tend to concentrate the emotion of the reader. For this to work effectively the reader has to be able to invest in the character – to care about what happens to him – and must understand the value of what's at stake. This is all more meat on the bones of the story.

The set-up – the character and the status quo – is usually fairly straightforward, and the thing that happens that sets the story on its way – often called the *inciting incident* – might again not prove too difficult to settle on. Next comes the 'middle bit' – the heart of the story, and the most challenging section to write. It is significant that we talk about events of a story *unfolding*; a story can run into trouble when this is not what is actually happening. The middle part of stories invented by young children is often characterised by the repeated connective 'and then': A happens and then B happens and then C happens. This is not the unfolding of a story but the chronological extending of a story by a process of simple addition: it's not a plot so much as a series of events. In a story that unfolds rather than extends, the events involve influence and consequence: A happens *but then* B happens *so then* C happens, for example. If your story has somehow become stodgy and directionless it has probably veered away from this dynamic of cause and effect and become bogged down in mere sequence.

You have a broad trajectory for your story when you start writing because you know the beginning and have a sense of an ending (the desirability of having an ending in mind will be discussed further in Chapter 9) but this trajectory will not be a straight line – the most direct journey from A to Z, where everything goes right, is the least interesting and probably not worth writing about. This is another thing which sets the naive stories made by young children apart from literary stories: they often focus on nice things happening to nice people and lack interest for that very reason. The interest in adult fiction lies in imperfect people attempting to overcome obstacles, having to negotiate unsatisfactory situations and, in many cases, losing their way.

This part of a novel, often defined through phrases such as 'progressive complications' or 'rising action' and representing the bulk of the story (diagrams and systems can obscure this important fact) is where a great deal of its tension and interest lies. Returning to *Jaws*, there's a circumstance that makes the situation of the police chief much more compelling than the need to vanquish the giant killer shark would be on its own. When he wants to close the beaches to protect the public he faces the opposition of the mayor, who knows the closure will affect tourism – the main economy of the town. This isolates the police chief: if he is to protect the townspeople he's going to have to tackle this thing on his own, and in the face of opposition. This adds jeopardy as he tries to do the right thing without the town's support, while the people remain vulnerable to the monster. Jeopardy, along with conflict and obstacles, helps keep the reader onside.

It's not helpful to systematise how this middle section might work: you need room for manoeuvre, not a bunch of rules. This is where your characters help you define plot developments, and help things happen more organically. We can usefully recall Ray Bradbury on plot: 'It cannot be mechanical. It can only be dynamic.'[49] As long as you know roughly where you're heading you will get there. Embrace the freedom brought by uncertainty as to what happens next. Give your characters interesting challenges and see what they do: you'll not only learn what they're made of by putting them under pressure, but their responses will direct the story. Make life difficult for them: impose boundaries and obstacles. If you give your protagonist unlimited wishes you have a character who can resolve any problem and, for that reason, you almost certainly have an uninteresting story; give a character three wishes and you have the basis of an interesting story, because you have given them a predicament.

This brings us on to the most basic story-shape of all, developed as a tool by improvisational theatre expert Kenn Adams in the 1990s – though it's arguable that we've all known this shape from infancy:

Once upon a time ... – establishes a person in a time/place
And every day ... – establishes the status quo
But one day ... – introduces the inciting incident which will set the story rolling
Because of that ...

Because of that …
Because of that … etc.
Until finally … – things come to a decisive head/crisis/climax/day
   of reckoning
And, ever since then … – resolution: our character/their world has
   changed, usually for the better in some way, even if not everyone lives happily ever after.[50]

This model can be surprisingly helpful because it gives us a
shape on which to hang our story without being prescriptive
about the function or the detail of 'the middle bit'. And while it's
not recommended that you write to a template, this simple shape
can be very useful, if your story has run into trouble, as a means of
quickly checking it over and getting it back on track.

Similarly useful is the visual model Kurt Vonnegut developed
for mapping plot. You can try this yourself. Take a sheet of A4
paper and turn it on its side (landscape, rather than portrait).
Draw a vertical line all the way down the page next to the far left-
hand edge of the paper. This is the axis of fortune. The top end
of that line represents good fortune (health, wealth, achievement,
happiness, etc.) and the bottom end represents ill fortune (disas-
ter, disgrace, dispossession, misery, etc.). Mark the halfway point
on this line and draw a horizontal line right across the page. This
line is the axis of time: its left-hand end is the beginning of the
story, its right-hand end the conclusion.

The line you are going to plot will follow the journey of your
character through time and fortune and, if the story is to have any
interest, it is unlikely to be a straight one. One of the examples
Vonnegut plots in this way is the story of *Cinderella*. Where does
he start? If he places Cinderella right in the middle of the line
of fortune, that would fix her state at the beginning of the story
as neither good nor bad: as 'OK'. But as he points out, she is *not*
OK at the beginning of the story: her mother has died, so you'd
start her below the midpoint. Her father then marries a horrible
woman with two horrible daughters, who make Cinderella's life

more miserable, so the line extends diagonally down and to the right. Then life goes on, no better, no worse. The line continues to the right horizontally. Then comes the inciting incident (the event which kicks off the story proper): the invitation to the ball at the palace. This brief glimpse of happiness is not to have any immediate effect – Cinderella is not to be allowed to go to the ball, so nothing changes. But then the fairy godmother appears and provides Cinderella with everything she needs – a dress, shoes, a coach, attendants – and she's off to the palace. Her line rises sharply, crossing the midway line of fortune. Her line continues to rise steeply as she is admired by all, and meets the prince; they dance, they fall in love: up, up, up. Then it's midnight and Cinderella has to flee as the magic wears off, losing her slipper in her haste. The line falls straight down again: in the time it takes the clock to strike twelve she is reduced from 'princess' to her former state – or is she? As Vonnegut points out, no one can take away the unforgettable night with the prince, so although she falls below the midway line, she doesn't fall as low as to her starting point. Again, life goes on (the line moves horizontally to the right) while the prince searches for the owner of the slipper. It starts to look unlikely that he will ever find her but eventually he does – the slipper fits and Cinderella's line goes sharply up again, past the previous highpoint at the ball, up as far as it can go until you run out of paper, an off-the-scale representation of enduring happiness.

Stories reveal a variety of different trajectories; however, what is key to most satisfying stories is not the exact shape of the storyline but the fact that it crosses and recrosses the line of fortune. As we've said, it's very difficult to interest a reader in stories where only good or only bad things happen. (A notable exception, as Vonnegut points out, is Franz Kafka's *The Metamorphosis* [1915], which starts below the line and goes relentlessly downhill.) But when we put our characters or their goals in jeopardy we ramp up the reader's interest in what happens.

Mapping your story onto Vonnegut's frame can alert you to where there might be problems. Where there are long periods of flatlining – in other words, nothing is changing substantially – you could usefully look at what job, if any, that part of the story is actually doing. If you find the whole story occupies the space above the midway line, or it all happens below the line, you might want to consider how interesting a reader will find a story in which everything's good and continues to be good, or everything's terrible and continues to be terrible. Ultimately a compelling story has to earn the satisfaction we feel at its conclusion by having taken us on an eventful journey.

It's worth acknowledging the limitations of Vonnegut's storyline graph. He does so himself, pointing out that 'This rise and fall is artificial and pretends we know more about life than we really do. And perhaps a true masterpiece cannot be crucified on a cross of this design.' He cites *Hamlet* as beginning, like *Cinderella*, below the halfway line. Like Cinderella, Hamlet is young, a parent has died, and the other parent has remarried. But, unlike in *Cinderella*, the events are not readily identifiable as 'good' or 'bad' for Hamlet, and finally he is killed in a duel. 'If he goes to heaven,' Vonnegut continues, 'he's off-scale happy like Cinderella; if he's going to hell he's off-scale unhappy like Kafka's cockroach, but *we don't know.*' Vonnegut believes *Hamlet* is respected as a masterpiece because in other stories 'we are so seldom told the truth. And in *Hamlet* Shakespeare tells us we don't know enough about life to know what the good news is and the bad news is.'[51]

Stories are not exactly like life; they are a response to life, a way of training the apparent randomness of reality into shapes which imply meaning. In real life we cannot identify the beginning, the middle or the end of our own stories – let alone what was the good news and what the bad. Fiction is consoling precisely because of its tendency to impose design on the uncertainties and disorder of life, but the greatest stories may be those whose designs in some way acknowledge life's inherent unruliness.

Hiding plot – putting doors in alleyways

In general an engaging plot needs to be (in a broad sense and within its own terms) both surprising and plausible. It's a tricky balancing act: the writer must ensure that readers have the information which makes a surprising turn of events plausible, but must also avoid alerting them to the likelihood of it happening. Bernard Cornwell, who has written several series of novels, of which the *Sharpe* series is best-known, observes that 'the mechanics of the plot have to be hidden. The reader must never see the way they're being manipulated.'[52] He explains that he spends much of his writing life doing what he calls 'putting doors in alleyways':

> I'll use *Sharpe* as an example. Say Sharpe, in Chapter 12, finds himself in a blind alleyway with high walls he can't climb and his sword is broken and his rifle is empty and there are 20 Frenchmen staring at him with loaded guns. They say, 'Aha! Mr Sharpe, we have got you at last!' and they are right. They have: he's dead. What you have to do at that point is go back to Chapter 3 and put a door in that alleyway. So when they say, 'We have you Mr Sharpe,' he's able to step through. Now if you did that in Chapter 12, no one would believe you because they'd think, 'Oh, come on, that door wouldn't be there.' [But] they do believe you if you establish the door very early in the book. So that's what I do.[53]

As Cornwell makes clear, it's not usually a door in an alleyway, and it needn't be a *thing* at all: it can be the creation of the possibility for a certain kind of behaviour in a character – behaviour which, when it finally manifests itself, takes the reader by surprise but nevertheless makes sense in the light of something we already know. As Cornwell's account suggests, these are often details that the writer adds retroactively, because the plot turn was not part of the original plan; but if he's a skilful writer there should be no sign in the finished work that the added material was an afterthought.

It's often more effective to achieve this 'seeding' of unexpected but credible events by providing two or three small references rather than planting a single large signpost. So if your character is a child who suddenly astonishes the family by providing them with an answer to all their problems, you might have that child earlier in the story unobtrusively engaged in problem-solving games in the background of scenes where she is not actively participating, in such a way that this detail seems part of the wallpaper, part of the general fabric of family life. When she delivers her amazing solution the reader will recall her helping Grandma with an anagram in the crossword, fixing the vacuum cleaner, playing with a Rubik's cube – all now clearly clues to her talent, even though they may not have been noticed at the time. Whether you're hiding evidence in plain sight or putting doors in alleyways, you're helping to make your surprising turn of events credible by unobtrusively weaving significant details into the tapestry of your story.

Narrative time

Novels and short stories have traditionally unfolded in broadly linear fashion: that is, the main events of the narrative are in chronological order. In *Jane Eyre*, for example, the main story is told in the order in which Jane experiences it. As we have seen, however, there may be other, hidden stories running alongside or underneath the one initially available to the reader. It is only when we learn of the existence of the mad woman in the attic of the house Jane is living in that we realise there has been another story all along, running parallel to the one we have been following. And we will go on to learn the beginning of this story – concerning Mr Rochester's first marriage – which predates Jane's arrival at Thornfield. Linear stories, though in broad terms unfolding sequentially, will often in this way revisit or refer to the events of the past.

Indeed, once we start to look closely at fictional narratives we shall see that narrative time is seldom merely linear. Whenever a character remembers a moment from her past, or anticipates a future event, there is a subtle chronological shift. And some writers accentuate this fluidity, deliberately and significantly breaking with simple linear chronology.

Kazuo Ishiguro's *The Remains of the Day* (1989) has a double time-frame. It begins with the heading: 'Prologue: July 1956 – Darlington Hall'. In a nominal 'now' the butler Stevens reflects on recent events and considers the journey he will take over the next six days. The next section is headed: 'Day One – Evening – Salisbury'. The account is presented almost as if Stevens is making regular entries in a journal. ('Tonight, I find myself in a guest house in the city of Salisbury. The first day of my trip is now completed, and all in all, I must say I am quite satisfied.')

In alternating chapters, the novel is then an account of his trip of a few days (which culminates in a meeting with an old colleague, Miss Kenton, whom he hopes to persuade to return to work at Darlington Hall) and recollections of events over a period of many years of service at the Hall. So there are two parallel narratives in the book: Stevens's journal-like account of his trip, which unfolds in chronological order over six days, and episodes from his past at Darlington Hall, not necessarily in chronological order, but unfolding alongside the account of the trip. The two narratives meet as Stevens, at the end of the outward leg of his journey, meets up with Miss Kenton, a significant character in the longer story of his working life, and the conclusion provides a double ending – that is, an ending to both narrative threads. This arrangement works particularly well because a major theme of the book is Stevens's attempt to come to terms with the fact that he has devoted a life of service to a foolish and misguided man, suppressing his own needs in the process. Now, at the end of the day, he finally sees this.

In *All the Light We Cannot See* (2014) Anthony Doerr tells the story principally through two characters who are about to meet at the beginning of the novel but do not finally do so until very near the end. In terms of time, the novel is organised along similar lines to *The Remains of the Day*: events of a few days (in this case

7–12 August 1944) alternate with sections which visit the characters' earlier lives. Finally, past and present meet as the trajectories of the two main characters collide. Doerr chose this method to stimulate the reader's interest in the improbable convergence of the paths of a young German soldier, schooled by the Hitler Youth, and a blind French girl in illegal possession of a radio (in the circumstances, a capital offence). He thinks the fact that the reader knows at the outset of the novel that they are destined to meet creates tension, explaining: 'It's more exciting if you know what's going to happen. If I have dinner with you and then at the end I pull out a gun and shoot you, that's surprise; if I put the gun on the table at the beginning of the meal, that's suspense.'[54] So there are good reasons for the way both Ishiguro and Doerr organise their time-frames.

The disposition of the four sections of William Faulkner's *The Sound and the Fury* (1929) suggests a similarly purposeful disruption of linear chronology. Although three of the sections chronicle the events of three consecutive days in 1928, the sections are not in chronological order – the sequence in the novel is 7, 6, 8 April – and they are interrupted by a section dealing with events that took place in 1910. But it's in the first of these sections that Faulkner's experiments with narrative time take their most radical and challenging form. The narrative voice follows, in impressionistic manner, the experience of Benjy, mentally disabled and unable to differentiate clearly between past events and present experience.

It can be difficult to grasp what is going on, particularly on a first reading of the novel. Faulkner gives the reader some assistance by the use of italics to indicate time-shifts, but his method isn't entirely consistent, and there's a continual blurring of the boundaries between one time-frame and another. This brief extract suggests the flavour and effect of Benjy's narrative:

> … we stopped in the hall and Caddy knelt and put her arms around me and her cold bright face against mine. She smelled like trees.

'You're not a poor baby. Are you. You've got your Caddy. Haven't you got your Caddy.'

Can't you shut up that moaning and slobbering, Luster said. Ain't you shamed of yourself, making all this racket. We passed the carriage house, where the carriage was. It had a new wheel.

'Git in, now, and set still until your maw come.' Dilsey said. She shoved me into the carriage. T. P. held the reins.[55]

Benjy's recollection of his sister, Caddy, belongs to the distant past; the italicised section represents, in this instance, the narrative present; and what follows represents another memory, sparked by the sight of the carriage – we understand from internal evidence that the second memory occupies a different time-frame from the first. If you think this is confusing you're absolutely right, but our difficulties as readers help us to empathise with Benjy's confusion and his largely incommunicable distress, and perhaps open us up to important questions concerning our own understanding of time.

Virginia Woolf's *The Years* (1937) is also, as its title suggests, centrally concerned with time. As with *The Sound and the Fury*, each of its sections is headed with a date, in this case from 1880 to the novel's present day. *The Years* is one of Woolf's less obviously experimental novels and the sequence of dates is conventionally linear, but the many gaps in the sequence highlight an important fact: it lies in the writer's power to control the flow of time within her narrative.

You'll know this, of course: it's obviously both inevitable and desirable that a narrative will compress or elide events. But the point is worth emphasising because many writers will at times experience the dulling effect of writing a passage merely or primarily in order to carry the narrative through to the next significant event. When that happens, it's worth considering ways of cutting more directly to the essential stuff. This can be done verbally – a sentence such as: 'By the time he reached the summit the sun was rising' might save you and your reader a long slog up a mountain; or you might use a chapter break (or the minor break represented on the page by an expanded space between the lines) to indicate the passage of time.

The decision to make a chronological leap may be planned, or it may arise, in the process of writing, from an instinctive feeling that not enough is happening to justify lingering on a particular scene or event. But you might usefully consider the possibility that you will be able to create the justification you need: suppose the journey up the mountain isn't a slog at all, but a period of visionary intensity during which your protagonist, acutely aware of every detail of his surroundings, arrives at a new understanding of the relationship between humankind and the natural world – wouldn't that give you reason to let the narrative unfold more slowly? In these, as in other matters relating to your fictional world, you are in charge.

– 6 –

Form and length

~

Definitions

When we first conceive of our work of fiction we may not be sure how long it is eventually going to be – not simply in the obvious sense of not knowing whether a novel is going to come in at 80,000 words or 90,000, but in a more significant way: we may not even know whether it's going to be a novel or a short story. When Joseph Conrad first wrote to his agent about *Lord Jim* (1900) he believed he would be submitting a story of about 20,000 words; as it turned out, he was actually embarking on a very substantial novel. The story, developing organically along unforeseen lines, resisted the form he had planned for it. This suggests the value of remaining open to the possibilities offered by a developing narrative, but it doesn't mean that there's no point at all in thinking about the length of our stories until they're finished; on the contrary, the more we understand about the various forms of fiction, as defined by length, the more likely we are to be in control of our effects.

Definitions vary but, broadly speaking, we might say that the typical contemporary novel will have a wordcount of somewhere between 80,000 and 100,000 (though longer novels are not uncommon, and any work of fiction above 50,000 words might reasonably be considered a novel); that the short story may be anything between 1,000 and 17,500 words long; and that the intermediate form, the novella, has been defined as a story of between 20,000 and 40,000 words. We needn't spend any time worrying about the 18,000-word story or the 45,000-word story, both of which fall between these categories: in matters of this kind, boundaries are almost always contentious and often arbitrary, and our concern here is simply to establish a working sense of the relationship between these three forms.

In recent years there has been considerable interest in fictions even shorter than the short story. Generally referred to as 'flash fiction', such stories may range from 6 to 1,000 words in length, and we shall be examining them in more detail later in this chapter.

Novels

The novel's length allows the writer to develop themes and characters over an extended period of narrative time. For example, D. H. Lawrence's *The Rainbow* (1915), chronicling the lives of three generations of a Nottinghamshire family, *needs* to unfold at length; it's very difficult to imagine it as a short story. And the lives of the Brangwen family spill over into a further novel, *Women in Love* (1920), more tightly focused in terms of its time-frame, but even more searching in its exploration of the theme that most obviously connects the two novels: the complex workings of human sexuality.

Stories have a natural tendency to grow beyond the framework we initially envisage for them: we may, for example, find that an event we had thought of as a minor episode takes on a new importance in relation to other events, and therefore requires expansion; or we introduce a new character to engage in debate with our protagonist, and then find that character developing in ways that bring her from the background of the story to the foreground. Knowing this (and perhaps knowing, too, that agents and editors are more likely to be interested in a good novel than a good collection of short stories) we may well be inclined to aim, in the first instance, for a novel, reckoning to adjust our expectations if the hoped-for content doesn't materialise. But we might save ourselves a good deal of time by familiarising ourselves with the characteristics of the short story: if we find that the story we have in mind can be matched up with those characteristics, this may direct us from the start to the shorter form and prevent us from embarking on an unnecessarily long journey.

Short stories

If you look at a range of short stories you'll find that they tend to share certain basic features; these features don't separate the short story neatly from the novel, but they do suggest significant differences. It's more helpful to speak in comparative terms than to set up sharp distinctions, so we might say that it's generally the case that, compared with a typical novel, a short story will:

− have fewer characters (often only two or three);
− unfold over a shorter time-frame (often in what is apparently real time);
− have fewer locations (often only one);
− have a single theme;
− have a single plot.

Each of these features might be presented as a constraint. A short story can't usually cope with a large cast of characters − there isn't time for the reader to get to know them all because there isn't room for the writer to develop them satisfactorily. Nor will it usually be able to deal with long time spans. (Maupassant's 'The Necklace' is unusual in covering ten years, but the decade separating the two parts of the story is summarised in a couple of hundred words.) It's also restricted in location and theme, and there's usually no scope for subplots. But these constraints may also be advantages: in each case their tendency to sharpen the writer's focus can be a source of narrative energy. Depending on the story we have to tell, the constraints of the short story may actually suit us very well, obliging us to strip away the inessential and concentrate on what is most important.

Although slackness should be avoided in all literary forms, a novel can afford to unfold at a more leisurely pace, allowing the novelist to accumulate detail in ways that, while adding to the general texture, may not be crucial to the story. In a short story any detail acquires heightened significance, because it occupies more space proportionate to the whole than it would in a novel. 'Her thumb and third finger were stained with ink' can occupy one ten-thousandth of a novel but can occupy one three-hundredth of a short story, so it inevitably acquires greater prominence in the latter context. When you introduce any detail into a short story you have to be aware of this difference of weight and effect.

Much of the above suggests parallels with poetry, and it's significant that discussions of short fiction are almost as likely to draw comparisons with poetry as they are to suggest contrasts with the novel. Alan Sillitoe observes that 'A [short] story is an encapsulated piece of work – it's short, it's poetic, it's high-powered, and it exists on its own. It's like a long poem used to be in the last century',[56] while for Frank O'Connor the short story is 'the nearest thing I know to lyric poetry'. He explains that 'a novel actually requires far more logic and far more knowledge of circumstances, whereas a short story can have the sort of detachment from circumstances that lyric poetry has'.[57] This 'detachment from circumstances', this singling out and focusing on one idea or moment, is the heart of the matter: it's not brevity alone that links the lyric poem and the short story, but concentration.

The compression of the short story presents particular challenges, and the demanding nature of the form has been remarked on by a number of writers, including V. S. Pritchett, who described it as 'exquisitely difficult', and Truman Capote, who observed: 'When seriously explored, the short story seems to me the most difficult and disciplining form of prose writing extant.'[58]

Should we, as writers, be deterred by the acknowledged difficulty of short fiction? Well, we need to recognise the challenges but, as Erskine Caldwell points out, the short story may offer tremendous advantages:

> To me, short-story writing is the essence of writing. I think a writer should always write short stories before he tries to write a novel. You have better control because a short story is concentrated into a small area. You also have better range because a short story can be anywhere from one to fifty pages long. You can mould it much better than you can a novel. A novel is a great, expansive thing. You can't make a change at one point without affecting something another fifty pages away.[59]

You don't have to accept every aspect of this assessment (why does a short story offer 'better range' at one to fifty pages than a novel at a hundred and fifty pages to a thousand?) to appreciate the essential argument, and to see the value of taking up the challenge.

The short story is, as Caldwell suggests, an excellent place for a developing writer to start, partly for practical reasons. Think of it this way: would you start out as an artist by embarking on a massive, densely populated canvas, or by painting a number of smaller portraits? If you were a composer, would your first work be a symphony, or might you learn the ropes by starting with a sonata, a sonatina, a song? Thinking along these lines, you might want to consider the practical reasons for serving an apprenticeship with the short story rather than starting with the novel.

As you may be aware from your own experience, developing writers will often keep rewriting the first few chapters of their novel, losing heart each time, trying to find the voice they want. Short stories give you the freedom to experiment with different voices, while increasing the chances that you'll complete one or more of the works you've begun. The satisfaction of completing something is important for your morale as a writer. If your drawers are already stuffed with uncompleted manuscripts, a good piece of advice might be: don't keep plugging away at an old novel, and don't start a new one; start (and finish) a short story. You don't need to have published something before you can call yourself a writer, but it might be fair to say that you need to have finished something.

Short stories enable you to test ideas, characters and situations without being committed to them long-term. If you realise, half-way through a novel, that you're flogging a dead horse and have to abandon the work, you'll have lost maybe hundreds of pages and a great deal of your time. You can afford to discard a couple of your first short stories with far less loss and yet have learnt as much, if not more, about writing.

Because a short story can be drafted and written relatively quickly, your ideas don't have time to go stale on you – you can get the words down while the initial inspiration is still fresh and interesting. And you might relish the sense of freedom that comes from being able to build on a small idea rather than trying to impose order on the large and often unruly collection of ideas that normally go into the making of a novel. You'll find it relatively easy to hold the whole shape of a short story in your head, and this makes it more manageable, both in the initial writing and the subsequent editing.

These practical considerations should prove helpful, but they shouldn't be seen as definitive. It may be that the story you want to tell actually demands the novel form, and it's certainly possible that your short story will, as you work on it, grow naturally into something larger. Take the considerations simply as guides and, above all, don't let their practical nature obscure the important artistic truth that the writing of short stories isn't *merely* a use-ful apprenticeship: the finest short stories can certainly stand, as works of art, alongside the finest novels – and possibly even, as William Boyd suggests here, above them:

> The short story can seem larger, more resonant and memorable than the shortness of the form would appear capable of delivering. ... The true, fully functioning short story should achieve a totality of effect that makes it almost impossible to encapsulate or summarise. For it is in this area, it seems to me, that the short story and the novel divide, where the effect of reading a good short story is quite different from the effect of reading a good novel. The great modern short stories

possess a quality of mystery and beguiling resonance about them – a complexity of afterthought – that cannot be pinned down or analysed. Bizarrely, in this situation, the whole is undeniably greater than the sum of its component parts.[60]

We don't have to subscribe entirely to Boyd's sharp sense of divergence to appreciate the essential point of his argument: that the short story may be particularly well suited to the communication, by suggestion, of the complex and elusive truths that lie at the heart of the greatest writing.

Flash fiction

How short can a story be? There's a famous micro-narrative, sometimes erroneously attributed to Hemingway, that runs, in its entirety, as follows: 'For sale: baby shoes; never worn.' Whatever we think the story is, there's no doubt that there's a story here. The trio of two-word phrases, not even amounting to a complete sentence, demonstrates the potential for extremely short fiction, though very few pieces as brief as this are anything like as satisfying.

The length of flash fiction (or the short short story) is understood slightly differently in different contexts (some competitions limit entries to 250 words; some anthologies set their limit at 750 words), but flash fiction is generally understood to mean a story of fewer than 1,000 words. Usually a work of flash fiction can be fitted onto two facing pages of a book – which of course can vary in what they can accommodate. Other definitions resist word-count as a measurement and describe such stories as 'smoke-long' – meaning that they take as long to read as it takes to smoke a cigarette – or 'palm-sized'.

Definitions are complicated by a profusion of subgenres. 'Microfiction', 'nanofiction' and 'sudden fiction' are terms used by some interchangeably with 'flash fiction', but by others to denote subcategories of flash with specific wordcounts. Other subcategories include the 'drabble' (100 words) and the 'dribble' or 'mini-saga'

(50 words). These very short forms are examples of 'constrained' writing – writing practised under strictly prescribed rules.

Although the term flash fiction is relatively new, the very short story has been around for a long time: Chekhov, Kafka and Hemingway all wrote what we would now call flash fiction. But we can go back much further than Chekhov to find very short stories. About 600 BC we find the storyteller Aesop; his very short moral stories are known as fables. Jump forward 600 years and we find another teller of very short moral stories, Jesus Christ; his stories are known as parables.

These early examples of flash fiction may be brief, but their implications are considerable. Behind each of them stands another, bigger story – a story that transcends the characters and the context of the one being told. We understand that Aesop's fable of the tortoise and the hare isn't simply about a race between two animals; it's also, and more importantly, about the value of diligence and perseverance as set against qualities that might look, at first sight, more impressive but which prove fragile. Similarly, we'll quickly see that the parable of the lost sheep has less to do with animal husbandry than with the desirability of concentrating effort and resources on those few people who have lost their way in life, rather than on the many who are managing pretty well.

The ability to suggest a big subject in a few words is also characteristic of contemporary flash fiction, which often implies a hinterland, a more expansive area behind the story's focal point. A story of this kind might, for example, capture a small but significant moment in a relationship, a moment that reveals, in condensed form, something essential to the relationship as a whole. Flash fiction can take as its focal point an incident as mundane as (to take four actual examples) throwing away food, cleaning the house, a change in the weather or swallowing a fishbone.[61] In each case the incident functions as a portal through which something much larger can be glimpsed. Joyce Carol Oates sees flash fiction as closely related to poetry, which often works in a similar way:

Very short fictions are nearly always experimental, exquisitely cali-
brated, reminiscent of [Robert] Frost's definition of a poem – a structure of words that consumes itself as it unfolds, like ice melting on a
stove ...[62]

We noted earlier in this chapter a relationship between the
short story and poetry, but it's unlikely that we'd ever confuse one
with the other; in the case of flash fiction, however, the resem-
blance may be so close that distinctions blur. Simon Armitage's
publishers categorise his collection *Seeing Stars* (2010) as poetry,
and Armitage himself describes the pieces in it as poems; yet if
the collection had been marketed as flash fiction, no one would be
asking for their money back. Here's an example from that collection, 'I'll Be There to Love and Comfort You':

The couple next door were testing the structural fabric
of the house with their difference of opinion. 'I can't
take much more of this,' I said to Mimi my wife. Right
then there was another almighty crash, as if every pan
in the kitchen had clattered to the tiled floor. Mimi said,
'Try to relax. Take one of your tablets.' She brewed a
pot of camomile tea and we retired to bed. But the
pounding and caterwauling carried on right into the small
hours. I was dreaming that the mother of all asteroids
was locked on a collision course with planet Earth,
when unbelievably a fist came thumping through the
bedroom wall just above the headboard. In the metallic
light of the full moon I saw the bloody knuckles and a
cobweb tattoo on the flap of skin between finger and
thumb, before the fist withdrew. Mimi's face was
powdered with dirt and dust, but she didn't wake. She
looked like a corpse pulled from the rubble of an
earthquake after five days in a faraway country famous
only for its paper kites.

I peered through the hole in the wall. It was dark on the
other side, with just occasional flashes of purple or green
light, like those weird electrically-powered life forms

zipping around in the ocean depths. There was a rustling
noise, like something stirring in a nest of straw, then a
voice, a voice no bigger than a sixpence, crying for help.
Now Mimi was right next to me. 'It's her,' she said. I
said, 'Don't be crazy, Mimi, she'd be twenty-four by
now.' 'It's her I tell you. Get her back, do you hear me?
GET HER BACK.' I rolled up my pyjama sleeve and
pushed my arm into the hole, first to my elbow, then as
far as my shoulder and neck. The air beyond was
clammy and damp, as if I'd reached into a nineteenth-
century London street in late November, fog rolling in up
the river, a cough in a doorway. Mimi was out of her
mind by now. My right cheek and my ear were flat to the
wall. Then slowly but slowly I opened my fist to the
unknown. And out of the void, slowly but slowly it
came: the pulsing starfish of a child's hand, swimming
and swimming and coming to settle on my upturned
palm.

This is set out exactly as in the collection, with justification only
of the left-hand margin and not the right, a pattern characteristic of poetry but not of published prose. However, the lineation
seems more arbitrary than is usual in poetry, even free verse –
would it matter if the lines were broken up differently? – and
it's evident that the piece straddles the hazy boundary between
poetry and prose. This isn't the place to discuss where poetry
ends and prose begins – not a particularly fruitful debate for
writers in any case – but what's clear from the collection as a
whole is that Armitage has very successfully occupied this rich
liminal area.

However we define it, Armitage's collection shows the advantages of thinking small. Flash fiction is able to exploit the fact
that there are styles of writing which would become tedious for
the reader at greater length, but that work effectively on a one-
off basis and a very small scale. It's an ideal vehicle for ideas and
effects which can't be sustained for long. For example, James
Claffey's 'Skull of a Sheep' (2011) begins: 'You are in a car speeding

through Dublin toward the West year after year … ' and goes on to describe a holiday journey annually undertaken by a child, encapsulating all of those journeys in one sentence which extends over two pages. Jamaica Kincaid's 'Girl' (1978) similarly uses a single long sentence to quite different effect, representing the relentless monologue of a mother's critical advice to her daughter: the momentum of the sentence propels the reader forward, bowling on with unstoppable force, revealing an increasingly dark and disturbing worldview.

Gregory Burnham's 'Subtotals' (1988) is a list, a record of the number of times the narrator calculates he has done certain things (or had certain things done to him). The miscellaneous nature of the things counted, the apparent lack of conscious organisation of the data, the things he chooses to provide a category for yet scores as zero, all contribute to our understanding of an individual life, an understanding which we revise with each new piece of information. What seems random is made sense of by the reader: Burnham's method actively invites us to contribute to the meaning of what he's written and make a story out of it ourselves. Lydia Davis's 'Problem' (1986) encourages the reader to see the complexity of family economic relationships by representing them as a mathematical problem to be solved. Such stories push at the boundary of narrative, offering considerable space for the reader to participate in the construction of their meaning. In 'The Interpreter for the Tribunal' (2007), Tony Eprile has the narrative voice slip unannounced between the interrogator and the person being interrogated, back and forth, blurring the boundary between the torturer and the tortured, conveying both the confusion of the situation and the sense in which both might be victims of the wider narrative, prisoners of the same system – might even be aspects of the same person. Such experiments can work beautifully in the very short form, and that may in fact be the only place they can work.

Just as the form is ideal for styles which are difficult to sustain over a longer piece, it's also the ideal place for the single brilliant idea: the 'what if … ' concept that really isn't big enough for a short story, let alone a novel. This may explain its attraction for writers of science fiction and magical realism – or speculative fiction in general – which are often concept-led (Arthur C. Clarke, Ray Bradbury and Kurt Vonnegut all contributed to the genre). Flash fiction allows Spencer Holst to wonder: what if some trained dancing bears escaped from a circus, bred and multiplied, set up their own community on a remote island where they and their descendants lived for many years undisturbed by humans until the arrival of naturalists who observed that 'on nights when the sky is bright and the moon is full, they gather to dance'? It allows Bruce Holland Rogers to wonder: what if when a baby learns language it forgets everything it knew before, things of great value that can't be put into language and so are lost forever? And it allows Luigi Malerba to wonder: what if the famous view of Rome afforded from the Gianicolo hill started to wear out just by being looked at by too many people?[63]

These are some of the joys of flash fiction: the severe constraint of the very short form can, paradoxically, prove wonderfully liberating. However, the form has its critics who see it very much as the poor relation of the short story. Its recent popularity has been ascribed to a cash-rich/time-poor economy. For those who worry about our diminishing attention spans, very short stories are 'signs of cultural decadence, bonbons for lazy readers, chocolates stuffed with snow', observes Charles Baxter, while reasonably countering that 'no-one ever said that sonnets or haikus were evidence of short attention spans'.[64] The best flash fiction is impervious to criticism of this kind. But the democratisation of communication offered by the internet means that there is a great deal of flash fiction out there, and the vast majority of it is simply not very good. The illusion that shorter must be easier may also play a part in this.

While a piece of flash fiction will take a lot less time to write than a novel, the flash fiction-writer may well labour longer over her two pages than a novelist will labour over any two pages of her novel. You are much more likely to produce a fine work of this kind if you are aware how difficult it is than if you think it's easy. Like a good lyric poem, a good piece of flash fiction will bear multiple readings, revealing something different each time. As with all writing, it will be as good as you make it.

– 7 –

Dialogue

~

Let's look at the first chapter of Jane Austen's *Pride and Prejudice* (1813). The opening sentence is, of course, one of the most famous in English literature – and, dazzled by this, we may not notice how cleverly the author uses the conversation that follows as a concise way of introducing the characters and setting the plot in motion. She manages the scene in such a manner as to deliver a great deal of important information in a credible and apparently natural way:

> It is a truth universally acknowledged, that a single man in possession of a good fortune must be in want of a wife.
>
> However little known the feelings or views of such a man may be on his first entering a neighbourhood, this truth is so well fixed in the minds of the surrounding families, that he is considered as the rightful property of some one or other of their daughters.
>
> 'My dear Mr. Bennet,' said his lady to him one day, 'have you heard that Netherfield Park is let at last?'
>
> Mr. Bennet replied that he had not.
>
> 'But it is,' returned she; 'for Mrs. Long has just been here, and she told me all about it.'
>
> Mr. Bennet made no answer.
>
> 'Do not you want to know who has taken it?' cried his wife impatiently.
>
> 'You want to tell me, and I have no objection to hearing it.'
>
> This was invitation enough.
>
> 'Why, my dear, you must know, Mrs. Long says that Netherfield is taken by a young man of large fortune from the north of England; that he came down on Monday in a chaise and four to see the place, and was so much delighted with it that he agreed with Mr. Morris immediately; that he is to take possession before Michaelmas, and some of his servants are to be in the house by the end of next week.'

'What is his name?'

'Bingley.'

'Is he married or single?'

'Oh! single, my dear, to be sure! A single man of large fortune; four or five thousand a year. What a fine thing for our girls!'

'How so? how can it affect them?'

'My dear Mr. Bennet,' replied his wife, 'how can you be so tiresome! You must know that I am thinking of his marrying one of them.'

'Is that his design in settling here?'

'Design! nonsense, how can you talk so! But it is very likely that he may fall in love with one of them, and therefore you must visit him as soon as he comes.'

'I see no occasion for that. You and the girls may go, or you may send them by themselves, which perhaps will be still better; for, as you are as handsome as any of them, Mr. Bingley might like you the best of the party.'

'My dear, you flatter me. I certainly have had my share of beauty, but I do not pretend to be any thing extraordinary now. When a woman has five grown up daughters, she ought to give over thinking of her own beauty.'

'In such cases, a woman has not often much beauty to think of.'

'But, my dear, you must indeed go and see Mr. Bingley when he comes into the neighbourhood.'

'It is more than I engage for, I assure you.'

'But consider your daughters. Only think what an establishment it would be for one of them. Sir William and Lady Lucas are determined to go, merely on that account, for in general, you know they visit no new comers. Indeed you must go, for it will be impossible for us to visit him, if you do not.'

'You are over-scrupulous, surely. I dare say Mr. Bingley will be very glad to see you; and I will send a few lines by you to assure him of my hearty consent to his marrying which ever he chooses of the girls; though I must throw in a good word for my little Lizzy.'

'I desire you will do no such thing. Lizzy is not a bit better than the others; and I am sure she is not half so handsome as Jane, nor half so good humoured as Lydia. But you are always giving *her* the preference.'

'They have none of them much to recommend them,' replied he; 'they are all silly and ignorant like other girls; but Lizzy has something more of quickness than her sisters.'

'Mr. Bennet, how can you abuse your own children in such a way? You take delight in vexing me. You have no compassion on my poor nerves.'

'You mistake me, my dear. I have a high respect for your nerves. They are my old friends. I have heard you mention them with consideration these twenty years at least.'

'Ah! you do not know what I suffer.'

'But I hope you will get over it, and live to see many young men of four thousand a year come into the neighbourhood.'

'It will be no use to us if twenty such should come, since you will not visit them.'

'Depend upon it, my dear, that when there are twenty I will visit them all.'

Mr. Bennet was so odd a mixture of quick parts, sarcastic humour, reserve, and caprice, that the experience of three and twenty years had been insufficient to make his wife understand his character. *Her* mind was less difficult to develop. She was a woman of mean understanding, little information, and uncertain temper. When she was discontented, she fancied herself nervous. The business of her life was to get her daughters married; its solace was visiting and news.

The first thing we might notice is that this chapter is predominantly dialogue – 80 per cent in fact. As the conversation proceeds we learn that the Bennets are to have a new neighbour (the wealthy, youthful and – crucially – single Mr Bingley) and that Mrs Bennet sees this event as a golden opportunity to marry off one of their five daughters. It's worth noting that if Mr Bennet were to agree immediately to go along with her to visit Mr Bingley the necessity for further conversation (and therefore the opportunity for Austen to give us further information) would end. His resistance leads to our being given further details about three of the daughters – one of whom will be the principal character in the story.

The scene works, despite the load of exposition it is carrying, because the dialogue isn't *merely* expository: the necessity for it is embedded in the narrative. It gives the impression of arising as much from the needs and tendencies of the characters as from Austen's authorial duty to convey necessary information to the reader. When dialogue feels unnatural it's often because it has obviously been introduced for the sole purpose of giving the reader information – because the writer has provided no good reason for the exchange to take place. Here, in this superbly crafted passage, Mrs Bennet is shown to have an agenda that she will relentlessly pursue. Mr Bennet is sceptical and only mildly interested but she needs to get him on board. So there's the motivation for the conversation. Equally importantly, she has information that he doesn't have, and that she is desperate to share with him; so it's both reasonable and realistic for him to ask her questions which enable her to deliver information, and natural for her to give him far more information than he actually requests.

The dialogue also works to develop character. Although Mr and Mrs Bennet speak roughly the same number of words, we get the impression that she is the more talkative of the two, because she is more willing to pursue the conversation. Her speech seems more urgent, even breathless – at one point she 'cries impatiently' and Austen gives her speeches seven exclamation marks whereas Mr Bennet's get none. We learn about her 'nerves' and also that Mr Bennet is capable of successfully flattering her. Long before we reach the last paragraph we are likely to have worked out for ourselves what that paragraph explicitly tells us about the characters of Mr and Mrs Bennet. Mrs Bennet's impetuous enthusiasm, her loquaciousness and her desperation to see her daughters married, as well as Mr Bennet's steadiness and scepticism, have already been revealed to us in the preceding dialogue.

It's worth noting that Austen doesn't go in for a lot of attribution here – that is, there isn't a great deal of 'he said/she said'. If we lop off the narrative comments at the top and bottom of the chapter we find only 33 words (out of 706) that aren't dialogue. And while these words are sometimes phrases attributing dialogue to the speaker ('said his lady to him one day'; 'cried his wife impatiently', etc.) they may stand instead of dialogue ('Mr Bennet replied that he had not'; 'Mr Bennet made no answer').

Austen has only two characters here and has sharply differentiated their voices, so she doesn't need to be constantly reminding the reader who is speaking. After '"My dear Mr. Bennet," replied his wife', the speaker changes eleven times before we're reminded who is speaking, and there are no reminders after that.

Before we unpack some of these strategies and move on to look in detail at how dialogue works – and how you can make it work for your writing – you might find it interesting to reread Austen's chapter with an enhanced alertness to the economy and efficiency with which she sets out her stall. It's not just the memorable opening sentence, at once emphatic and questionable, that reveals her mastery; from a technical point of view the whole chapter is a triumph.

Dialogue matters

If, as a reader, you have ever skimmed through parts of a novel, you might be able to confirm Elmore Leonard's belief that readers tend to skip 'thick paragraphs of prose' but not dialogue.[65] This may be as true of non-fiction as of fiction: when we read a newspaper article we may find ourselves paying particular attention to quotes – what people have actually said – and rather less to the journalist's summaries or analyses. Words matter, and speech, whether in life or in fiction, often seems to matter most.

Before we look at how we can make dialogue work for our stories it's worth considering when we need it – and when we don't. In comparison with reported speech, dialogue will often give greater vitality to a scene. First, consider this passage:

After we'd gone to bed I read for a while. I thought Jonathan was asleep but after a while he sat up and said we needed to talk – he had something to tell me. He had been seeing someone and he wanted a divorce. I asked him what he meant. I asked how long it had been going on and he made out it didn't matter and tried to play it down but I begged him just to tell the truth – the truth couldn't be worse than me knowing he was lying. At first he said it had started three years ago, then five years ago, and finally admitted it was ten years ago. I guessed it was my sister but eventually it turned out it was my brother. Charlotte woke up and came in and asked why we were shouting. I tried to explain but Jonathan said she was just a child and told me to have more self-discipline. I covered Charlotte's ears and told Jonathan what I thought of him.

Summary has its place, but this scene is crying out for dramatisation: we want to hear the characters' voices. As soon as we make them speak we find them doing all sorts of other things too. Now look at this version of the same events:

After we'd gone to bed I read for a while. I was just about to put the light off when Jonathan sat up.

'We need to talk,' he said. That's when I began to panic. That's my line. Jonathan never needs to talk. 'I've got something to tell you.'

I laid my book down on the duvet, face down, open at my place, carefully. I had the feeling that everything from here on had to be done carefully.

'I've been seeing someone,' he said, staring steadily at the book. 'I want a divorce.'

'What do you mean?' My voice sounded odd. Not mine. Feeble and whining. 'Who is it?'

'It doesn't matter.'

'It does matter.'

He ran his hand over his face.

'How long has this been going on?'

'It doesn't matter. It's not important. I want to leave anyway.'

A cold fury started to seep through me. My hands were shaking. 'I need to know,' I said slowly. 'I need to know how long you've been lying to me. I need to know the truth.'

'It really doesn't matter.'

I jumped out of bed. I wanted somehow to make it different. 'How can you possibly know what matters to me? How dare you decide what matters? It matters. Tell me. Now.'

He sighed, covered his face with both hands. 'It started three years ago.'

'Liar.' He covers his face when he's lying. Like a child. 'You bloody liar.'

'Five years ago.'

'Tell me the truth!' My throat hurt from the effort of not screaming at him.

He dropped his hands to the duvet. 'Ten years,' he said.

Ten years? 'Ten years matters,' I said. 'Ten years really matters.' I started crying. I wanted it all to stop. I wanted to pick up my book where I had left off and everything to go back to how it was. 'Who is it? Is it Ann?'

'Since you must know,' Jonathan said, 'it's James.'

'Jesus Christ. You're gay? You've always been gay?' I was screaming now. 'Which James? James at work?'

He shook his head. He looked straight at me. 'Your brother. I'm sorry.'

I couldn't begin to think what this meant. I just felt the shock of it. 'How could you do this to us?'

Charlotte was standing in the doorway.

'Darling ... '

'Why are you shouting? Mummy, why are you crying?'

'Because your father – '

'Nicky! She's a child! Have some discipline for God's sake!'

'Discipline?' I shrieked. 'You bloody hypocrite! Where was your discipline when you were fucking my brother? For ten years! Where was your discipline then?'

It's true that these changes involve something more than the simple substitution of dialogue for reported speech, but the act of realising a scene in dialogue inevitably forces the writer into closer relationship with his characters. In entering their space and giving them voice he can create a dynamic tension far greater than is usually provided by reported speech.

It's worth remembering, however, that there are situations in which dialogue is definitely not required:

'Where to?'

'King's Cross, please,' Duncan replied.

'Return or single?'

'Return please.'
'Underground?'
'Sorry?'
'Do you want it to include the Underground?'
'Er, yes I think so. Yes please.'
'So you're returning today.'
'No, no, Tuesday. I need a return – coming back on Tuesday.'
'Then you can't include the Underground. You can only include the Underground if you're coming back the same day.'

While this dialogue may be realistic, it's also inert; it would probably be much kinder to your reader to replace the whole lot with: 'Duncan bought a ticket to London.' Even if one or more of these details is significant in terms of your plot, there are more economical (and therefore less tedious) ways of showing the transaction.

Dialogue matters, and its content has to matter. Like any other part of a narrative, dialogue can be a waste of the reader's time if it doesn't progress plot or illuminate character in some way. And while whole stories can be told through dialogue, we have to be careful that there *is* a story. Lengthy conversations about the meaning of life or the nature of evil don't usually make for engaging fiction; energy of dialogue and energy of plot are intimately related.

Carrying information in dialogue

We have to be very careful when using dialogue to convey information to the reader. If it's too heavily weighted with exposition it quickly becomes artificial; the reader can immediately see what we're up to and the illusion of realism is shattered:

'Where to?'
'Kings Cross,' replied Duncan. 'I need to get to London urgently – my mother has just died in mysterious circumstances and I need to find a 24-hour dry cleaner.'

'Return or single?'

'Return please. I have to get back for the funeral although I am not looking forward to meeting my relations who clearly find my behaviour highly suspicious.'

'Underground?'

'Sorry? I am finding it hard to concentrate on account of the terrible thoughts which haunt my every waking moment.'

'Do you want it to include the Underground?'

'Er, yes I think so. Yes please. Although generally I do suffer from a fear of confined spaces. So if she had had an accident in the cellar at the remote house where she lived alone that would have had nothing to do with me.'

'So you're returning today.'

'No, no, Tuesday. I need a return – coming back on Tuesday. For the funeral, in case you missed that the first time I said it.'

'Then you can't include the Underground. You can only include the Underground if you're coming back the same day. Are you feeling alright, sir? Your hands are shaking, you are sweating profusely and you appear to have a gash on your head as though you had been stabbed by a crochet-hook or something similar.'

While dialogue can usefully advance the reader's understanding of unfolding events, it can prove alienating if it seems to be relentlessly prosecuting plot at the expense of realism. Dialogue can be used to convey all kinds of information to the reader but, as we have seen with Mr and Mrs Bennet, there has to be a reason why A is conveying all this information to B. If you have to explain some historical situation or give some technical details which the reader needs to know in order to understand what's going on, you may end up with A delivering a long explicatory speech which feels more like a passage from a textbook than anything a person might really say. Realising its unnaturalness, you may be tempted to fix this after the event by having B exclaim 'You've done your homework!' or 'Quite a speech!' or something similar. But you're not fixing it because the speech has already been boring and artificial and you can't undo its shortcomings by acknowledging and implicitly apologising for them. Writers need to fix things that don't work before the reader sees them.

There are strategies to help you avoid temporarily reducing a character to a mere channel for data. The first question you might ask yourself is: is dialogue really the best way to deliver this information? If B needs this information are there other means by which she could get it? If it's the reader, rather than B, who needs the information, are there other means by which he could get it? If you have decided dialogue is definitely the way to go you need to find a reason why A would tell B. If you can't find a good reason, invent one. Your characters exist, in part at least, to serve the story, so give A a reason to tell B, or B a reason to want or need to know.

In *Wolf Hall* (2009) Hilary Mantel needs both the reader and her protagonist, Thomas Cromwell, to gain insight into Anne Boleyn's agenda. If our grasp of Tudor history is a little shaky, this doesn't matter: Mantel has made sure we know by now that Henry VIII hopes to discard his Spanish wife, Katherine of Aragon, and to marry Anne. Mantel has Anne's sister, Mary Boleyn, literally run into Cromwell at court: 'She puts one hand against the panelling, catching her breath, and the other against his shoulder, as if he were just part of the wall.' Mary is friendly ('I like your grey velvet, where did you find that?') and in the mood for gossip. She says:

> 'When the king turned his mind to Anne, he thought that, knowing how things are done in France, she might accept a ... a certain position, in the court. And in his heart, as he put it. He said he would give up all other mistresses. The letters he has written, in his own hand ... '
>
> 'Really?'
>
> The cardinal always says that you can never get the king to write a letter himself. Even to another king. Even to the Pope. Even when it might make a difference.
>
> 'Yes, since last summer. He writes and then sometimes, where he would sign Henricus Rex ... ' She takes his hand, turns up his palm, and with her forefinger traces a shape. 'Where he should sign his name, instead he draws a heart – and he puts their initials in it. Oh,

you mustn't laugh … ' She can't keep the smile off her face. 'He says he is suffering.'

He wants to say, Mary, these letters, can you steal them for me?

'My sister says, this is not France, and I am not a fool like you, Mary. She knows I was Henry's mistress and she sees how I'm left. And she takes a message from it.'

He is almost holding his breath: but she's reckless now, she will have her say.

'I tell you, they will ride over Hell to marry. They have vowed it. Anne says she will have him and she cares not if Katherine and every Spaniard is in the sea and drowned. What Henry wants he will have, and what Anne wants she will have, and I can say that, because I know them both, who better?'[66]

Mary is the perfect authority on the matter and therefore Mantel has deliberately chosen her – and not just any court tattler – as the conduit for the information. And she takes the opportunity to have Cromwell process the news as he learns it – the significance of the king writing a letter himself; the value to Cromwell of possession of such a letter – which also tells us about *his* agenda. It all seems to happen so naturally, and it's partly because Mantel has more going on in this little scene than the mere conveying of information. She puts Mary physically close to Cromwell, has her touching his shoulder, stroking his velvet sleeve, tracing a heart in his palm – her gestures tell another story about her potential availability to Cromwell, which runs alongside the story coming from her lips. Mantel has engineered this meeting beautifully to advance the reader's knowledge as it advances Cromwell's, in a way which simultaneously speaks volumes and is completely believable.

Capturing character in dialogue

In examining the opening of *Pride and Prejudice* we saw how Austen uses dialogue to establish and differentiate character, and it's worth thinking further about the ways in which our characters' speech might reflect their personalities. Shirley Jackson's short story 'Charles' (1948) shows how effectively dialogue can be used to establish character, even as it advances plot:

> The day my son Laurie started kindergarten he renounced corduroy overalls with bibs and began wearing blue jeans with a belt; I watched him go off the first morning with the older girl next door, seeing clearly that an era of my life was ended, my sweet-voiced nursery-school tot replaced by a long-trousered, swaggering character who forgot to stop at the corner and wave good-bye to me.
>
> He came home the same way, the front door slamming open, his cap on the floor, and the voice suddenly become raucous shouting, 'Isn't anybody *here?*'
>
> At lunch he spoke insolently to his father, spilled his baby sister's milk, and remarked that his teacher said we were not to take the name of the Lord in vain.
>
> 'How *was* school today?' I asked, elaborately casual.
>
> 'All right,' he said.
>
> 'Did you learn anything?' his father asked.
>
> Laurie regarded his father coldly. 'I didn't learn nothing,' he said.
>
> 'Anything,' I said. 'Didn't learn anything.'

Only 160 words into the story and we know there is trouble brewing for Laurie and his parents; we are alerted to this both through the content of his speech and its tone. As the story unfolds Jackson exploits Laurie's role as the conduit of all information from school to great effect: the story is told almost entirely through conversations, delivering a real surprise at the end, all the more effective because the 'reveal' is delivered in a single line of dialogue, simultaneously shocking to the mother and the reader.

We need to think as carefully about our characters' voices as we do about their actions. Are their basic speech-patterns crude or elaborate, uncertain or forthright, measured or slapdash? Consider this passage from Charles Dickens's *The Posthumous Papers of the Pickwick Club* (1837). Mr Pickwick and Mr Wardle are at a cricket match and can't help noticing the frequent loud remarks of a fellow spectator on the game – 'ejaculations which seemed to establish him in the opinion of all around, as a most excellent and undeniable judge of the whole art and mystery of the noble game of cricket':

'Capital game – well played – some strokes admirable,' said the stranger as both sides crowded into the tent, at the conclusion of the game.

'You have played it Sir?' inquired Mr. Wardle, who had been much amused by his loquacity.

'Played it! Think I have – thousands of times – not here – West Indies – exciting thing – hot work – very.'

'It must be rather a warm pursuit in such a climate,' observed Mr. Pickwick.

'Warm! – red hot – scorching – glowing. Played a match once – single wicket – friend the Colonel – Sir Thomas Blazo – who should get the greatest number of runs. – Won the toss – first innings – seven o'clock, A.M. – six natives to look out – went in; kept in – heat intense – natives all fainted – taken away – fresh half-dozen ordered – fainted also – Blazo bowling – supported by two natives – couldn't bowl me out – fainted too – cleared away the Colonel – wouldn't give in – faithful attendant – Quanko Samba – last man left – sun so hot, bat in blisters, ball scorched brown – five hundred and seventy runs – rather exhausted – Quanko mustered up last remaining strength – bowled me out – had a bath, and went out to dinner.'

'And what became of what's-his-name, Sir?' inquired an old gentleman.

'Blazo?'

'No – the other gentleman.'

'Quanko Samba?'

'Yes, Sir.'

'Poor Quanko – never recovered it – bowled on, on my account – bowled off, on his own – died Sir.' Here the stranger buried his countenance in a brown jug, but whether to hide his emotion or imbibe its contents, we cannot distinctly affirm.[67]

'Ejaculations' and 'loquacity' are useful hints but it is, of course, the dialogue itself that gives us the fullest sense of Jingle's speech. The short phrases, separated by dashes and unencumbered by connective tissue, vividly convey the quality of his headlong discourse and, by extension, his impulsive and unreliable character.

In Flannery O'Connor's 'A Circle in the Fire' (1954) three boys appear on Mrs Cope's remote farm. It's not clear what they want and she is finding their presence unsettling. Mrs Pritchard, who works for her, alarms her by relating a conversation her husband, Hollis, had with the boys:

> This morning Hollis seen them behind the bull pen and that big one ast if it wasn't some place they could wash at and Hollis said no it wasn't and that you didn't want no boys dropping cigarette butts in your woods and he said, 'She don't own them woods,' and Hollis said, 'She does too,' and that there little one he said, 'Man, Gawd owns them woods and her too,' and that there one with the glasses said, 'I reckon she own the sky over this place too,' and that there littlest one says, 'Owns the sky and can't no airplane go over here without she says so,' and then the big one says, 'I never seen a place with so many damn women on it, how do you stand it here?' and Hollis said he had done had enough of their big talk by then and he turned and walked off without giving no reply one way or the other.

We'll perhaps recognise the basic speech-patterns as those of an uneducated woman with a tendency to garrulousness, but we'll also notice that Mrs Pritchard's discourse is shaped by circumstances. The dialogue comes to us indirectly: the boys spoke to Hollis, who relayed the conversation to his wife, who is in turn repeating it to Mrs Cope. A great deal of ground is covered, not without detail but at breathless speed: as reported, the conversation with the boys starts as a request for somewhere to wash and quickly escalates into a challenge to Mrs Cope's authority which also deprecates her gender. Mrs Pritchard's delivery of her report in a single extended sentence illuminates her fundamental character but it also communicates something of the disturbance created by the boys' threatening presence.

Although dialogue normally conveys the character and emotions of the speaker, it may also on occasion be used to tell us something about the listener. You may have noticed, in our earlier discussion of Faulkner's *The Sound and the Fury*, that the punctuation of dialogue in Benjy's section of the novel is unconventional: questions don't have question marks and attributions are cut off with full stops from the speech to which they refer. Here's another passage from the same section:

> 'Is you all seen anything of a quarter down here.' Luster said.
> 'What quarter.'
> 'The one I had here this morning.' Luster said. 'I lost it somewhere. It fell through this here hole in my pocket. If I don't find it I can't go to the show tonight.'
> 'Where'd you get a quarter, boy. Find it in white folks' pocket while they ain't looking.'
> 'Got it at the getting place.' Luster said. 'Plenty more where that one come from. Only I got to find that one. Is you all found it yet.'[68]

All dialogue, as Benjy conceives it, has the finality of a statement. Other people's speech strikes his ear as a series of separate announcements. He doesn't seem to perceive the cause-and-effect aspect of conversation; to him the back-and-forth is just some-then-some. The unconventional representation of dialogue here emphasises the alienation of a character who doesn't contribute to discussion and is repeatedly spoken of as if he is absent. Throughout Benjy's section of the novel, Faulkner challenges the reader to hear dialogue as Benjy hears it.

Writing between the lines

Plot and character may be revealed not only through what characters say but through what they don't say. The spoken words are the surface, the declared element, of an interaction, but it's possible to suggest to the reader that beneath the surface of a conversation something else is going on.

In her short story 'Here We Are' (1931), Dorothy Parker describes a young couple spending a considerable time settling into a railway carriage before they finally speak:

'Well!' the young man said.

'Well!' she said.

'Well, here we are,' he said.

'Here we are,' she said. 'Aren't we?'

'I should say we were,' he said. 'Eeyop. Here we are.'

'Well!' she said.

'Well!' he said. 'Well. How does it feel to be an old married lady?'

'Oh, it's too soon to ask me that,' she said. 'At least – I mean. Well, I mean, goodness, we've only been married about three hours, haven't we?'

The young man studied his wrist-watch as if he were just acquiring the knack of reading time.

'We have been married,' he said, 'exactly two hours and twenty-six minutes.'

'My,' she said. 'It seems like longer.'

'No,' he said. 'It isn't hardly half-past six yet.'

'It seems like later,' she said. 'I guess it's because it starts getting dark so early.'

'It does, at that,' he said. 'The nights are going to be pretty long from now on. I mean. I mean – well, it starts getting dark early.'

If getting straight to the point were Parker's aim in this story, a great deal of this dialogue could be cut. However, the purpose of the banal exchange is to show that these young newly-weds don't yet know how to speak to each other: they fill up the space between them with words, but they don't communicate. These apparently empty phrases are doing an important job, defining the uneasy relationship of the two characters.

As the story unfolds, the content of their dialogue continues to be a less than reliable indicator of the couple's feelings. Their discussion of the day's events spirals into disagreements when the bride asks her new husband whether the bridesmaids didn't look 'perfectly lovely'? He agrees that Louise looked a 'knock-out', which his bride takes as a criticism of the other bridesmaid (her own sister). She then asks him what he thinks of her new hat. While he likes it, he confesses to liking her blue one too – a bad move:

'It's too bad,' she said, 'you didn't marry somebody that would get the kind of hats you'd like. Hats that cost three ninety-five. Why didn't you marry Louise? You always think she looks so beautiful. You'd love her taste in hats. Why didn't you marry her?'

'Ah, now, honey,' he said. 'For heaven's sakes!'

The argument expands into new territories, but they finally make peace, only a few minutes before they arrive at their honeymoon destination. And by this time we have realised that the argument isn't really about bridesmaids or hats – they are simply convenient pegs on which an argument can be hung. Right from those early lines, when the husband comments that 'the nights are going to be pretty long from now on' and hurriedly explains the exact sense in which he meant it – or thought he meant it – there is evidence that both characters are anxiously attuned to the distance rapidly closing between them and the terrifying double bed awaiting them in a New York hotel room.

By telling the story almost exclusively in dialogue, Parker encourages us to read what's going on *behind* the spoken words: the immediate anxiety about sex and the general anxiety about the commitment to one person for life. The quarrel stands in place of the conversation they can't have. Parker's approach allows her to suggest, without specifying, the truths the characters conceal from each other: we have to work out for ourselves the facts and feelings that underlie their evasive talk. As readers, we are encouraged to participate imaginatively in the storytelling – filling in the gaps the writer has left for us – and we will almost certainly find that this enriches our reading.

Ernest Hemingway's 'Hills Like White Elephants' paints a picture of a couple sitting at a table in the hot sunshine at a remote railway junction, waiting for the connecting train to Madrid – a picture so compelling that we might easily finish the story without realising that we've been given hardly any direct information about the characters; we've had to rely almost entirely on the words they speak to each other. We've been told nothing about their appearance except that she has taken off her hat. They talk about the landscape and about their drinks, and while there's a hint of tension between them, we're a couple of pages into the story before we find this:

'It's really an awfully simple operation, Jig,' the man said. 'It's not really an operation at all.'

The girl looked at the ground the table legs rested on.

'I know you wouldn't mind it, Jig. It's really not anything. It's just to let the air in.'

The girl did not say anything.

'I'll go with you and I'll stay with you all the time. They just let the air in and then it's all perfectly natural.'

When the girl doesn't reply, it's significant: her silence is tacit resistance. She isn't buying into the terms in which the man is describing the abortion (which we now guess is the purpose of their journey to the city – although the 'operation' is never named) but she isn't arguing with them either. This has a much more profound effect on the reader than if she were to answer him, as each of us imaginatively participates in what's going on in that silence – each reader bringing her own world of experience to the possibilities of that moment. This is also why Hemingway doesn't tell us *how* anything is said, absolutely trusting his dialogue – and us – to do that job for him: we imaginatively construct the tone in which the man is speaking precisely because we are not told what it is. Let's pick up the story again from where we left off:

'Then what will we do afterward?'

'We'll be fine afterward. Just like we were before.'

'What makes you think so?'

'That's the only thing that bothers us. It's the only thing that's made us unhappy.'

The girl looked at the bead curtain, put her hand out and took hold of two of the strings of beads.

'And you think then we'll be all right and be happy.'

'I know we will. You don't have to be afraid. I've known lots of people that have done it.'

'So have I,' said the girl. 'And afterward they were all so happy.'

Hemingway's skill is such that we know with absolute certainty that the girl doesn't mean what she's just said. The man's next words imply that he, too, recognises this:

> 'Well,' the man said, 'if you don't want to you don't have to. I wouldn't have you do it if you didn't want to. But I know it's perfectly simple.'
>
> 'And you really want to?'
>
> 'I think it's the best thing to do. But I don't want you to do it if you don't really want to.'

We know that what he really means is that he wants her to want to, and that what she really means is she wants him *not* to want her to. We've noted earlier that the word 'abortion' is never mentioned, and the characters' real wants are also skirted around or stepped over; each hopes the other will say the thing they need to hear. This is the tragedy of the story: the things that are said are not always true and the important things are too hard to say at all. This lends real poignancy to the closing lines:

> 'Do you feel better?' he asked.
>
> 'I feel fine,' she said. 'There's nothing wrong with me. I feel fine.'

Nothing, we might say, could be further from the truth, yet the truth has been revealed.

As human beings we have a tendency to neaten the disorderly, to follow and make patterns, to prefer the logical to the inconsequential. So when one character asks a question it can seems natural to have another character answer it straightforwardly. However, our own experience tells us this is by no means necessarily true to life. When A asks B a question in real life, B may: answer it truthfully; answer it with a lie; answer it in a way which shows they have misunderstood the question; answer it in a way which shows they resent the question; buy time by repeating the question; answer it with another question; change the subject; say nothing; burst into tears; be interrupted by C before they can say anything at all – and you can easily imagine other responses. Any of these examples may open up interesting possibilities while also imparting greater realism to our dialogue.

Dialogue in fiction is, of course, an artificial construct. It's not simply that it serves, and is affected by, our wider narrative purposes; there's also the fact that if it faithfully reproduced real-life speech our writing would often be boring – full of repetitions, non sequiturs, digressions, irrelevancies, trivia and hesitations; it would also take up far too much space. The writer's aim is to make the dialogue *appear* authentic.

Attributing dialogue

Like Austen in the opening chapter of *Pride and Prejudice*, Hemingway tells us who is speaking only when absolutely necessary, yet we never struggle to work out who it is. (In both cases there are only two people in the scene, which makes this easier for the writer.) If you look again at the original dialogue where Duncan buys a ticket you'll notice its sole merit regarding style: the dialogue is only attributed once to one speaker:

'King's Cross please,' Duncan replied.

It's clear that there are only two people involved in the exchange and that one of them sells tickets, so there is no need to clutter it up with unnecessary attributions. It's worth remembering the function of explicit attributions: they are there simply to help the reader. If it's obvious who's speaking you can – and generally should – omit the attribution.

There are two rules commonly given concerning the use of 'said' to attribute dialogue:

1. The word 'said' should hardly ever be used.
2. No word other than 'said' should ever be used.

Confused? Let's look at the competing arguments.

The origin of 'said is dead' seems to be the classroom, and a drive by teachers to encourage students to use a more varied vocabulary in their creative writing. While this may indeed have helped children meet their literacy test targets it was not advice designed for grown-up writers, yet it has somehow been taken up, largely unexamined, as a credible tenet. Search the web for 'said is dead' and you'll find lists of words which could be used instead of 'said'. Applying this advice can produce absurd results:

> 'Where to?' the clerk demanded.
> 'King's Cross, please,' Duncan rejoined.
> 'Return or single?' she enquired.
> 'Return please,' he retorted.
> 'Underground?' she quizzed.
> 'Sorry?' he posed.
> 'Do you want it to include the Underground?' she urged.
> 'Er, yes I think so. Yes please,' he beseeched.
> 'So you're returning today,' she ordained.
> 'No, no, Tuesday. I need a return coming back on Tuesday,' he retaliated.
> 'Then you can't include the Underground. You can only include the Underground if you're coming back the same day,' she alleged.

While 'said is dead' is pleasing on the ear, it's worse than useless on the page. *What* is said is usually of primary importance and anything else that draws attention to itself draws attention away from the spoken words. The insistence on finding substitutes for 'said' results in writing which does exactly this, refocusing the reader's attention on the way something is being said – persistently and largely unnecessarily. If we're going to use a word other than 'said' it ought to be doing the job *better* than said.

But 'said' is boring, isn't it? Well, it is if you're expecting it to do a job above its pay grade. Like 'did' and 'had' (which no one ever accuses of being boring), 'said' is a humble but indispensable tool of storytelling, so much so that most of the time we are unaware of the frequency with which it occurs. Like the inverted commas which commonly frame dialogue, 'said' is part of the wallpaper of fiction, quietly getting on with its job without really being noticed.

So what about the case for *only* using 'said'? Elmore Leonard's opinion is often quoted:

> Never use a verb other than 'said' to carry dialogue. The line of dialogue belongs to the character; the verb is the writer sticking his nose in. But 'said' is far less intrusive than 'grumbled'; 'gasped'; cautioned'; 'lied'.[69]

And Leonard goes further: he also outlaws words qualifying 'said':

> Never use an adverb to modify the verb 'said' … To use an adverb this way (or almost any way) is a mortal sin. The writer is now exposing himself in earnest, using a word that can distract and interrupt the rhythm of the exchange.[70]

This hard line is, as we said, widely quoted; what is much less widely quoted is what Leonard says by way of introduction to his 'rules':

> These are rules I've picked up along the way to help me remain invisible when I'm writing a book, to help me show rather than tell what's taking place in the story. If you have a facility for language and imagery and the sound of your voice pleases you, invisibility is not what you are after …[71]

We discuss the relative merits of showing and telling in several other places, but it's clear that Leonard intends his rules for writers who want to write the way he writes. What Leonard calls 'the sound of your own voice' was a kind of vanity as far as his own writing was concerned, because he actively sought to remove the authorial voice from his work, allowing the reader to experience an apparently unmediated relationship with the story and characters – one reason, perhaps, that his books were so often made into films. (Of course no reading experience is unmediated by the author, but this was the illusion he sought to create.) If that's the agenda, the writer's insistence on *how* something is said can be seen as interfering with the supposedly unmediated reader-text relationship.

Your choices will depend on your agenda. If you want to write like Elmore Leonard, follow his rules; if you want a narrative voice to supply more than basic stage directions, don't. You may well settle on a less prescriptive mixture. If you look back at the extract from 'Here We Are' you'll see that Dorothy Parker deliberately makes liberal use of plain 'said', allowing the characters' words to speak entirely for themselves. If, however, you revisit the extract from 'Charles' you'll observe that Shirley Jackson can't give us the full sense of the family dynamic in the mother's question: 'How *was* school today?' without describing the 'elaborately casual' tone in which it is asked. So it's up to you. See what suits your story. And of course you don't have to choose *only* 'said' or *never* 'said' – most writers employ whatever works best in the context.

Finally, it's worth remembering that there are ways of avoiding the issue completely, by focusing on what's going on around the dialogue:

'Where to?' The woman behind the counter sounded as though she couldn't care less.

'King's Cross, please.' Duncan hazarded his brightest smile – well, brightest for 7am.

'Return or single?' She didn't look up from her screen.

'Return please.' Duncan decided to waste no more smiles. Too much effort.

'Underground?'

'Sorry?'

Finally she looked up. 'Do you want it to include the Underground?' She mouthed the words clearly, as though he were hard of hearing.

'Er, yes I think so. Yes please.'

'So you're returning today.' She emphasised *today*, her index finger tapping on the counter between them, as if the gesture were universal sign language for 'this moment in time'. Did she think he might be foreign as well as deaf?

'No, no, Tuesday. I need a return coming back on Tuesday.'

She looked back at the screen and sighed. 'Then you can't include the Underground. You can only include the Underground if you're coming back the same day.'

Not deaf, not foreign; just an idiot.

Embedding the dialogue in other aspects of the characters' interaction can obviate the need for direct attribution altogether, while adding value to the exchange.

Punctuating dialogue conventionally

All punctuation is a code which enables the reader to understand how the writer intends his or her words to be understood and its conventional use in dialogue needs to be properly understood. We don't have to be taught how to *read* dialogue – we pick it up as we learn to read – but many people struggle with the punctuation when *writing* dialogue, as we can easily navigate everyday life without ever being required to do so. If you are confident you know how to punctuate dialogue please feel free to skip to the next section; if not, this might be helpful:

'So how should I punctuate dialogue?' asked Nicky.

'Well, you should start by indenting it, as if it's a new paragraph,' Marion replied.

'Yes,' agreed Denise, 'and then when someone else starts speaking you need to start a new paragraph and indent again. That tells the reader the speaker has changed, even if the writer hasn't told you who's speaking.'

'Like this?'

'Exactly. Also, all the punctuation in the words spoken should remain with the words spoken – inside the speech marks.'

'Got it,' said Nicky. 'Related to that: I've noticed that when someone speaks a whole sentence, instead of ending with a full stop it often ends with a comma, as in Marion's advice about indenting.'

'That happens when the dialogue is followed by more writing that is, when you read it, part of the same sentence,' Marion replied. 'So lots of dialogue ends with a comma where in ordinary prose the sentence would end with a full stop,' she added. 'Like just then.'

'OK. So we use a comma in place of a full stop when the speech has ended but the sentence hasn't. What about question marks?' asked Nicky.

'All the punctuation in the words spoken should remain with the words spoken – inside the speech marks,' Denise patiently repeated.

'And that includes exclamation marks!' added Marion, less patiently.

'But supposing,' said Nicky, 'you split a sentence and have the person who is speaking designated in the middle of the spoken sentence?'

'What? Do you mean like you just did there?' asked Denise.

'Aw, you guys.' Nicky blushed. 'Hey! There was no comma after you guys!'

'That's because *Nicky blushed* is a complete sentence on its own and doesn't relate directly to the words spoken. And while I'm – '

'Thanks! I was just about to ask how you show that the speaker is interrupted, rather than … '

'Just trailing off?'

'Exactly! So a dash means the speaker's being interrupted before they've finished and three dots means they don't quite finish what they were going to … '

When in doubt, pick up a good book and reacquaint yourself with the conventions you automatically understand as a reader.

Alternative ways of punctuating dialogue

Some writers have chosen ways of presenting dialogue which don't involve using inverted commas at all. Here's an excerpt from Simon Burt's short story 'Wh'appen?' (1986) as it would conventionally be punctuated.

'Div!' Farley said.

'Who's a div?' Salimi said.

'You're a div, div!' Farley said.

'I'm not a div,' Salimi said.

The words didn't seem to mean much, apart from their tone. The tone conveyed what they meant. So did the punch to the shoulder that accompanied them.

'Div!' Farley said. 'Tramp! Pouf! Flid! Plonker! Paki! Cunt! Dildo!'

'I'm not,' Salimi said.

But Burt doesn't punctuate it like that. This is how the same excerpt appears in print:

> Div! Farley said.
> Who's a div? Salimi said.
> You're a div, div! Farley said.
> I'm not a div, Salimi said.
> The words didn't seem to mean much, apart from their tone. The tone conveyed what they meant. So did the punch to the shoulder that accompanied them.
> Div! Farley said. Tramp! Pouf! Flid! Plonker! Paki! Cunt! Dildo!
> I'm not, Salimi said.

Even without the inverted commas it's abundantly clear who is speaking, because Burt keeps telling us; the repeated attributions become part of the rhythm of the writing. It might strike you, however, that the clarity of this passage depends on the simplicity of the dialogue and the spareness of the attributions, as well as on the fact that the boys' invective is radically different in tone from the intervening descriptive material: a different text might not lend itself so readily to this treatment.

Here's a passage from Niall Griffiths's *Runt* (2007):

> I felt my head go funny. All kind of floppy and wobblesome like mud and I felt worried.
> —Uncle …
> The mountain flopped from side to side. Bad taste sicky feeling in my mouth.
> —Uncle …
> —What, bach? What's happening?
> Drunkle held my moving head in his hands and I could see his face all big and close but not like Arthur's I *liked* Drunkle's face being big and close it made me better and it wasn't like Arthur's, no.
> —What, bach? Tell me what's wrong. Are you going away? Are you having a Time?[72]

Griffiths's reduced punctuation here includes the substitution of a single introductory dash for the more usual inverted commas as a means of indicating dialogue. This particular use of the dash is hardly new – James Joyce used it as early as 1916 in *A Portrait of the Artist as a Young Man* – and its use has increased significantly in recent years, but it would still be considered non-standard.

The essential purpose of punctuating dialogue is twofold: to separate speech from narrative, and to separate the speech of one character from that of another. The standard method of punctuating dialogue has proved durable because it provides the most effective safeguard against confusion. Both Burt and Griffiths avoid confusion, but it's worth reflecting that, while very few agents, editors or readers will object to the conventional punctuation of dialogue, many will have reservations about unconventional punctuation.

Accent and dialect

This has been a vexed issue throughout the history of the novel: Sir Walter Scott's rendering of Scottish dialect in his novels met with resistance from some readers, while Charlotte Brontë rewrote some passages of dialect in *Wuthering Heights* (1847) after Emily Brontë's death, making it more accessible to readers. Yet many of us will feel the need at times to give some indication, in our writing, of alternative forms of English.

Let's look at a passage of dialogue from D. H. Lawrence's short story, 'Odour of Chrysanthemums' (1911), considering our response to his representation of the Nottinghamshire dialect spoken by most of the mining families among whom Lawrence grew up:

> ''Asna 'e come whoam yit?' asked the man, without any form of greeting, but with deference and sympathy. 'I couldna say wheer he is – 'e's non ower theer!' – he jerked his head to signify the 'Prince of Wales'.
>
> ''E's 'appen gone up to th' "Yew",' said Mrs Rigley.
>
> There was another pause. Rigley had evidently something to get off his mind:
>
> 'Ah left 'im finishin' a stint,' he began. 'Loose-all 'ad bin gone about ten minutes when we com'n away, an' I shouted, "Are ter comin',

Walt?" an' 'e said, "Go on, Ah shanna be but a'ef a minnit," so we com'n ter th' bottom, me an' Bowers, thinkin' as 'e wor just behint, an' 'ud come up i' th' next bantle – '

How difficult do you find this? If you come from Nottinghamshire, maybe not very difficult at all, but if your own speech is that of another region, or if it falls into the broad and debatable category of 'received pronunciation', you are likely to find *some* difficulty in reading the passage. Let's distinguish, first of all, between accent (and its representation on the page) and dialect: 'whoam' and 'wheer' simply show, through their spelling, how familiar words are pronounced by these characters; 'loose-all' and 'bantle' are dialect terms, probably unfamiliar to most modern readers ('loose-all' meaning the end of work as signalled by the pit hooter and 'bantle' meaning a batch, in this case a group of men). Provided accent is more or less unambiguously rendered (not always an easy matter, though Lawrence manages it skilfully) the problems it poses will usually be overcome in the course of our reading – particularly if we read aloud; dialect terms, on the other hand, may interrupt our reading by sending us to a dictionary.

Why create the difficulty at all? If we frame this question as 'Why not have all these characters speaking standard English?' we may put ourselves well on the way to answering it. These characters wouldn't have spoken standard English, and if Lawrence wants to create authentic-sounding dialogue he must acknowledge that fact in his rendering of it. As readers, we may well feel that the apparent authenticity of the speech of Lawrence's characters contributes importantly to the story's power, and we may, for that reason, be willing to accept a certain amount of difficulty.

Even so, many writers, recognising that some readers are intimidated by dialogue of this kind, prefer a lighter touch, gesturing towards localised forms of English without attempting to replicate them. A lot can be achieved by attention to syntax: think about how sentences are – often quite subtly – structured differently in different parts of the English-speaking world. Here's a snippet of conversation from *I Know Why The Caged Bird Sings* (1969) by Maya Angelou:

> 'Well, how is it up North?'
> 'See any of them big buildings?'
> 'Ever ride in one of them elevators?'
> 'Was you scared?'
> 'Whitefolks any different, like they say?'[73]

This captures the rhythm and feel of local usage without making any significant demands on the non-local reader.

The examples we've given so far are of dialogue embedded in a framing narrative that is written in a more conventional version of the English language, but some fiction is written entirely in an alternative English. A good example is Trinidad-born Sam Selvon's ground-breaking 1956 novel, *The Lonely Londoners*. Selvon began writing the framing narrative in what he referred to as 'straight English', but hit his stride when he began to set it in the dialect he was already using for the dialogue. Here's Henry Oliver, nick-named Galahad, newly arrived in London from Trinidad and suddenly brought up short by a sense of his own vulnerability:

> Galahad make for the tube station when he left Moses, and he stand up there on Queensway watching everybody going about their business, and a feeling of loneliness and fright come on him all of a sudden. He forget all the brave words he was talking to Moses, and he realise that here he is, in London, and he ain't have money or work or place to sleep or any friend or anything, and he standing up here by the tube station watching people, and everybody look so busy he frighten to ask questions from any of them. You think any of them bothering with what going on in his mind? Or in anybody else mind but their own?[74]

This is a distinctive form of English, but there's nothing here that is likely to impede the understanding of any non-Trinidadian English speaker. Trinidadian English is rich in terms that might challenge the non-Caribbean reader, but Selvon tends largely to avoid them: it's mainly through a finely modulated verbal patterning that runs consistently through both narrative and dialogue that the novel achieves its immersive effect.

Writers will approach these matters in a variety of different ways, but here are a few considerations by way of guidance. Firstly, a work of fiction should be able to stand on its own feet, and this might steer us away from writing dialogue or narrative that requires a glossary or footnotes in order to be understood; secondly, rendering a dialect you know intimately will produce better results than attempting to mimic one with which you have only a nodding acquaintance; and thirdly, compromise in this matter, as in many other aspects of writing, isn't a mark of failure, and may be, in practical terms, a necessity.

Other worlds, other times

Writers of speculative fiction set in a future or otherwise 'other' world, tend to suppose, quite reasonably, that speech in other worlds will be different from speech in our own. A common approach to this matter is to give characters dialogue that sounds vaguely archaic ('Come, child, these people know not our ways'), but this has been widely and often thoughtlessly used, and can seem both tiresome and absurd: it's worth observing that the ease with which a style can be parodied is usually a reliable warning against adopting it. The device was perhaps most charmingly handled in the *Star Wars* films, where part of the appeal of the tiny alien Yoda lies in his use of archaic inversions, such as 'the last of the Jedi will you be'. The problem of preserving a sense of this oddness when translating Yoda's speech into foreign languages has been the subject of serious debate, a matter that has drawn some criticism: 'A fucking break, give me,' one linguist remarked. Undoubtedly Yoda's inverted speech patterns contribute to his aura of wisdom, and give his pronouncements a poetic quality – we'll recognise their parallels in Shakespearean lines such as 'A glooming peace this morning with it brings' (*Romeo and Juliet*) or 'For them the gracious Duncan have I murdered' (*Macbeth*); but turning to archaic language patterns can be problematic when we're trying to imagine the language of alternative worlds. We shall look later, in our discussion of other-world narrative voices, at more inventive approaches to linguistic otherness, but we'll move on now to consider dialogue in relation to historical fiction.

When William Golding was writing *The Inheritors* (1955) he had no idea how his characters, who are Neanderthals, might have communicated. So he chose to have them speak in very clear and unambiguous modern English, using short words and simple sentences, for example: 'Ha and Nil have brought many days' wood back. Fa and Lok have brought many days' food back. And soon the warm days will be here.'[75] The strategy is highly effective in context, but this unusual novel is, technically, *pre*-historical fiction, and the picture becomes more complicated when we're setting our story in a literate age: we face the problem of reconciling evidence of the speech of the period in question with what will be intelligible to a twenty-first-century reader.

The most reliable way to get a feel for the speech of a particular period is to read widely in material written at the time (or, in the case of more recent history, to consult audio and video resources). While dialogue in novels and plays may not exactly represent everyday speech, it can often provide a sense of the vocabulary, as well as nuances associated with region or social class. Best of all, however, is anything you can get hold of which has real people's speech transcribed verbatim. Letters, diaries, court records, newspaper reports of court proceedings and other documentary evidence can be excellent sources. If you wanted to develop an ear for a Victorian working-class voice, for example, you could immerse yourself in Henry Mayhew's *London Labour and the London Poor* (1851). Mayhew conducted hundreds of interviews with the city's poorest inhabitants which he transcribed and then edited with a commentary. Consider what useful scraps can be culled from this excerpt, on the wives of 'ballast-heavers and coal-whippers':

> They were next asked, who had suffered from want owing to their husbands drinking their earnings ...
>
> 'Starvation has been my lot,' said one. 'And mine,' added another. 'My children,' said a third, 'have often gone to bed at night without breaking their fast the whole length of the day.' 'And mine,' said one, 'have many a time gone without a bit or sup of anything all the day, through their father working for the publican.'
>
> 'I cannot,' exclaimed the next, 'afford my children a ha'porth of milk a-day.'
>
> 'Many a time,' said one, who appeared to be very much moved, 'have I put my four children to bed, when the only meal they have had the whole day has been 1lb. of bread; but it's of no use opening my mouth.'[76]

First-hand testimonies (or, in this last case, something close to first-hand testimonies) convey the texture of the language, as it was spoken. While diaries, letters and reportage may stand at a little distance from daily conversation, they are nevertheless likely to bring us very close indeed to the speech of the period in which they were written.

We need to bear in mind, however, that the writer of historical fiction isn't required to *replicate* the speech of another age but to *suggest* that speech. If you return to the passage from *Wolf Hall* quoted earlier in this chapter, it might strike you that Cromwell's interjected 'Really?' sounds a little too modern for the period; if you then turn to the *Oxford English Dictionary* you'll see that the earliest recorded example of this interrogative use of the word occurs more than 200 years later. It seems probable that nobody used the word in this way in Cromwell's time, but only the most pedantic reader would object to its use here. Mantel has spoken in an interview of her own finely balanced approach to dialogue:

> Everything must be clear from the context, and so what you are after is a suggestion of the language of the time. You don't want pastiche,

which can be grim, false and very often embarrassing. You want what you write to be accessible, and while I do pay a lot of attention to individual words and when they were first used, I'm not as much concerned with every single word as I am with thoughts and with habits of thought. The basic question is not 'Did they say this?' but 'Could they have thought this?', and I think that's what you use as a guide. So many words have changed their meaning or taken on different nuances, that it's impossible to be authentic. That is why I favour an idiom that has a suggestion of the era rather than trying to imitate it slavishly.[77]

Mantel isn't suggesting that the writer can take outrageous liberties – it's hard to imagine her having Anne Boleyn say 'OK', or Henry VIII complain that he's feeling stressed to the max – but she is arguing for a degree of flexibility, on the grounds both that the novelist can't get it absolutely right and that, even if she could, the resulting novel might prove inaccessible to her readers.

How do we show a character's thoughts?

The obvious answer is that we show his thoughts through what he says and that is, of course, one possibility; but as we've seen, some thoughts are not spoken. There are no firm rules for representing unspoken thought, so it's up to the writer to choose a way of making a character's thoughts distinguishable from both dialogue and narration. You might try something like this:

> 'Where to?'
> 'Paddington, please,' Mike replied. Didn't she recognise him? he wondered. She must recognise him.
> 'Return or single?'
> I do this every day, he reflected. She sees me every day.
> 'Return please.'
> What a cow, he thought.

Or what about this?

> 'Where to?'
> 'Paddington, please.'

Doesn't she recognise him? She must recognise him.
'Return or single?'
He does this every day. She sees him *every* day. The cow!
'Return please.'

Or this?

'Where to?'
'Paddington, please,' I replied.
Do you recognise me? You must recognise me.
'Return or single?'
I do this every day! You see me every day!
'Return please.'
Cow.

All of these variants convey unspoken thought, and none is likely to confuse the reader. Here thought operates in quick alternation with speech, but sometimes thought is protracted, and unaccompanied by speech, as in this passage from Thomas Hardy's *Jude the Obscure* (1895). Jude is reflecting on the horror of life as he has come to see it:

Growing up brought responsibilities, he found. Events did not rhyme quite as he had thought. Nature's logic was too horrid for him to care for. That mercy towards one set of creatures was cruelty towards another sickened his sense of harmony. As you got older, and felt yourself to be at the centre of your time, and not at a point in its circumference, as you had felt when you were little, you were seized with a sort of shuddering, he perceived. All around you there seemed to be something glaring, garish, rattling, and the noises and glares hit upon the little cell called your life, and shook it, and scorched it.

If he could only prevent himself growing up! He did not want to be a man.[78]

Here the writer introduces the notion of thought-process by means of the indicative phrase 'he found'. He doesn't need to indicate the status of the observations with each new sentence, but slips in a reminder a few lines further on ('he perceived'). A passage of this kind can be extremely useful for providing insight into a character's worldview or his motivation, but if carried on for too long it may have a deadening effect on a narrative, impeding its progress.

The early twentieth century saw a surge of interest in the workings of the human mind, and the rise of a type of fiction at once more centrally concerned with the thought-processes of its characters and more intimate in its rendering of those processes. Virginia Woolf's *To the Lighthouse* (1927) runs to a couple of hundred pages, yet its plot (as the term is conventionally understood) can be summarised quite adequately in a hundred words; much of the novel's 'action' is actually thought. Here Mrs Ramsay is thinking about two young friends, Paul and Minta – will he propose to her? – and her thoughts accompany her reading of the folk tale, 'The Fisherman and His Wife', to her children:

> Minta Doyle and Paul Rayley had not come back then. That could only mean, Mrs. Ramsay thought, one thing. She must accept him, or she must refuse him. This going off after luncheon for a walk, even though Andrew was with them – what could it mean? except that she had decided, rightly, Mrs. Ramsay thought (and she was very, very fond of Minta), to accept that good fellow, who might not be brilliant, but then, thought Mrs. Ramsay, realising that James was tugging at her to make her go on reading aloud the Fisherman and his Wife, she did in her own heart infinitely prefer boobies to clever men who wrote dissertations ...[79]

You'll realise at once that Woolf's text works in more complex ways than Hardy's, using an unusually fluid syntax to represent the movement of Mrs Ramsay's mind, and showing how her thoughts interact with what's going on immediately around her. To say that Woolf's treatment of thought is more lively than Hardy's isn't of course to say that she's a better writer than Hardy, but it's fair to say that her overriding interest in the thoughts of her characters has led her to refine the ways in which those thoughts can be represented.

Woolf's technique might be described as more immersive than Hardy's. James Joyce's *Ulysses* (1922) immerses us still more deeply in the thoughts of one of its characters, Molly Bloom:

> Yes because he never did a thing like that before as ask to get his breakfast in bed with a couple of eggs since the *City Arms* hotel when he used to be pretending to be laid up with a sick voice doing his highness to make himself interesting to that old faggot Mrs Riordan that he thought he had a great leg of and she never left us a farthing all for masses for herself and her soul greatest miser ever was actually afraid to lay out 4d for her methylated spirit telling me all her ailments she had too much old chat in her about politics and earthquakes and the end of the world let us have a bit of fun first God help the world if all the women were her sort down on bathingsuits and lownecks of course nobody wanted her to wear I suppose she was pious because no man would look at her twice I hope Ill never be like her a wonder she didnt want us to cover our faces but she was a welleducated woman certainly and her gabby talk about Mr Riordan here and Mr Riordan there I suppose he was glad to get shut of her ....[80]

Here we have the impression of having been plugged directly into the flow of Molly's thoughts: there's no authorial intervention ('she thought', 'she reflected') to tell us that we're in her mind, though it's clear enough what's happening as Joyce moves into a mode often described as 'stream of consciousness', with the words seeming to tumble out in unmediated form; the absence of punctuation in this particular case heightens the effect. Molly's long, discursive monologue plunges the reader deeply into her mind, into her individual point of view – and this brings us to the subject of our next chapter.

– 8 –

Narrative viewpoint and narrative voice

～

Where do we stand?

When we speak nowadays about someone's point of view we generally mean a mental position or attitude adopted in relation to a subject; historically the phrase has also been used in a more physical sense to suggest the spatial relationship of the observer to the thing observed. For the writer of fiction, both senses are important.

'All description is an opinion about the world,' says Anne Enright, advising: 'Find a place to stand.'[81] Almost all description comes through the narrative voice, so whatever point of view the narrative voice is representing is the point from which anything is perceived and the point from which everything is described. That is your place to stand.

Ask four writers to describe a particular place as an omniscient third-person narrator – let's say the main concourse at King's Cross station – and you'll certainly get a variety of descriptions. But ask each of the four to describe the scene from the point of view of one of the following and the descriptions are likely to be much more strongly differentiated:

– a beggar sitting on the pavement at the entrance to the station
– a short-sighted elderly lady about to meet a friend she hasn't seen for forty years
– a police officer who has just been alerted to a suitcase left unattended on a platform
– a man mending the station clock from a scaffold high above the concourse.

The differentiation arises both from the individual's outlook (which we can understand either as a fundamental matter of character or as a result of the particular circumstances in which he finds himself) and from his physical location. The beggar may be intent on getting enough money to pay for his next meal – he may be scanning the faces of the passers-by for any sign of sympathy; his physical location significantly restricts his view of the concourse. The lady is (let us imagine) anticipating her friend's arrival with a mixture of anxiety (will she recognise her? might she miss her completely?) and pleasure (she has so much to tell her); she needs to get close to the barrier, but she's frail and can't push through the crowd. The police officer hurries towards the platform where the suitcase was seen; the crowd parts to let her through but she barely notices her immediate surroundings because her mind is racing ahead, thinking about the decision she may have to make. The man on the scaffold has a unique bird's-eye view of all the activity below him; he sees the police officer hurrying towards the far side of the station and momentarily wonders what is going on, but he's not a naturally curious person and the repair is more difficult and time-consuming than he'd anticipated, so he turns back to his work.

These aren't the only stories that might arise from the given information, but the fundamental point should be clear: the story we tell is significantly affected by the narrative point of view. For each character, different details are prioritised or escape notice; different details take on significance, meaning or potential. Whatever our story is, it can't be told without a point of view of some kind, and we need to discover the point of view that best serves its needs.

Author and narrator – knowing and telling

How do you decide the point of entry for your reader? First person or third person? Reliable or unreliable narrator? One point of view or several? Whose voice do you want the reader to hear?

Most stories pivot on the question of which character knows what and – crucially – what your reader knows and when you let them know it. The choice of narrative voice and point of view defines how much the reader can know.

To clarify an important matter: there is a difference between the author and the narrator. The author creates the story and controls how the events unfold; the narrator is the voice in which the story is told. The difference between the two is easy to discern when the narration is in the first person. We can be sure that while Günter Grass wrote *The Tin Drum* (1959), it's not Grass's own voice which addresses the reader at the opening of the novel:

> Granted: I am an inmate of a mental hospital; my keeper is watching me, he never lets me out of his sight; there's a peephole in the door, and my keeper's eye is the shade of brown that can never see through a blue-eyed type like me.

Here it's clear that the narrator is telling his story, and that the narrator is a creation of the author. But often the narrator's voice is less clearly distinguishable from the author's; when, for example, the narrator of Jane Austen's *Emma* (1815) remarks that 'Human nature is so well disposed towards those who are in interesting situations, that a young person, who either marries or dies, is sure of being kindly spoken of',[82] we recognise the wry humour of the observation but we can't easily gauge the distance between Jane Austen's view and that of her narrator.

Whether or not the opinion of a narrator at a given moment in the text reflects the opinion of the author, the narrative voice in a good novel needs to be carefully constructed. It can allow writers to indulge in grand observations or amusing generalisations which, in their own everyday lives, they might never express – or, indeed, in the fullest sense subscribe to. All narratives stand at *some* distance from the author; the author projects the narrator as a *persona*. If you think of the novel as a puppet show, the narrator is equivalent to the puppet, foregrounded on the stage, while the author is equivalent to the puppeteer, hidden from view but actually masterminding the operation.

A first-person narrator is usually a character in the story and the reader will of course get to know her as the story unfolds. With a third-person narrator, describing events and characters as a non-participant observer, the narrative voice will still have characteristics which differentiate it from other narrative voices in other books, and the reader gets to know that voice too. Although a third-person narrator can't accurately be described as *being* a character in the novel, it's true to say that she *has* character. Whether her voice is quirky, irreverent, authoritative or poetic, ideally your reader will want to spend time in her company and will be receptive to the story she tells.

As readers, we tend not to question in what time-relationship the narrator stands to the story. In real life when someone tells you a story about something significant that has happened to him, he will usually start with the big event ('I'm getting married'; 'My father died'; 'I've lost my job'). Then they will track back and relate the succession of events which led to this result. The narrator in a novel often works quite differently, saving the big news for the end of the narrative. The narrator is not your close friend and can't presume on your goodwill, patience or interest in the details of a story in which you initially have no investment. So we could say that the narrative is a story told by a stranger, and that stranger is going to have to work a lot harder to gain your sympathy and interest than a friend does. For this reason he is unlikely to tell you the big news up front; he is going to hold it back, building your appetite for the outcome, letting you know it's there without letting you know what it is until the author judges the moment to be right.

The success of the relationship usually depends in part on the reader being prepared not to notice that a narrator is telling the story as if she doesn't already know how it turns out, though logically, in any past-tense narrative, she must know. Sometimes a narrator does indicate that she has foreknowledge, with observations such as: 'How keenly Margaret would come to regret that moment of indecision!' or 'Little did I know that was the last time I would see my brother.' Far more often, however, the narrator gives no suggestion, as the narrative unfolds, of knowing how things will turn out in the end.

Past-tense narratives don't often specify the time-lag between the events of the narrative and the narrator's recording of those events, usually relying on nothing more than a tacit understanding that the events have already happened. Present-tense narratives (which are much less common) operate differently, under the terms of a different understanding: there, we accept the convention that the action and the narrator's recording of the action are happening simultaneously, even while knowing that this couldn't possibly be the case.

First- and third-person narratives: the basics

If Jonathan Swift's *Gulliver's Travels* (1726) had been written in the third person, it might have begun:

> Lemuel Gulliver's father had a small estate in Northamptonshire; Lemuel was the third of five sons.

But as it is, *Gulliver's Travels* is written in the first person and begins:

> My father had a small estate in Northamptonshire; I was the third of five sons.

We can make some general observations about the advantages and disadvantages of each kind of narrative. A first-person voice seems direct – there's nothing apparently between the character and the reader. Imbued with the personality of the character, it will perhaps give more colour and flavour to the narrative. It encourages a more intimate relationship between narrator and reader: the reader sees the world through the narrator's eyes. The disadvantage, however, is that the reader can *only* see the world through the narrator's eyes. A third-person narrative, while perhaps lacking some of the immediacy of the first-person voice, can range more widely; it can offer a *meanwhile* or an *elsewhere* in a story, showing events that take place outside the purview of the protagonist. The first-person narrator can only know or surmise other characters' experience from evidence provided by his own observation (he sees a character blush or weep or smile) or by second-hand means (he hears of events through the dialogue of other characters, he is sent a letter, he discovers a diary) and this limitation can sometimes create plot difficulties; the third-person narrator can see as widely as the author needs him to.

So your choice between first and third person may be summarised as a choice between specific viewpoint and wider viewpoint, idiosyncratic voice or more neutral voice. Yet there is a spectrum of third-person narrative, from the *omniscient* (all-knowing) third person to the *tight* third person which is only a small step away from first person. Tight third person has a restricted viewpoint, similar to that of the first person; the narrator is not the story's protagonist, but shares the protagonist's perspective. As in the case of a first-person narrator, a tight third-person narrator must interpret the world of the story in the light of the protagonist's experience of it.

How perspective changes the story

You can see how close the relationship is between a first-person narrative and a tight third-person narrative by comparing these two passages:

First person

The receptionist told me that Ella would be late so I took a seat facing the revolving glass doors and picked up a magazine. I didn't have to wait long.

Ella looked elegant in a long black coat, a fedora and quite unnecessary sunglasses. The skirt of the coat, lifting in the draught from the door, momentarily revealed a shocking pink satin lining and impossibly shiny black patent leather riding boots. She moved with easy confidence towards the welcome desk, spoke briefly with the receptionist and then slowly tilted her head in my direction. An old sensation immediately resurfaced: I wanted to look away from the directness of her gaze, but couldn't.

She took off her hat as she walked towards me, allowing her golden curls to tumble round her shoulders; her bright smile and look of delighted surprise announced, I suspected, a premeditated charm offensive.

Only very slight changes are required to move from the first-person narrative to a tight third-person report of the experience of the observer – let's call him Joe:

Tight third person

The receptionist told Joe that Ella would be late so he took a seat facing the revolving glass doors and picked up a magazine. He didn't have to wait long.

Ella looked elegant in a long black coat, a fedora and quite unnecessary sunglasses. The skirt of the coat, lifting in the draught from the door, momentarily revealed a shocking pink satin lining and impossibly shiny black patent leather riding boots. She moved with easy confidence towards the welcome desk, spoke briefly with the receptionist and then slowly tilted her head in Joe's direction. An old sensation immediately resurfaced: he wanted to look away from the directness of her gaze, but couldn't.

She took off her hat as she walked towards him, allowing her golden curls to tumble round her shoulders; her bright smile and look of delighted surprise announced, he suspected, a premeditated charm offensive.

When a first-person or tight third-person narrative is working well we're not usually conscious, as readers, of how it's done, or of the conventions which are being adhered to. However, these conventions quickly reveal themselves when we try to rewrite the passage, making Ella the first-person narrator. Firstly, we need to remove references unique to Joe's perspective. How Joe has spent his time waiting for her, what he feels when she looks at him, his interpretation of her demeanour – all this has to go, of course, because Ella can't know it. Let's try writing it without implying knowledge of what Joe feels or thinks:

> I'd called ahead to say I'd be late.
>
> I looked elegant in a long black coat, a fedora and quite unnecessary sunglasses. The skirt of my coat, lifting in the draught from the door, momentarily revealed the shocking pink satin lining and impossibly shiny black patent leather riding boots. I moved with easy confidence towards the welcome desk, spoke briefly with the receptionist and then slowly tilted my head in Joe's direction.
>
> I took off my hat as I walked towards him with a bright smile and a look of delighted surprise, allowing my golden curls to tumble round my shoulders.

You'll realise that we haven't yet done enough. The passage feels very peculiar because we're still seeing Ella, rather than seeing what she sees. Both in her references to her clothes and to her own behaviour, she is describing things she knows intimately (and would therefore probably not mention) as if she were watching herself from outside. Let's now edit out all the stuff Ella wouldn't be likely to say about her own appearance:

> I'd called ahead to say I'd be late.
>
> When I arrived I asked for Joe at the desk and the receptionist pointed him out. I approached him, smiling.

Now all we have is her actions: what's missing is her experience. If we try to supply that experience, strictly from her perspective, we might come up with something like this:

> I was late and went straight to the desk to ask whether Joe had arrived. The receptionist pointed him out; he was sitting facing the door, looking at me over the top of a magazine. Same old Joe. Same old jacket. And, going by the magazine, same old politics.
>
> Suddenly I felt ridiculous. We used to mock mercilessly anyone who wore sunglasses indoors. And the hat – what had possessed me? I pulled it off and went towards him, trying to look more pleased than I felt.

The point of view is now securely Ella's – it doesn't refer to anything except what she might be strongly aware of or likely to notice, and that's a reliable guiding principle, whether you're writing in the first or tight third person; as you'll see, it still applies when the passage is flipped into tight third:

> Ella was late and went straight to the desk to see whether Joe had arrived. The receptionist pointed him out; he was sitting facing the door, looking at her over the top of a magazine. Same old Joe. Same old jacket. And, going by the magazine, same old politics.
>
> Suddenly she felt ridiculous. They used to mock mercilessly anyone who wore sunglasses indoors. And the hat – what had possessed her? She pulled it off and went towards him, trying to look more pleased than she felt.

What these examples show is that the point of view you choose dictates the terms in which the scene is described. Think of your main character as filming what's going on around her. Where is she looking? What does she notice, and what does she think or feel when she notices it? Although the story may be largely about *her*, if it's told from her point of view the focus is on what's around her and who's interacting with her, not on the way she appears from outside. First-person or tight third-person narrative voice becomes insecure when the writer isn't inside the character, seeing the world through her eyes. If you are truly entering the mind of that character – *inhabiting* the character – you won't make the mistake of having her know what she can't realistically know, or see what she can't feasibly see. If you, the writer, are walking through the revolving door with Ella, or waiting in reception with Joe, your account of their experiences is more likely to be believable and to feel authentic to the reader.

Multiple-viewpoint narratives

You need a very good reason to tell a story from more than one perspective because the format makes added demands on the reader. Yes, you the writer are doing the hard work, keeping all these balls in the air, but the reader is also required to follow the juggling, to keep each ball in play mentally, to take on board and then 'park' one version of the story (or part of it) while she attends to another. And it's not just a matter of making intellectual demands: you might also consider the possibility that bustling too briskly between different vantage-points will have the effect of reducing the reader's emotional engagement with any one of them. So the decision to use multiple viewpoints shouldn't be made for merely superficial reasons; there needs to be some added value for the reader in return for this added effort, and this added value needs to arise directly from the unique possibilities this form offers.

Wilkie Collins, a colleague and professional rival of Charles Dickens, was, like Dickens, a game-changer in terms of the development of the novel. *The Woman in White* (1859) is widely regarded as one of the first and best mystery novels, while *The Moonstone* (1868) is widely regarded as one of the first and best detective novels. Setting aside the difficulties attendant on 'first' and 'best', we can see that both books clearly represented significant steps forward in fiction, and it's interesting to note that both novels are similarly constructed, each consisting of a series of purportedly first-hand accounts from the points of view of different characters. Introducing the first of these accounts at the beginning of *The Woman in White*, Collins has his narrator explain:

> ... the story here presented will be told by more than one pen, as the story of an offence against the laws is told in court by more than one witness – with the same object in both cases, to present the truth always in its most direct and most intelligible aspect; and to trace the course of one complete series of events, by making the persons who have been most closely connected with them, at each successive stage, relate their own experience, word for word.

While the courtroom analogy breaks down under close examination, it's still possible to appreciate the general idea that readers might gain a fuller understanding of events by seeing them from a variety of angles.

More recently, writers have used the device less to pin down a definitive version of events than to cast doubt on the idea that there is any such thing. Each character's version of the story will prioritise certain events and neglect others, depending on their position within it. Their view may challenge or subvert another view; the onus is more on the reader to sift and interpret what may be anything from slightly nuanced differences to competing or even irreconcilable versions of events and their meaning.

In *We Were the Mulvaneys* (1996), which charts the disintegration of a seemingly ideal family, Joyce Carol Oates uses a third-person narrator for much of the book which takes, at different points, various members of the family as its centre of consciousness; but she also has some chapters in the first-person voice of Judd, the youngest son of the family. Ali Smith's *The Accidental* (2006) tells the story of an uninvited visitor's effect on a family. Various sections of the novel use a tight third-person perspective to focus on the experience of individual members of the Smart family, and there is also a first-person narrative from the point of view of the visitor. Barbara Kingsolver does something similar in *The Poisonwood Bible* (1998): she too devotes most of the book to interleaving the separate perspectives of members of the same family – four sisters in this case, with each of them as first-person narrator of her section. The majority of Toni Morrison's *Beloved* is told in the third person, sometimes tight third person, but shifts to first person at one point in the novel as each of the three main characters voices her view.

In all these books the approach enables us to appreciate and interpret the story from different perspectives, sifting different versions and readings, partly assembling the story for ourselves while deepening our understanding of the characters' relationships to each other. This strategy of mobilising more than one point of view can be taken further by adding in other materials. In *Alias Grace* (1996) Margaret Atwood uses both present and past tense and has two principal narrative voices: Grace's first-person voice and a third-person voice centred on the doctor Simon Jordan's experience; but the novel also includes letters and extracts from factual sources (events are based on a historical double murder). It's also possible to create faux-factual sources, as Stephen King does in *Carrie* (1974), which intersperses third-person narration with purportedly factual material, including newspaper and magazine articles, academic papers, excerpts from reference books, song lyrics and even graffiti.

A particularly ambitious example of the multiple-viewpoint narrative is Marlon James's *A Brief History of Seven Killings* (2014). With twelve different first-person narrators, the majority of whom speak in forms of Jamaican dialect, the book is by any standards demanding, and particularly so for a non-Caribbean reader. But if it had been written in any other way its force would have been diminished: James is intent on giving a fictive platform to those whose voices have been marginalised, and in doing so he creates the effect of immediacy that is one of the sources of the novel's power.

The narrative is loosely organised around the attempted assassination of a reggae star (here called simply 'The Singer', but readily identifiable as Bob Marley) and presents the lives and thoughts of its varied cast of actors against a background of US-fomented civil unrest in Jamaica. One of these is Demus, who makes plain his own wish to speak directly to his audience, without mediation. Projecting into the future from 1976 he imagines a writer attempting to speak for him, setting down his experience 'maybe forty years later':

> Somebody going to write about this, sit down at a table on a Sunday afternoon with wood floor creaking and fridge humming but no ghost around him like they around me all the time and he going write my story. And he won't know what to write, or how to write it because he didn't live it, or know what cordite smell like or how blood taste when it stay stubborn in your mouth no matter how much you spit. He never feel it in the one drop.[83]

The writer of Demus's story some forty years after the events described at this point in the narrative is, of course, James himself, and the words he puts into Demus's mouth suggest his own inadequacy to the task he has set himself. At the same time, however, James strains towards what we might call the illusion of authenticity, asking us to believe (on some level, at least) that what we are hearing is indeed the unmediated voice of the character: 'This is what I want to say before the writer say it for me.'[84]

This is what justifies the narrative's multiple viewpoints. Much of the novel's energy is derived from the impression we have of hearing each separate voice speaking directly to us, and as with the work of Faulkner – whose influence James acknowledges – we engage with the novel's demands in the knowledge that these are intimately bound up with its strengths.

The range of perspectives

It might be helpful here to look very briefly at the development of the novel, both in order to give a context to our own writing and to give some sense of the variety of perspectives available to the writer of fiction. You may be surprised to discover how early in the history of the novel writers were experimenting with a range of narrative viewpoints.

The book with the strongest claim to being the first novel in English is *Love-Letters Between a Nobleman and His Sister* (1684), attributed to Aphra Behn. As the title suggests, it takes the form (largely) of a correspondence between two characters. The epistolary novel (a novel consisting of letters) offers the opportunity to have more than one first-person narrator – indeed, as many first-person narrators as there are fictional letter writers.

It wasn't until the appearance of Daniel Defoe's *Robinson Crusoe* (1719) that the new long-form fiction hit its stride. Defoe followed up with *Captain Singleton* (1720), *Colonel Jack* (1722), *Moll Flanders* (1722) and *Roxana* (1724) – all, like *Robinson Crusoe*, written in the first person, as though they were autobiographies. Following on from Behn's first venture in the genre, Samuel Richardson went on to popularise the epistolary novel in *Pamela* (1740), *Clarissa* (1748) and *The History of Sir Charles Grandison* (1753), while in novels such as *Tom Jones* (1749) Henry Fielding used the third-person omniscient narrative voice with great success. Jane Austen began developing the tight third in *Sense and Sensibility* (1811) and had come close to perfecting it by the time she wrote *Emma*.

Apart from Charlotte's *Shirley* (1849), the seven completed novels by the Brontë sisters are written in variants of the first person. Charlotte's *Jane Eyre*, *Villette* (1853) and *The Professor* (1857) and Anne's *Agnes Grey* (1847) each have a single narrator (the character of the title), while Anne's *The Tenant of Wildfell Hall* (1848) is framed as a sequence of letters from Gilbert Markham to his brother-in-law, but incorporates the diary of Helen Graham, which she gives to Markham, and which forms the centre of the novel. Emily's only novel, *Wuthering Heights*, significantly complicates the first-person narrative: its frame narrator, Lockwood, incorporates in his own narrative what is essentially a first-person account by the housekeeper, Nelly Dean – though Lockwood claims a degree of narratorial control, explaining at one point that he will continue Nelly's account 'in her own words, only a little condensed'. The reader's general experience is of hearing Nelly's voice, but here the text draws attention to the fact that her account is mediated by Lockwood.

The novels of Charles Dickens are remarkably inventive in their treatment of viewpoint. *The Old Curiosity Shop* (1841) begins in the first person ('Although I am an old man, night is generally my time for walking'), but at the end of the third chapter the unnamed first-person narrator – who has already begun to recede from the action of the novel – announces a shift:

> And now that I have carried this history so far in my own character and introduced these personages to the reader, I shall for the convenience of the narrative detach myself from its further course, and leave

those who have prominent and necessary parts in it to speak and act for themselves.

The original narrator then disappears, not, as the phrase 'speak … for themselves' might suggest, in order to give way to other first-person narrators, but to allow the novel to continue with an omniscient third-person narrator. In *Bleak House* (1853) we find the process reversed, with the third-person narrative of the novel's opening giving way at the beginning of the third chapter to a first-person narration by the novel's protagonist, Esther Summerson. But perhaps the most striking of Dickens's shifts occurs in *Our Mutual Friend* (1865). Here's the opening of the novel:

> In these times of ours, though concerning the exact year there is no need to be precise, a boat of dirty and disreputable appearance, with two figures in it, floated on the Thames, between Southwark bridge which is of iron, and London Bridge which is of stone, as an autumn evening was closing in.
>
> The figures in this boat were those of a strong man with ragged grizzled hair and a sun-browned face, and a dark girl of nineteen or twenty, sufficiently like him to be recognizable as his daughter. The girl rowed, pulling a pair of sculls very easily; the man, with the rudder-lines slack in his hands, and his hands loose in his waistband, kept an eager look out. He had no net, hook, or line, and he could not be a fisherman; his boat had no cushion for a sitter, no paint, no inscription, no appliance beyond a rusty boathook and a coil of rope, and he could not be a waterman; his boat was too crazy and too small to take in cargo for delivery, and he could not be a lighterman or river-carrier; there was no clue to what he looked for, but he looked for something, with a most intent and searching gaze. The tide, which had turned an hour before, was running down, and his eyes watched every little race and eddy in its broad sweep, as the boat made slight head-way against it, or drove stern foremost before it, according as he directed his daughter by a movement of his head. She watched his face as earnestly as he watched the river. But, in the intensity of her look there was a touch of dread or horror.

It's a gripping opening, intriguing and atmospheric, but the second chapter opens with a very different viewpoint and a dramatic change of tone, as Dickens introduces us to a family whose lives seem far removed from those of the two figures out on the river in their dirty boat under a darkening sky:

> Mr and Mrs Veneering were bran-new people in a bran-new house in a bran-new quarter of London. Everything about the Veneerings was spick and span new. All their furniture was new, all their friends were new, all their servants were new, their plate was new, their carriage was new, their harness was new, their horses were new, their pictures were new, they themselves were new, they were as newly married as was lawfully compatible with their having a bran-new baby …

Both passages are written in the third person, but you'll see immediately that the differences between them are significant, and affect our position as readers in relation to their subjects. The description of the Veneerings is essentially omniscient, slyly judgemental and sure of its judgements, while the novel's opening seems uncertain in ways we might normally associate with the tight third-person narrative – that is, a narrative circumscribed by the particular position of a character involved in the action, though the narrator here will not, in fact, prove to be one of the novel's characters. Within a few paragraphs the narrative has moved into rather more conventional territory, but not before the reader has registered the disturbing implications of the narrator's baffled gaze as he looks out on a scene he lacks the understanding and authority to explain.

The suggestions of narratorial bafflement in this passage prefigure the sense of uncertainty that informs so many aspects of modernist fiction. In *Jacob's Room* (1922) Virginia Woolf experiments with narrative viewpoint in ways at once playful and serious, at one stage deliberately circumscribing her third-person narrator's range of perception and understanding before throwing off the constraint in tacit acknowledgement of the overriding power of the creative imagination. The novel's protagonist, Jacob

Flanders, is at this point in the narrative a student at Cambridge, and the narrator observes his life there from a distance that perhaps reflects Woolf's own vexed relationship with the university:

> There was a sofa, chairs, a square table, and the window being open, one could see how they sat – legs issuing here, one there crumpled in a corner of the sofa; and, presumably, for you could not see him, somebody stood by the fender, talking. Anyhow, Jacob, who sat astride a chair and ate dates from a long box, burst out laughing. ...
>
> The laughter died in the air. The sound of it could scarcely have reached anyone standing by the Chapel, which stretched along the opposite side of the court. The laughter died out, and only gestures of arms, movements of bodies, could be seen shaping something in the room. Was it an argument? A bet on the boat races? Was it nothing of the sort? What was shaped by the arms and bodies moving in the twilight room?
>
> A step or two beyond the window there was nothing at all, except the enclosing buildings – chimneys upright, roofs horizontal; too much brick and building for a May night, perhaps. And then before one's eyes would come the bare hills of Turkey – sharp lines, dry earth, coloured flowers, and colour on the shoulders of the women, standing naked-legged in the stream to beat linen on the stones.[85]

Arguably more knowing than the description that opens *Our Mutual Friend*, the passage plays similarly on the notion of a narrator whose physical position prevents her from seeing clearly the events she would like to understand and describe more fully. The exclusion is artificial, of course: the novelist doesn't require the window to be open in order to see what her imaginary characters are doing, and she can, if she wishes, invent the conversations she affects not to be able to hear. Woolf knows this perfectly well, and demonstrates the point by launching us out beyond the college walls to a scene geographically distant, far beyond sight, yet suddenly more immediate than Jacob's Cambridge surroundings. The passage neatly exemplifies an obvious but important truth: as writers we choose not only the stories we tell but the vantage-points from which we tell them.

Two general points are worth considering here. Firstly, the merits of any given viewpoint are determined by the nature of the particular story we want to tell and the experience we want the reader to have: playing around with narrative viewpoint simply because we can is unlikely to produce good results (though this isn't an argument against focused experimentation as part of the writing process). Secondly, as in all matters relating to writing, we need to be in control of our effects: accidental slippage between one point of view and another is a common error, and it will be perceived as an error by any attentive reader.

Centres of consciousness in the third-person narrative

Whatever quarter a narrative comes from, it reflects what Henry James called 'a centre of consciousness' – a position from which the events of the story are perceived. Let's look again, with this in mind, at the tight third person, a narrative viewpoint which, in Chris Power's useful definition, 'confers the intimacy and inflection of first-person storytelling on third-person narration'.[86]

Here's the opening of Katherine Mansfield's short story, 'An Ideal Family' (1921):

That evening for the first time in his life, as he pressed through the swing door and descended the three broad steps to the pavement, old Mr Neave felt he was too old for the spring. Spring – warm, eager, restless – was there, waiting for him in the golden light, ready in front of everybody to run up, to blow in his white beard, to drag sweetly on his arm. And he couldn't meet her, no; he couldn't square up once more and stride off, jaunty as a young man. He was tired and, although the late sun was still shining, curiously cold, with a numbed feeling all over. Quite suddenly he hadn't the energy, he hadn't the heart to stand this gaiety and bright movement any longer; it confused him. He wanted to stand still, to wave it away with his stick, to say, 'Be off with you!' Suddenly it was a terrible effort to greet as usual – tipping his wideawake with his stick – all the people whom he knew, the friends, acquaintances, shopkeepers, postmen, drivers. But the gay glance that went with the gesture, the kindly twinkle that seemed to say, 'I'm a match and more for any of you' – that old Mr Neave could not manage at all. He stumped along, lifting his knees high as if he were walking through air that had somehow grown heavy and solid like water.

Here we're *with* Mr Neave, sharing his thoughts and sensations: we know what he feels about his ageing body, and what he feels about spring and his own inadequacy to meet its challenge; we're privy to his sense of fatigue and confusion in the face of a fast-moving and indifferent world. Compare the opening of Virginia Woolf's *Mrs Dalloway* (1925):

Mrs. Dalloway said she would buy the flowers herself. For Lucy had her work cut out for her. The doors would be taken off their hinges; Rumpelmayer's men were coming. And then, thought Clarissa Dalloway, what a morning – fresh as if issued to children on a beach.

What a lark! What a plunge! For so it had always seemed to her, when, with a little squeak of the hinges, which she could hear now, she had burst open the French windows and plunged at Bourton into the open air. How fresh, how calm, stiller than this of course, the air was in the early morning; like the flap of a wave; the kiss of a wave; chill and sharp and yet (for a girl of eighteen as she then was) solemn, feeling as she did, standing there at the open window, that something awful was about to happen; looking at the flowers, at the trees with the smoke winding off them and the rooks rising, falling; standing and looking until Peter Walsh said, 'Musing among the vegetables?' – was that it? – 'I prefer men to cauliflowers' – was that it? He must have said it at breakfast one morning when she had gone out on to the terrace – Peter Walsh. He would be back from India one of these days, June or July, she forgot which, for his letters were awfully dull; it was his sayings one remembered; his eyes, his pocket-knife, his smile, his grumpiness and, when millions of things had utterly vanished – how strange it was! – a few sayings like this about cabbages.

Again, we're *with* the character, privy to her thoughts, sensations and – in this case – memories. We can imagine almost all of this in Mrs Dalloway's voice as her mind darts through sound and sensation, time and place. Together Mansfield and Woolf, writing at about the same time, took to a new level the idea of a third-person narrative voice that intimately knows and follows the movements of a character's mind. Such a voice often seems more rambling and less organised, and therefore more realistic – more like the way we experience our own thought-processes. An interlocutor (someone to whom these words are addressed) need not be implied: these thoughts often appear to be sealed inside the head of the character rather than actually expressed.

Another kind of narrator figures herself as a member of the community of the story, without participating, or having only a peripheral role. Elizabeth Gaskell uses this method in order to draw us in as indulgent observers of the parochial community of *Cranford* (1853). The novel is narrated mainly in the third person, but notice the use of 'I' and 'we' in this extract from the first chapter:

> I imagine that a few of the gentlefolks of Cranford were poor, and had some difficulty in making both ends meet; but they were like the Spartans, and concealed their smart under a smiling face. We none of us spoke of money, because that subject savoured of commerce and trade, and though some might be poor, we were all aristocratic. The Cranfordians had that kindly *esprit de corps* which made them overlook all deficiencies in success when some among them tried to conceal their poverty. When Mrs Forrester, for instance, gave a party in her baby-house of a dwelling, and the little maiden disturbed the ladies on the sofa by a request that she might get the tea-tray out from underneath, everyone took this novel proceeding as the most natural thing in the world, and talked on about household forms and ceremonies as if we all believed that our hostess had a regular servants' hall, second table, with housekeeper and steward, instead of the one little charity-school maiden, whose short ruddy arms could never have been strong enough to carry the tray upstairs, if she had not been assisted in private by her mistress, who now sat in state, pretending not to know what cakes were sent up, though she knew, and we knew, and she knew that we knew, and we knew that she knew that we knew, she had been busy all the morning making tea-bread and sponge-cakes.

The narrator doesn't obtrude in the novel that follows, but has established herself as being in the place (she is, we discover, an occasional visitor) and, more importantly, in the know. She seems to be saying 'come and sit beside me and I will show you how things are done here'. Earlier we discussed Mary Mann's 'Little Brother', which is one of a sequence of short stories Mann wrote in the 1890s. In the stories, which are set in the fictional village of Dulditch, the narrator is figured as the rector's sister; positioned at the heart of the community yet at the periphery of the featured events, she is ideally placed to be our window on this particular world. As with Gaskell's *Cranford* narrator, a first-person voice is present on occasion, but the character represented by that voice doesn't significantly intrude: she exists to tell other people's stories.

Character and state of mind as revealed in first-person voices

So far in this chapter we've been speaking mainly of the viewpoint implied in a narrative. It's easy enough in theory to distinguish between viewpoint and voice, but in practice it's very difficult to consider one in the absence of the other. We might also note that any discussion of narrative voice is likely to be linked to our discussion of character in Chapter 3. Let's move on now to examine a variety of first-person narrative voices, bearing in mind the close relationship of voice to viewpoint, as well as to the character and mental state of the narrator.

The first-person narrative allows the writer the fullest opportunity to give an individual flavour to the narrative voice. Peter Carey's *True History of the Kelly Gang* (2000), a novel based on the life of the Australian outlaw Ned Kelly, purports to be a transcript of 'thirteen parcels of stained and dog-eared papers, every one of them in Ned Kelly's distinctive hand'. The narrative tells us that they have been written for the benefit of Kelly's daughter, who is addressed directly in the novel's opening paragraph:

> I lost my own father at 12 yr. of age and know what it is to be raised on lies and silences my dear daughter you are presently too young to understand a word I write but this history is for you and will contain no single lie may I burn in Hell if I speak false.

In order to convey an impression of Kelly's limited education Carey significantly reduces punctuation and keeps his speech simple, while Kelly's address to his daughter (whose place we, as readers of the text, can be said to occupy) produces a startling sense of intimacy. The result is a highly individual narrative voice: John Updike described the work as a 'feat of imposture', powerfully persuading the reader that it is Kelly, rather than Carey, who is its author.[87]

Eight years after the success of *The Adventures of Tom Sawyer* (1876), which was written in the third person, Mark Twain took the character of Tom's best friend in that novel and made him the first-person narrator of *The Adventures of Huckleberry Finn* (1884). Here's how that story begins:

> You don't know about me, without you have read a book by the name of *The Adventures of Tom Sawyer*; but that ain't no matter. That book was made by Mr. Mark Twain, and he told the truth, mainly. There was things which he stretched, but mainly he told the truth. That is nothing. I never seen anybody but lied one time or another, without it was Aunt Polly, or the widow, or maybe Mary. Aunt Polly – Tom's Aunt Polly, she is – and Mary, and the Widow Douglas is all told about in that book, which is mostly a true book, with some stretchers, as I said before.

Again we see the use of a fairly basic vocabulary coupled with a casual, conversational tone; the narrator rambles a little, as people often do in conversation – he hasn't got to the end of the paragraph before he repeats himself – and his self-introduction gives a strong sense of a lively, undisciplined character who is going to tell us his story without literary frills or flourishes. We see particularly clearly here the distinction between character and author: Finn refers to his creator by name, amusingly suggesting that Twain may have departed from the truth in his earlier novel, and this adds to the illusion that the character is a real person, living and moving in the same world as the author, and therefore in the same world as the author's readers.

In creating appropriately unsophisticated voices for their narrators both Carey and Twain have chosen to operate within certain linguistic constraints. In *Runt*, Niall Griffiths takes things a step further. The average vocabulary of a native English speaker is 20,000–35,000 words; an eight-year-old is likely to know about 10,000 words, a four-year-old about 5,000. So when Griffiths decided to limit the vocabulary of his first-person narrator in his novel *Runt* to under 1,000 words he was making life very difficult for himself. However, the constraints under which he chose to write produced a remarkably engaging narrative voice.

Runt isn't like most sixteen-year-olds; he's barely literate and is a kind of savant. Griffiths's decision to place a very low cap on the vocabulary at his disposal meant that he had to be extremely inventive with what he did have, and the result is that, as one reviewer wrote, his prose 'enchants you: within a page the rhythm and syntax of Runt's idiolect have taught you how he thinks'.[88] Here's the opening of the novel:

> Last summer it was not like any other summer of my life it was when so many things happened to go Crash in my head. When I said tara to the school and laughed and did a dance on my own and NotDad pushed me out and up to Drunkle's house because He Needed Me they said, Them Two, He Needed Me is what They said cos Auntie Scantie was found up in the tree like they found the ripped sheep but *she* wasn't ripped or not in a way that could be eyed and he's lonely They said and He Needed Me but They were going to Go Their Separate Ways and wanted me gone, My Mam Bethan and that dark bastard NotDad.

By restricting Runt's lexicon Griffiths makes the words available in new ways, in new relationships to each other, creating a voice unique to Runt but essentially accessible to the reader.

Charlie Gordon, the protagonist in Daniel Keyes's novel, *Flowers for Algernon* (1966), is classed as a 'retarded adult'. Motivated by his desire to become 'smart', he allows himself to become the first human subject of a new surgical procedure designed to boost intelligence. The surgery has previously been performed on a mouse, Algernon, whom Charlie observes as his own intelligence rockets. The whole story is told through the journal the researchers ask him to keep, and the narrative, which begins with a limited range of expression, becomes increasingly sophisticated as his mental powers improve. After a while, however, Algernon's intelligence declines, and the reader soon notices evidence of the same reversal in Charlie, whose changing voice mirrors his mental deterioration. Keyes has hit on a highly original way of communicating the horror of Charlie's situation by binding the reader up in his shifting world as he experiences and describes it.

There's a difference in theory between the fundamental character of a narrator and the way a narrator responds to the particular circumstances set up by the narrative, though it's often difficult in practice to separate the two: in fiction, as in life, character is partly determined by circumstance (Ned Kelly's character might have been very different if he hadn't been born into an impoverished and persecuted Irish family; Charlie's mental powers rise and fall under the influence of the scientific experiment to which he is subjected) and fundamental characteristics may determine how a character responds to the events of a narrative. In the act of writing we may not need to worry very much about the distinction, but it's worth touching on it here. If we compare the voice of Huckleberry Finn, in the passage we've just discussed, with that of the narrator of Dorothy Parker's short story, 'A Telephone Call' (1930), we'll see that Finn's voice is predominantly indicative of his basic character while that of Parker's narrator primarily reveals her response to a specific situation. She's waiting for a phone call:

> Please, God, let him telephone me now. Dear God, let him call me
> now. I won't ask anything else of You, truly I won't. It isn't very much

to ask. It would be so little to You, God, such a little, little thing. Only let him telephone now. Please, God. Please, please, please.

If I didn't think about it, maybe the telephone might ring. Sometimes it does that. If I could think of something else. If I could think of something else. Maybe if I counted five hundred by fives, it might ring by that time. I'll count slowly. I won't cheat. And if it rings when I get to three hundred, I won't stop; I won't answer it until I get to five hundred. Five, ten, fifteen, twenty, twenty-five, thirty, thirty-five, forty, forty-five, fifty … Oh, please ring. Please.

The narrative voice, raw and unselfconscious, reveals the narrator's desperation in all its nakedness. Ostensibly the address is initially to God, and subsequently ('Oh, please ring') to the telephone, but she's really talking to herself, attempting, through her words, to manipulate events that are actually beyond her control. While we might surmise that certain fundamental characteristics (neediness, the desire for control) underlie the desperate monologue, we can also imagine this narrator turning up for work on the following day in a very different state of mind and communicating with her colleagues in a very different voice.

We could hardly say the same about the narrator of Edgar Allan Poe's 'The Tell-Tale Heart' (1843), whose agitation seems to come from a deeper and darker source than that of Parker's narrator:

True! – nervous – very, very dreadfully nervous I had been and am; but why will you say that I am mad? The disease had sharpened my senses – not destroyed – not dulled them. Above all was the sense of hearing acute. I heard all things in the heaven and in the earth. I heard many things in hell. How, then, am I mad?

Hearken! and observe how healthily – how calmly I can tell you the whole story.

It is impossible to say how first the idea entered my brain; but once conceived, it haunted me day and night. Object there was none. Passion there was none. I loved the old man. He had never wronged me. He had never given me insult. For his gold I had no desire. I think it was his eye! Yes, it was this! He had the eye of a vulture – a pale blue eye, with a film over it. Whenever it fell upon me, my blood ran cold; and so by degrees – very gradually – I made up my mind to take the life of the old man, and thus rid myself of the eye forever.

Now this is the point. You fancy me mad. Madmen know nothing. But you should have seen me. You should have seen how wisely I proceeded – with what caution – with what foresight – with what dissimulation I went to work! I was never kinder to the old man than during the whole week before I killed him. And every night, about midnight, I turned the latch of his door and opened it – oh so gently! And then, when I had made an opening sufficient for my head, I put in a dark lantern, all closed, closed, that no light shone out, and then I thrust in my head. Oh, you would have laughed to see how cunningly I thrust it in! I moved it slowly – very, very slowly, so that I might not disturb the old man's sleep. It took me an hour to place my whole head within the opening so far that I could see him as he lay upon his bed. Ha! would a madman have been so wise as this?

There's a disturbing energy in this agitated narrative voice, an energy achieved partly by Poe's use of short phrases, sometimes separated by dashes rather than being brought to rest on a full stop. We'll also notice the insistency of the voice – this is a speaker working with a kind of desperation not merely to inform his listener but to *persuade* him; and there's something worryingly erratic in his line of reasoning – he seems to feel that he's advancing a logical argument, but the logic is so deeply flawed that the argument falls apart as he presents it. And this brings us to the subject of narratorial unreliability.

The unreliable narrator

We might reasonably ask ourselves whether any first-person narrator is truly reliable. A well-conceived narrator will be a product of his background and his experience, and his outlook will be influenced by both; the lens through which he perceives the world will affect his shaping of the story he has to tell. But the term 'unreliable narrator' usually implies a narrator whose telling of the story leads us actively to question some of the story's details.

The narrator may be telling us one thing, yet he has given us information which in some way undermines, challenges or contradicts his own presentation of events; there's usually a strong sense that he's unaware of any interpretation other than his own.

Let's stay with 'The Tell-Tale Heart' in order to see how this particular narrative sets up a tension between what the narrator tells us and what the reader might understand from the telling. The insistency we've just noted relates to one matter in particular, the question of the narrator's sanity. The events themselves must make us question his mental state. He has, after all – if his story is to be believed at all – recently killed an old man, a crime arguably unjustifiable for any reason, and certainly not justified by the reason the narrator gives. As he continues his disjointed explanation of the killing, we become increasingly suspicious of his version of events. If it's true that he is, as he tells us at the beginning of the story, 'very, very dreadfully nervous' and also the victim of an unspecified disease that affects his perception, then we will surely ask ourselves how this squares with the injunction to 'observe how healthily – how calmly I can tell you the whole story'. (As we noted earlier, the voice in this story is distinctly agitated, so what we observe is something quite different from what the narrator imagines us to be observing.) When he tells us that, under the influence of his disease, 'I heard all things in the heaven and in the earth. I heard many things in hell', most rational readers will have a ready response to the question that follows: 'How, then, am I mad?' And how do we respond to his description of creeping into the old man's room? As if the act itself isn't weird enough, the narrator says it takes him an hour to get his head through the door. We recognise that either his perception or his behaviour is extremely odd, and we are on our guard, conscious of the tension between his insistence that he isn't mad and our own increasing certainty that he must be.

Unreliable narratives don't necessarily draw attention to their unreliability in such obvious ways as this; nor is the sanity of the narrator necessarily in question. It may simply be that the narrator's subjective view of the world doesn't match the facts as revealed in the narrative. Dowell, the narrator of Ford Madox Ford's *The Good Soldier* (1915), discovers in the telling of his story that his version of events has been based on false impressions. He lived for years in ignorance of his wife's affair with his best friend, and even though his narrative has been written subsequently, some of his earlier impressions have persisted, against the evidence that should have destroyed them. Early in his narrative, he tells us: 'I don't believe that for one minute she [his wife] was out of my sight, except when she was safely tucked up in bed' – a revealing exception, we might think. Dowell later offers a dramatic correction:

> But, looking over what I have written, I see that I have unintention-
> ally misled you when I said that Florence was never out of my sight.
> Yet that was the impression that I really had until just now. When I
> come to think of it she was out of my sight most of the time.[89]

This isn't the only thing the narrator has got wrong, and it's argu-able that Dowell never fully grasps the truths that the attentive reader gleans from his narrative.

Dowell gives misleading information not because he's a liar, but because he has only a limited understanding of what he has wit-nessed. Something similar might be said of Stevens, the narrator of Kazuo Ishiguro's *The Remains of the Day*, a man who appears not to understand himself. Like Dowell, Stevens is a narrator who, even as he tells his story, seems to stand at a distance from his own experience, failing fully to understand the implications of his own narrative: the significance of certain actions or reactions is revealed to the reader *through* Stevens but not *to* him. Stevens clearly believes that any display of emotion is inappropriate to his role as butler, and he is so reticent about his feelings that we don't know – as he himself seems not to know – what they are until a fragment of external evidence brings them to our attention.

Even though he knows his father (also a butler) is dying upstairs in the servants' quarters, Stevens is carrying on in characteris-tically professional fashion, coping admirably with an extremely demanding and politically significant dinner at Darlington Hall, smiling and chatting with guests as he goes about his work. He is serving port to a group of gentlemen when, we are told:

> I felt something touch my elbow and turned to find Lord Darlington.
> 'Stevens, are you alright?'
> 'Yes, sir. Perfectly.'
> 'You look as though you're crying.'
> I laughed and taking out a handkerchief, quickly wiped my face.
> 'I'm very sorry, sir. The strains of a hard day.'[90]

Stevens is showing himself here to be the consummate professional, but there's also a suggestion that he doesn't recognise his grief for what it is. The fact that he hardly ever acknowledges – let alone reflects on – his own feelings means that on the extremely rare occasions when he does, the acknowledgement hits the reader with extraordinary force. Towards the close of the novel, Mrs Benn – with whom, when she was Miss Kenton, Stevens had worked at the Hall some years before – talks candidly about her life since then, and about how she has come to terms with her often unsatisfactory marriage:

> Miss Kenton fell silent again for a moment. Then she went on:
> 'But that doesn't mean to say, of course, there aren't occasions now and then – extremely desolate occasions – when you think to yourself: "What a terrible mistake I've made with my life." And you get to thinking about a different life, a *better* life you might have had. For instance, I get to thinking about a life I might have had with you, Mr Stevens. And I suppose that's when I get angry over some trivial little thing and leave. But each time I do so, I realize before long – my rightful place is with my husband. After all, there's no turning back the clock now. One can't be forever dwelling on what might have been. One should realize one has as good as most, perhaps better, and be grateful.'
> I do not think I responded immediately, for it took me a moment or two to fully digest these words of Miss Kenton. Moreover, as you might appreciate, their implications were such as to provoke a certain

degree of sorrow within me. Indeed – why should I not admit it? – at that moment, my heart was breaking.'[91]

It is because Stevens has never acknowledged any sense of feeling for Miss Kenton beyond professional friendship, nor any real sense of regret about how he has spent his life – though the attentive reader will have seen ample evidence of these possibilities – that this revelation is so powerful. The reader responds to this momentary glimpse of the secret the narrator has been keeping from himself for years, but Stevens is unable to contemplate it. The next sentence runs on, without so much as a paragraph break:

> Before long, however, I turned to her and said with a smile:
> 'You're very correct, Mrs Benn. As you say, it is too late to turn back the clock.'[92]

'Very correct': the phrase seems in context to mean 'absolutely right', but it isn't usually used in that sense, and we might conclude that Stevens is also drawing attention to the need, as he perceives it, for people to deny their feelings in the interests of correct behaviour.

Muriel Spark gives us a very different character as the unreliable narrator of her short story 'You Should Have Seen the Mess' (1958), which begins:

> I am now more than glad that I did not pass into the grammar school five years ago, although it was a disappointment at the time. I was always good at English, but not so good at the other subjects!!

The double exclamation mark confirms the youth – and the unsubtlety – of our narrator who goes on to tell us about her life, clearly unaware that the impression she means to give is at variance with the considerably less appealing one we actually get.

We quickly realise that she places a particularly high value on cleanliness. The grammar school does not come up to standard in any case (dusty, untidy, chipped paintwork) and when she gets a job in an office she is very upset by the cracked cups and lack of saucers: 'We never keep a cracked cup, but throw it out, because those cracks can harbour germs. So Mum gave me my own cup to take to the office.' We also note that she is quick to perceive slights and to take offence where none may be intended:

> … at the end of the week, when I got my salary, Mr Heygate [her employer] said, 'Well, Lorna, what are you going to do with your first pay?' I did not like him saying this, and I nearly passed a comment, but I said, 'I don't know.' He said, 'What do you do in the evenings, Lorna? Do you watch Telly?' I did take this as an insult, because we call it TV, and his remark made me out to be uneducated. I just stood, and did not answer, and he looked surprised.

Mr Heygate's attempts to draw out his new employee are taken amiss, and Lorna clearly doesn't realise her own behaviour is both odd and rude. Her mother decides she should leave that job ('Also, the desks in the general office were rickety') and she goes for an interview at a publisher's ('One look was enough!!') before winding up at a chemical company, where it is clean and modern and the boss dresses smartly.

Lorna has been taken under the wing of the local doctor and his wife, and while they are 'very kind' to her she is appalled by what she considers to be their casual and disreputable domestic arrangements ('they did not have twin beds, although he was a doctor'). Dr Darby and his wife, Mavis, introduce her to their friends, who are always 'coming and going, and they had interesting conversation, although sometimes it gave me a surprise, and I did not know where to look'; she takes up with one of them, a talented young artist ('It was always unhygienic when I went to Willy's place, and I told him so once, but he said, "Lorna, you are a joy"'). Willy is wealthy and generous – they are clearly keen on each other and there is talk of marriage. The last paragraph of the story is, in its way, tragic:

> One night, when I went home, I was upset as usual, after Willy's place. Mum and Dad had gone to bed, and I looked round our kitchen which

is done in primrose and white. Then I went into the living-room, where Dad has done one wall in a patterned paper, deep rose and white, and the other walls pale rose, with white woodwork. The suite is new, and Mum keeps everything beautiful. So it came to me, all of a sudden, what a fool I was, going with Willy. I agree to equality, but as to me marrying Willy, as I said to Mavis, when I recall his place, and the good carpet gone greasy, not to mention the paint oozing out of the tubes, I think it would break my heart to sink so low.

We often talk about 'reading between the lines' and this is very much what an unreliable narrator has us doing: we see that the things that Lorna thinks keep her safe actually hold her back. She conflates her fear of dirt, disorder and difference with respectability and security, so when a door leading out of her world opens, she shuts it, believing that she has had a lucky escape. Her worldview is dependent on keeping the door closed: she sees that other people live their lives differently, but can't see that to live differently isn't necessarily to live wrongly. The narrator shows us the world as she sees it, naively assuming that we see it in the same way; the author works on the assumption that her reader has a wider and deeper understanding than Lorna's. It's in the tension between the narrator's view on the one hand and the writer's and reader's on the other that we find the narrative's energy and meaning.

First-person plural narration

Extremely rare and very difficult to manage, the first-person plural narrative is ostensibly told by a group of people. In *The Virgin Suicides* (1993), Jeffrey Eugenides tells a story about a family of girls who all individually and for no apparent reason committed suicide; the story is told from the point of view of a group of local boys (sometimes referred to as 'we' and sometimes as 'the boys'). Now middle-aged men, they have conducted interviews and pieced together various items of evidence which they present to the reader ('Please don't touch. We're going to put the picture back in its envelope now'),[93] hoping to solve the mystery, though they ultimately conclude:

> It didn't matter in the end how old they had been, or that they were girls, but only that we had loved them, and that they hadn't heard us calling, still do not hear us, up here in the tree house, with our thinning hair and soft bellies, calling them out of those rooms where they went to be alone for all time, alone in suicide, which is deeper than death, and where we will never find the pieces to put them back together.[94]

The boys' collective infatuation with the girls, we come to understand, prevents them from really knowing them, and we come to see that Eugenides may be using the plural first person to raise questions less about a particular boy and a particular girl, but about boys and girls, collective experience of otherness and even, perhaps, the unconscious tyranny of the male gaze. Joshua Ferris uses the same device in *Then We Came to the End* (2007) where the camaraderie of a bunch of stressed-out employees in an advertising agency seems the only way to survive the toxic mix of boredom and anxiety. Ferris plays on the collective experience of office life, where he emphasises a sense of 'them' and 'us' by telling the story not from 'my' but from 'our' point of view.

The rarity with which we encounter a choral first person suggests its limited usefulness; however, both these examples demonstrate that it can be successfully deployed by skilled writers in the right context.

Second-person address

We've already seen, in our discussion of the first-person narrative as a means of conveying character, several examples of this – the narrator addressing a 'you' – and it may be helpful to think a little further about this. The first thing we might notice is that in each of those cases the narrator stands in a slightly different relationship to the 'you' of his narrative: Huckleberry Finn is addressing himself

directly to the supposed reader of the book; Ned Kelly is addressing the daughter for whose benefit he is setting down his 'true history' (and over whose shoulder, as it were, the reader of the book
is looking); the narrator of 'The Tell-Tale Heart', more complicat-
edly, is addressing a reader who may also be an implied character in
the story – an interlocutor whose doubts about the narrator's sanity
have just been expressed at the point at which the narrative opens.

Perhaps the most famous of direct addresses is Jane Eyre's
announcement: 'Reader, I married him.' In explicitly acknowledging the reader's presence, Charlotte Brontë's narrator-protagonist
sets up a connection between narrator and reader – though the
reader in this instance is a more or less abstract entity, standing
outside the frame of the narrative.

Anne Brontë's *The Tenant of Wildfell Hall* opens with a similarly
direct address to the reader ('You must go back with me to the
autumn of 1827. My father, as you know, was a sort of gentleman
farmer in –shire … ') – figuring the reader as a passenger on a
journey through time and space, and the narrator as guide. You'll
notice that the addressee is represented as already knowing some
of the facts of the story, and you'll understand from this that
there's a difference in this case between the hypothetical reader
of the narrative and the actual reader of the novel; but you'll also
see how this approach draws us, the actual readers, into the story.
We can imagine ourselves as taking part in the narrative itself,
entering its space at the invitation or insistence of the narrator.

Involvement of the reader can be taken a step further. Let's
return to the opening of J. D. Salinger's *The Catcher in the Rye*:

> If you really want to hear about it, the first thing you'll probably want
> to know is where I was born, and what my lousy childhood was like,
> and how my parents were occupied and all before they had me, and
> all that David Copperfield kind of crap …

In this address to his readers, the narrator comes close to turning them into characters in the novel. We have, it appears, been
pressing him to tell us about himself; he's going to do so, but on

his own terms. He assumes we'll want him to tell his life story in traditional form, but we know at once from the way he frames that assumption ('all that David Copperfield kind of crap') that he wants to tell it in a different way. We experience the opening of the novel as an ill-tempered and uninterruptable monologue, yet it's perversely engaging in its involvement of its readers, implying that we have the power to talk back to him even as it forbids us to do so: 'If there's one thing I hate, it's the movies. Don't even mention them to me.'

And one step further still: the first-person narrator of Mohsin Hamid's *The Reluctant Fundamentalist* (2007) addresses his story to a shadowy second person who is not (or is not simply) the reader, but an active presence in the narrative. Although his actions, like his words, are mediated by the narrator (we never hear his voice directly, and his actions and feelings have to be deduced from what the narrator says to him) this figure is, in a way that will prove crucially important, a character in the novel. Hamid establishes the dynamic in the novel's opening paragraphs:

> Excuse me, sir, but may I be of assistance? Ah, I see I have alarmed you. Do not be frightened by my beard: I am a lover of America. I noticed that you were looking for something; more than looking, in fact you seemed to be on a *mission*, and since I am both a native of this city and a speaker of your language, I thought I might offer you my services.
>
> How did I know that you were American? No, not by the colour of your skin ... Instead, it was your *bearing* that allowed me to identify you, and I do not mean that as an insult, for I see your face has hardened, but merely as an observation.

It's a difficult act to sustain, and some readers may be troubled by the unnaturalness of phrases such as 'You would rather wait, you say' or 'Is he praying, you ask', but the second-person address is an important source of the novel's power. The sense of approaching danger and the suspense as we wait to see what the danger is, and from what direction it might come, are given a sharper edge by a device which narrows the gap between the reader and the action.

These are all first-person narratives, but the narrator of a predominantly third-person narrative can also use the first-person/ second-person dynamic to establish intimate terms with the reader. The omniscient narrator of Charlotte Brontë's *Shirley* occasionally assumes first-person status in order to address the reader directly, as in the novel's opening paragraphs, where she asserts a degree of intimacy while also suggesting (rather like the narrator of *The Catcher in the Rye*, though far more decorously) that we may need to adjust our expectations concerning the kind of story she is about to tell:

> Of late years, an abundant shower of curates has fallen upon the north of England: they lie very thick on the hills; every parish has one or more of them; they are young enough to be very active, and ought to be doing a great deal of good. But not of late years are we about to speak; we are going back to the beginning of this century: late years – present years are dusty, sun-burnt, hot, arid; we will evade the noon, forget it in siesta, pass the mid-day in slumber, and dream of dawn.
>
> If you think, from this prelude, that anything like a romance is preparing for you, reader, you never were more mistaken. Do you anticipate sentiment, and poetry, and reverie? Do you expect passion, and stimulus, and melodrama? Calm your expectations; reduce them to a lowly standard. Something real, cool, and solid lies before you; something unromantic as Monday morning, when all who have work wake with the consciousness that they must rise and betake themselves thereto.

The voice is engaging, nudging us gently and with subtle humour into agreement with the implied idea that the ordinary ('something as unromantic as Monday morning') may be not only more 'real' than romance but also of greater interest.

Direct address may draw us into a work of fiction, but it may also have the effect of reminding us that what we are reading *is* a work of fiction – an artificial construct. For the postmodern writer this may be a desirable effect. Here's the opening of Italo Calvino's *If on a winter's night a traveller* (1979):

> You are about to begin reading Italo Calvino's new novel, *If on a winter's night a traveller*. Relax. Concentrate. Dispel every other thought. Let the world around you fade. Best to close the door; the TV is always on in the next room. Tell the others right away, 'No, I don't want to watch TV!' Raise your voice – they won't hear you otherwise – 'I'm reading! I don't want to be disturbed!' Maybe they haven't heard you, with all that racket; speak louder, yell: 'I'm beginning to read Italo Calvino's new novel!' Or if you prefer, don't say anything; just hope they'll leave you alone.

Readers eager for immersion in a story may find this approach frustrating; others will enjoy the playfulness of a narrative centrally concerned with the act of reading. Whether or not we want, as writers, to work in this vein, we'll find it useful to see how it might be done.

Other-world narrative voices

'What's it going to be then, eh?'

There was me, that is Alex, and my three droogs, that is Pete, Georgie, and Dim, Dim being really dim, and we sat in the Korova Milkbar making up our rassoodocks what to do with the evening, a flip dark chill winter bastard though dry. The Korova Milkbar was a milk-plus mesto, and you may, O my brothers, have forgotten what these mestos were like, things changing so skorry these days and everybody very quick to forget, newspapers not being read much neither. Well, what they sold there was milk plus something else. They had no licence for selling liquor, but there was no law yet against prodding some of the new veshches which they used to put into the old moloko, so you could peet it with vellocet or synthemesc or drencrom or one or two other veshches which would give you a nice quiet horrorshow fifteen minutes admiring Bog And All His Holy Angels and Saints in your left shoe with lights bursting all over your mozg.

> Or you could peet milk with knives in it, as we used to say, and this would sharpen you up and make you ready for a bit of dirty twenty-to-one, and that was what we were peeting this evening I'm starting off the story with.

The opening of Anthony Burgess's novel *A Clockwork Orange* (1962) plunges the reader into the world – and language – of its characters. The language Burgess developed for the book, Nadsat (a cocktail of Russian, Romany, Cockney-rhyming and other slang culled from the army and the criminal underworld), has the effect of separating Burgess's dystopia from our own time, or, indeed, any fixed time or place.

Burgess wanted readers to learn the argot as they progressed through the novel; he later wrote that Nadsat 'was meant to turn *A Clockwork Orange* into a brainwashing primer. You should read the book and at the end you should find yourself in possession of a minimal Russian vocabulary – without effort, with surprise.'[95] It was important to him that readers learnt the language themselves, with no support outside the text itself: 'The novel was to be an exercise in linguistic programming, with the exoticisms gradually clarified by context: I would resist to the limit any publisher's demand that a glossary be provided. A glossary would disrupt the programme and nullify the brainwashing.'[96] His editor felt that the early version of the book was, in fact, too demanding, and Burgess was persuaded to begin it with relatively few unfamiliar words, gradually increasing the proportion of them, and also having Alex, the narrator, help the reader a little – as when he describes the designs on their 'jelly moulds', which we understand to be decorated codpieces:

> I had one in the shape of a spider, Pete had a rooker (a hand, that is), Georgie had a very fancy one of a flower, and poor old Dim had a very hound-and-horny one of a clown's litso (face, that is) ...[97]

Readers did find it hard, and initial sales were poor; however Stanley Kubrick's film of the book generated interest in it and *A Clockwork Orange* is now widely regarded as a modern classic.

It's clear from Burgess's own account that his choice of this demanding strategy was not merely intended to defamiliarise the text, emphasising the otherness of this world, but to demonstrate to the reader that we can unconsciously absorb language; that in turn may imply that we can unconsciously absorb culture through language, and that it's possible that we – or people like us – could, with worrying ease, buy into the violent culture of the book's characters. Burgess's choice of narrative voice on the one hand emphasises the foreignness of the society described – it is emphatically *not* here and now – but it also suggests how easily that society might cease to be foreign to us.

Burgess's *Nothing Like the Sun* (1964), a fictional account of the life of William Shakespeare, is a very different novel, yet the challenge it presented was related to that of *A Clockwork Orange*. We discussed with reference to dialogue in historical fiction the difficulty of representing the speech of the past, suggesting the need to strike a compromise between historical accuracy and reader accessibility. A writer choosing to put the narrative, as well as the dialogue, in a more or less authentic period voice faces this problem on a vast scale. Burgess developed a voice which was an 'approximation to Elizabethan English', a voice constructed out of words and phrases drawn from Shakespeare's own writing and that of his contemporaries, but largely avoiding vocabulary which would merely bewilder the modern reader. As in *A Clockwork Orange* Burgess was careful to provide contexts from which the meaning of unfamiliar words could be deduced.

Later novelists writing in some kind of 'other' language have sometimes seemed less confident about the reader's ability to interpret unfamiliar words – or perhaps less resistant to their editors' demands. Russell Hoban in *Riddley Walker* (1980) and Paul Kingsnorth in *The Wake* (2014) both offer glossaries (though, to be fair, Hoban's is more of a sample). *Riddley Walker* is set in post-nuclear holocaust Kent, so Hoban is relatively free to speculate how his characters might communicate in that imagined future, and no one can call him out because there is no measure against which its seeming authenticity can be judged. Hoban has explained that 'language went through a near-total breakdown in a dark age after the destruction of civilisation', so the language of the time of the book is part reconstructed, part residual. Some words are corruptions (*pirntowt* for *printout*), others are reworkings (*berstin fyr* for *explosives*) and the whole language is presented phonetically (so *wud* stands both for *wood* and *would*). Hoban explains: 'Riddley-speak is only a breaking down and twisting of standard English, so the reader who sounds out the words and uses a little imagination ought to be able to understand it.' Like Nadsat for Burgess, Riddley-speak performs a function additional to its role as a tool of communication: 'Technically it works well with the story because it slows the reader down to Riddley's rate of comprehension.'[58] Here's a taste of Riddley-speak, from the opening of the novel:

> On my naming day when I come 12 I gone front spear and kilt a wyld boar he parbly ben the las wyld pig on the Bundel Downs any how there hadnt ben none for a long time befor him nor I aint looking to see none agen. He dint make the groun shake nor nothing like that when he come on to my spear he wernt all that big plus he lookit poorly. He done the reqwyrt he ternt and stood and clattert his teef and made his rush and there we wer then. Him on 1 end of the spear kicking his life out and me on the other end watching him dy. I said, 'Your tern now my tern later.' The other spears gone in then and he wer dead and the steam coming up off him in the rain and we all yelt, 'Offert!'

Kingsnorth's *The Wake* is set not in the future but a thousand years ago, in eleventh-century Lincolnshire. Knowing that very few of his readers will have knowledge of Old English (OE), he compromises with what he calls a 'pseudo-OE'. As far as possible he uses only words which originate in OE, OE spelling and no letters which didn't exist in OE (no k, v, j or q). However, he builds in flexibility:

To achieve the sound and look I wanted on the page I have combined Old English words with modern vocabulary, mutated and hammered the shape of OE words and word endings to suit my purpose, and been wanton in combining the Wessex dialect with that of Mercia, Anglia and Northumberland – and dropping in a smattering of Old Norse when it seemed to work. ... There was one final rule I set myself, and it was this: all of the previous rules could be overridden, if necessary, by a meta-rule, which functioned as a kind of literary thegn: do what the novel needs you to do. This, in the end, was a matter of instinct ...'[99]

Here's a sample:

Loc it is well cnawan there is those wolde be tellan lies and those with only them selfs in mynd. There is those now who specs of us and what we done but who cnawan triewe no man cnawan triewe but i and what i tell i will tell as I sceolde and all that will be telt will be all the triewth. Triewth there is lytel of now in this half broc land our folc wepan and greotan and biddan help from their crist who locs on in stillness saen naht. And no triewth will thu hiere from the hore who claims he is our cyng or from his biscops or those who wolde be his men by spillan anglisc guttas on anglisc ground and claiman anglisc land their own.[100]

When Hoban says, of the language of *Riddley Walker*, 'some words that look strange will explain themselves when sounded out; others may require a little more work',[101] he could just as easily be talking about *The Wake* – although the latter is certainly easier if you have a grasp of OE pronunciation, which Kingsnorth helpfully explains in an endnote.

Like Burgess and Hoban, Kingsnorth has more than one reason for his decision about the language of the book. Firstly, he dislikes historical novels written in modern language, because our worldview is specific to our time and place and this is implicit in our language: 'To put 21st-century sentences into the mouths of eleventh century characters would be the equivalent of giving them iPads and cappuccinos: just wrong.' Secondly, he wanted to convey 'the sheer alienness of Old England':

The early English created the nation we now live in. They are, in a very real sense, the ancestors of all of us living in England today, wherever our actual ancestors come from. Despite this link, though, their world was distant from ours; not only in time but in values, understanding, mythopoesis. Language seemed the best way to convey this.

This novel was written in a tongue which no one has ever spoken, but which is intended to project a ghost image of the speech patterns of a long-dead land: a place at once alien and familiar. Another world, the foundation of our own.[102]

The phrase 'at once alien and familiar' usefully describes the function of all these dialects, whatever time and place the writer imagines. Burgess, Hoban and Kingsnorth use language to insist on the otherness of the world their characters inhabit, while immersing the reader in that world to a point where its language and values become familiar. The challenge the writers face (and offer) involves pushing the alien to a point just within the reader's capacity to accommodate it. This is where Kingsnorth's 'instinct' comes in – the writer has to judge how far he can go before the unknown reader feels insufficiently rewarded for the extra effort she is putting in and wants to give up and do something else.

As with so many aspects of writing, the author using other-world speech is constantly negotiating, trading one thing for another. Careful in his choice of unfamiliar language, introducing new words gradually and in a context which allows the reader to understand their meaning, he tries to map out a path which simultaneously remains true to his intentions and keeps the reader fully on board. Such a balancing act is fraught with difficulty and is a high-risk enterprise for a writer, but when done successfully may result in genuinely new and exciting work.

– 9 –

Beginnings and endings; tension and pace

∼

A good enough beginning

If you have difficulty starting a writing project you're not alone. It's significant that when those who have trouble starting something find themselves in a structured teaching session, working with a clearly stated prompt, they may often produce good writing, so the problem is not that they can't write, but that when they are defining their own goals they are dissatisfied with much of what they write. When a developing writer says 'I can't get started' what they usually mean is not that they stare at the naked page or the blank screen and are unable to make a single mark on it, but that they do start and are disappointed with their efforts; they start, but they start over and over again. It is as if they believe that until they can get that first paragraph perfect there's no point going on. In reality, unless you are prepared to tolerate an imperfect opening at the start of the writing process, there's a good chance that you'll never make any significant progress at all.

While perfectionism can hinder progress, the emphasis on (eventually) getting the opening right is not misplaced. The beginning of a story often introduces the main character and/or theme and may set the plot ticking; it establishes a narrative voice and sets up reader expectation. It's the opening gambit in establishing an implicit contract between the reader and writer as they set out together on a journey. Imagine a reader in a bookshop deciding whether to put the book in her hand back on the shelf or take it to the till: your opening paragraphs are likely to represent your opportunity to persuade her to buy a ticket for the journey. And it's precisely because an opening has to do so much that you need to step back and look at this logically. There's a good argument that it's difficult to write a final draft of an opening before you have written a provisional draft of the whole narrative. The opening of your story will very likely need to be rewritten, mainly because you don't know enough about the story until you have completed a first draft.

Understand that you are needlessly sabotaging your chances of getting a story written if you fixate, at too early a stage in the writing of it, on creating the perfect opening. You may torment yourself by comparing your own beginnings with the openings of works by the authors you most admire. However, quite apart from the fact that nobody can write quite like (say) Virginia Woolf, it's unreasonable to expect the opening of the first draft of your story to compare favourably with material which has almost certainly been through several drafts, first by the (already experienced) writer alone, and then influenced by feedback from any combination of trusted friends, other writers, agents and editors.

Experienced writers know that their original opening is unlikely to survive unmodified in subsequent drafts of the story. They understand that the concern to perfect the first part of a narrative is actually irrational and counterproductive. It's like saying you can't build a house until you've found the perfect front door. Just get on with building the house. Once you've done that, you'll be able to see much more clearly what kind of door it needs.

Another analogy that may be helpful in this context: think of the mess you make in the kitchen while you're cooking. That's not what the guests at your dinner party are going to see on the table; they're going to see the results of that messy process. Just as your cooking will, hopefully, produce something good to eat, so your writing may eventually produce something good to read.

When you've finished your short story or novel you'll probably need to revisit its opening several times. In doing so you may find that the opening is basically sound but needs minor tweaks in the light of the experience you have gained writing the whole story; or perhaps that you need to write a new opening; or even that the opening is now superfluous and that you can cut it altogether. William Golding's early versions of *Lord of the Flies* (1954) began on the plane, prior to the crash that strands the boys on an island. When the manuscript was completed this was axed: the classic novel as we know it begins on the island, as the survivors find each other and take stock of the situation. The crash is an event which marks a turning point in the boys' lives – there's a 'before the crash' and an 'after the crash' and Golding's final version located itself exclusively in an 'after', where there are, significantly, 'No grown-ups!' It can be extremely helpful to examine how much 'before' your story needs. If you can lop off your opening and everything still makes sense, it's obviously redundant.

Whatever you conclude about your opening, the important point is that problems, here as in other parts of your narrative, are fixable. If you bear this in mind when you start writing you'll be freeing yourself to get on and do the work, without the burden of trying to achieve the ideal opening at an unrealistically early stage in the writing process.

Now that we've established these important practical matters, let's look at a few successful openings with a view to understanding how they work. An opening will often suggest the subject and setting of a book, while also introducing one or more of its characters, as in the opening of D. H. Lawrence's *Women in Love*:

Ursula and Gudrun Brangwen sat one morning in the window-bay of their father's house in Beldover, working and talking. Ursula was stitching a piece of brightly-coloured embroidery, and Gudrun was drawing upon a board which she held on her knee. They were mostly silent, talking as their thoughts strayed through their minds.

'Ursula,' said Gudrun, 'don't you *really want* to get married?' Ursula laid her embroidery in her lap and looked up. Her face was calm and considerate.

'I don't know,' she replied. 'It depends how you mean.'

Gudrun was slightly taken aback. She watched her sister for some moments.

'Well,' she said, ironically, 'it usually means one thing! But don't you think anyhow, you'd be –' she darkened slightly – 'in a better position than you are in now.'

A shadow came over Ursula's face.

'I might,' she said. 'But I'm not sure.'

Again Gudrun paused, slightly irritated. She wanted to be quite definite.

Look how economically Lawrence works, firstly setting the scene through a brief descriptive passage: the phrase 'in their father's house' strongly suggests that these are unmarried women, makes it absolutely clear that they are sisters, and obliquely hints at something a little unsatisfactory in their circumstances. We might also surmise from their activities that the women have a degree of leisure, and this, in turn, broadly defines their social status. The dialogue that follows provides confirmation of their marital status and the unsatisfactoriness of their present circumstances, while neatly establishing character and suggesting significant differences between the sisters. Ursula, with her 'calm and considerate' expression – 'considerate' here meaning simply 'thoughtful' – thinks and speaks in a noticeably different way from Gudrun: her response to Gudrun's first question isn't so much an answer as a recognition of the question's complexity, while Gudrun considers the question to be straightforward – 'it usually means one thing'; Ursula expresses herself in hesitancies and uncertainties – 'I might … I'm not sure' – while Gudrun, we are explicitly told, 'wanted to be quite definite'. And the subject of their discussion is the subject of the novel: the quest for fulfilment in human relationships, in particular the relationships between men and women.

There will be dramatic moments in this novel, but Lawrence leads us in gently. The opening of Zadie Smith's *White Teeth* (2000) thrusts us directly into a dramatic scene:

Early in the morning, late in the century, Cricklewood Broadway. At 06.27 hours on 1 January 1975, Alfred Archibald Jones was dressed in corduroy and sat in a fume-filled Cavalier Musketeer Estate face down on the steering wheel, hoping the judgment would not be too heavy upon him. He lay forward in a prostrate cross, jaw slack, arms splayed either side like some fallen angel; scrunched up in each fist he held his army service medals (left) and his marriage licence (right), for he had decided to take his mistakes with him. A little green light flashed in his eye, signalling a right turn he had resolved never to make. He was resigned to it. He was prepared for it. He had flipped a coin and stood staunchly by its conclusions. It was a decided-upon suicide. In fact it was a New Year's resolution.

The scene may be dramatic, but the tone isn't: the first part of this description is factual and precise, reading very like an account read out in court by a police officer – place, time, date, name, type of car, position of human figure; we seem to be watching Jones from outside. But we quickly establish a rather more intimate relationship with him – his hopes for a light judgement, his resignation, his preparedness. The medals and marriage licence are, it's suggested, emblematic of his mistakes, and they function as a 'hook' – a device to draw us into the story. We understand immediately that they mean something and that the narrative that follows will help us to understand their meaning.

Let's turn now to the opening of Robert Graves's *I, Claudius* (1934):

> I, Tiberius Claudius Drusus Nero Germanicus This-that-and-the-other (for I shall not trouble you yet with all my titles) who was once, and not so long ago either, known to my friends and relatives and associates as 'Claudius the Idiot,' or 'That Claudius,' or 'Claudius the Stammerer,' or 'Clau-Clau-Claudius' or at best as 'Poor Uncle Claudius,' am now about to write this strange history of my life; starting from my earliest childhood and continuing year by year until I reach the fateful point of change where, some eight years ago, at the age of fifty-one, I suddenly found myself caught in what I may call the 'golden predicament' from which I have never since become disentangled.

The most obvious hook in this long opening sentence comes at its end: a predicament is a difficult situation, usually requiring some

kind of resolution (we might say that predicament, broadly understood, is the mainspring of most novelistic plots) and we'll probably want to know what this particular predicament is, particularly
since it's qualified by an adjective which is certainly surprising
and perhaps even contradictory: 'golden opportunity' is a phrase
we readily understand, but 'golden predicament' seems to offer
something more puzzling, and therefore more intriguing.

There are smaller hooks along the way – 'strange' and 'fateful'
are terms that naturally make us want to know more – and the
voice itself is also intriguing. Claudius begins his supposed autobiography as if making a formal proclamation, before lapsing into
the informal and casually dismissive 'This-that-and-the other',
undermining himself even as he tells us what an important person
he is. The sentence as a whole, at once elaborate and conversational, is the perfect introduction to a man ill-suited to public life
who has nevertheless risen to become ruler of the Roman empire.

The voice to which we're introduced in the opening of Vladimir
Nabokov's *Lolita* (1955) is very different, but equally arresting:

> Lolita, light of my life, fire of my loins. My sin, my soul. Lo-lee-ta:
> the tip of the tongue taking a trip of three steps down the palette
> to tap, at three, the teeth. Lo. Lee. Ta. She was Lo, plain Lo, in the
> morning, standing four feet ten in one sock. She was Lola in slacks.
> She was Dolly at school. She was Dolores on the dotted line. But in
> my arms she was always Lolita.

Rhythmical, alliterative, seductively musical, this is prose that
seems to be pushing towards poetry. Its ostensible subject is the
school-age girl who is the focus of the narrator's transgressive
passion, but we're actually learning at least as much about the
narrator himself. His riffing on variants of her name may suggest something fluid about her personality but it also suggests
the obsessive nature of his own interest in her, particularly in the
detailed physicality with which he renders the way the syllables
feel in his mouth. This is the gateway to a disturbing narrative,
but the voice draws us in.

As you'll understand from this selection, openings have a variety of functions: they can (in any combination) introduce character, suggest a theme or subject, set the plot rolling, indicate time and place, or intrigue us with the promise of what is to come; they can also, particularly in the case of first-person narratives, establish an interesting or inviting narrative voice. The crucial thing in your own writing is to check that your opening does actually have a function – that it's doing a necessary job. A description of weather that has no real bearing on the narrative, an account of a place which is not substantially important to the story, the introduction of a character who plays no significant part in the action – any of this is likely to be just so much dead material, suggesting that the writer is writing herself into the story, warming up in front of the reader. By all means warm up, but be sure to cut these passages later so the reader begins reading at the point where the real story begins. You could usefully ask yourself: how late in the sequence of events can I begin the story?

Exposition and starting *in medias res*

One common way of starting a story is with some exposition – this is the set-up, the way things are, the 'once upon a time there was ... '. This can be done in straightforward fashion, or more artfully, as in the opening of Rudyard Kipling's 'Mary Postgate' (1915):

> Of Miss Mary Postgate, Lady McCausland wrote that she was 'thoroughly conscientious, tidy, companionable, and ladylike. I am very sorry to part with her, and shall always be interested in her welfare.'

This single hardworking sentence, which consists largely of quotation from what is clearly a job reference, gives us a character for Mary Postgate (from Lady McCausland's perspective), implies that Mary is leaving her job for a new one, and tells us the class of person she works for. (She is, we soon learn, a professional 'companion'.) As it turns out, tragic events will later lead Mary to behave in an entirely unexpected fashion, forcing us to question Lady McCausland's initial assessment of her.

Letters can be very useful when you want to convey information it might prove awkward to present otherwise. E. M. Forster's *Howards End* (1910) begins (after a single brief sentence of introduction by the primary narrator) with a letter from Helen Schlegel to her sister, Margaret:

Howards End,

Tuesday.

Dearest Meg,

It isn't going to be what we expected. It is old and little, and altogether delightful – red brick. We can scarcely pack in as it is, and the dear knows what will happen when Paul (younger son) arrives tomorrow. From hall you go right or left into dining-room or drawing-room. Hall itself is practically a room. You open another door in it, and there are the stairs going up in a sort of tunnel to the first floor. Three bedrooms in a row there, and three attics in a row above. That isn't all the house really, but it's all that one notices – nine windows as you look up from the front garden.

'Then there's a very big wych-elm – to the left as you look up – leaning a little over the house, and standing on the boundary between the garden and meadow. I quite love that tree already. Also ordinary elms, oaks – no nastier than ordinary oaks – pear trees, apple trees, and a vine. No silver birches, though. However, I must get on to my host and hostess. I only wanted to show that it isn't the least what we expected. Why did we settle that their house would be all gables and wiggles, and their garden all gamboge-coloured paths? I believe simply because we associate them with expensive hotels – Mrs. Wilcox trailing in beautiful dresses down long corridors, Mr. Wilcox bullying porters, etc. We females are that unjust.

In line with what we've already said about dialogue, a letter should be written for a reason and should avoid telling the fictional recipient what he is already likely to know. Forster works skilfully here to provide the reader with important information about the house while maintaining our sense of Helen's need to convey that information to her sister in a letter. It's not simply that Margaret has never seen Howards End, but that the house is utterly different from 'what we expected': Helen is writing to correct a view based on previous acquaintance with Mr and Mrs Wilcox, a view she now regards as unjust as well as erroneous. And along with the description of the house, Forster provides the reader, through Helen's excitable account, with details that will prove significant in the larger narrative of the novel: the imminent arrival of the Wilcoxes' younger son, the emblematic wych-elm and the bullying behaviour of Mr Wilcox.

In both of these cases the narrative begins at a moment of transition: Mary is about to start a new job, while Helen has arrived for the first time at the house which – as the novel's title suggests – will provide an important focus for the narrative. Starting your story at a point where change is occurring can be helpful. Zee Edgell's *Beka Lamb* (1982) begins:

> On a warm November day Beka Lamb won an essay contest at St. Cecilia's Academy, situated not far from the front gate of His Majesty's Prison on Milpa Lane. It seemed to her family that overnight Beka changed from what her mother called a 'flat-rate Belize creole' into a person with 'high mind'.

It's a moment of transition for Beka (or at least her family thinks so), and we also have information about her age (roughly), ethnicity and nationality, and even a sense of period (Belize was a British colony until 1981, and there's a king on the throne).

Alice Munro starts her short story 'The Turkey Season' (1980) apparently straightforwardly:

> When I was fourteen I got a job at the Turkey Barn for the Christmas season. I was still too young to get a job working in a store or as a part-time waitress; I was also too nervous.
>
> I was a turkey gutter. The other people who worked at the Turkey Barn were Lily and Marjorie and Gladys, who were also gutters; Irene and Henry, who were pluckers; Herb Abbott, the foreman, who superintended the whole operation and filled in wherever he was needed. Morgan Elliott was the owner and boss. He and his son, Morgy, did the killing.

A lot of people are introduced – perhaps too many for a reader to be expected to remember them all, but the list gives us a sense of the relatively small size of this outfit. An interesting piece of information about the narrator is also slipped in: she's too nervous to get a job serving the public but will be comfortable enough with turkey slaughter. We don't quite know what to make of that yet, so we store it away for later. And we're brought up short by the final line. So Munro turns the spadework of setting the scene into something more nuanced, which makes us think it's worth our while to read on.

Munro's stories often start with a simple sentence from which a narrative unfolds. It may be something such as 'I don't keep up with Hugo's writing' or 'I think of my mother sometimes in department stores' – which begins to unravel a train of thought on the narrator's part, leading into the story. Or it may state a fact which takes us straight there: 'Flo said to watch for White Slavers' or 'My father came across the field carrying the body of the boy who had been drowned.'[103] There is something arresting about the baldness of these statements that makes us want to read on.

Another way of starting a story is to begin *in medias res* – in the midst of things. Of course, all stories have an implied or explicit 'before' and 'after', but there's a particular sense in certain narratives of our having entered in the middle of an episode, conversation or thought-process. Katherine Mansfield makes good use of this device, as in 'The Garden Party' (1922), which begins: 'And after all the weather was ideal.' 'And' is a conjunction, and therefore should link back to something that has gone before, though what that might be isn't, in this instance, entirely clear. A pedantic grammarian would argue that 'and' shouldn't even be used to start a sentence; here Mansfield audaciously uses it to start a story. Similarly, 'A Dill Pickle' (1917) begins: 'And then, after six years, she saw him again', while the opening sentence of 'The Daughters of the Late Colonel' (1921) is: 'The week after was one of the busiest of their lives.' The week after what? Whose lives? In this case, the clues are in the title, but you'll see how this opening sweeps us into a story which has already begun, pulling us along in its wake.

A similar energy is created when Mansfield starts her stories, as she often does, with a character in motion: 'On his way to the station William remembered with a fresh pang of disappointment ... '; 'And when they came out of the lace shop there was their own driver ... '; 'With despair – cold, sharp despair – buried deep in her heart like a wicked knife, Miss Meadows in cap and gown and carrying a little baton, trod the cold corridors that led to the music hall.'[104] The character in motion draws us along with them; the narrative feels reassuringly purposeful – we're going somewhere, or something's about to happen.

However – and wherever – you choose to start your story, your opening is an opportunity to recruit your reader. 'A great writer,' said Vladimir Nabokov, 'is always a great enchanter'[105] and there is certainly a sense in which we beguile or seduce our reader into the world of our narrative. We suggested at the beginning of this chapter that you shouldn't spend too long on your opening at too early a stage, but eventually you may want to give it particularly close attention. And when you've found the right front door for your purposes, you'll know it.

A sense of an ending

As readers we've probably all had experience of unsatisfactory endings. Sometimes a book just ends. We might have had an uneasy premonition this was going to happen when we noticed there were only a couple of pages to go and we couldn't imagine how it could all be wrapped up in time. 'But what happened about this problem, and that character, and how ... ?' We feel short-changed, cheated of an ending.

On the other hand, endings can go on too long. The story ends – and then there's more ending, and then perhaps a bit more ending after that. Inexperienced writers often don't know when to stop. They've enjoyed writing the story, they've enjoyed writing the ending, but they haven't used up all their writing yet so they keep going until there's nothing more they can think of to say.

Consider the ending of Dawn Powell's *My Home Is Far Away* (1944). Marcia (who wants to be a writer) is on a train, finally escaping her home town (London Junction), her psychotic stepmother and a father who seems unable or unwilling to protect her. She hopes to make her own way in the world:

> The rain came louder, beating across the window. Marcia rubbed a spot on the pane and saw they were already at Union Falls, miles and miles from London Junction. The rain covered the spot, and Marcia took her forefinger and wrote 'MARCIA WILLARD' across the foggy pane.

It's a good ending, leaving the reader speculating about Marcia's future, and perhaps taking comfort from the suggestion that, in writing her name (in capitals) on the window, she is boldly asserting her own identity. But an inexperienced writer might have continued beyond the point at which Powell stopped, perhaps along the lines of the italicised passage below:

> … Marcia took her forefinger and wrote 'MARCIA WILLARD' across the foggy pane.
>
> *It reminded her who she was – she resolved never to forget again. This was a new chapter in her life – the whole world lay before her. Marcia had decided she was never going back to London Junction, not if you paid her a million dollars. She had her freedom and that was priceless.*

This addition to the ending doesn't contribute anything of substance; in fact it dilutes the power of that final image. It exemplifies a habit very common in developing writers: they don't trust their readers to understand what they've been shown, so they tell them as well. Writers who keep adding words after they've finished telling the story are often unaware that by writing more they're actually dissipating the impact of what they've already written.

So what we're looking for in an ending is something that falls between no ending at all and an unnecessarily protracted and insistent ending. As with every aspect of writing, arriving at a satisfactory conclusion is the result of a balancing act.

We've already discussed the value of beginning your story relatively late in the sequence of events, and we can now see that getting out early often makes for a more powerful, more satisfying or more nuanced reading experience. But where exactly to end a story is a matter of fine judgement: where do you want to leave the reader?

On the one hand you want to leave enough room for the reader to participate imaginatively in the ending (as in the real ending of *My Home Is Far Away*); on the other, you don't want to leave them baffled or confused by giving them too little to work with. If you have underwritten an ending, readers will usually be quick to tell you. One of the great advantages of working within a community of writers (whether in a class or in an informal writers' circle) is the opportunity it offers to test your work and receive feedback from a variety of perspectives. If one person tells you he doesn't understand your ending, you're no wiser: it could be a failure on his part. But if three people tell you they don't understand your ending there's a strong chance you have work to do.

An overwritten ending is slightly harder to reach consensus on, as it may seem to work at a basic level – it's an ending, after all, that readers are likely to understand. But try cutting progressively back from the end and seeing how the conclusion reads with each new cut. Wherever the cut improves the story, you know those extra words have to go. Improvement may, of course, be understood differently by different writers, and it's up to you to decide the balance that works best for you and for your narrative: do you want your ending to deposit the reader safely back on dry land at the end of the voyage, or to drop them at the mouth of the harbour so they have a short swim to the shore?

It can be helpful, when ending a story, to think not only in terms of *where it ends* but also *how it lands* and, relatedly, where its readers are likely to land. In other words, think about how you want the reader to respond when she closes the book: what thoughts and feelings do you want her to be left with?

Let's consider this idea in relation to Joseph Conrad's *Heart of Darkness* (1899). One of the characters, Marlow, has just finished telling a very dark story – a story that occupies most of the novel – and the novel's conclusion reminds us that he has been telling it to a group of men who sit in a boat close to the mouth of the River Thames, waiting for the tide to turn:

> Marlow ceased, and sat apart, indistinct and silent, in the pose of a meditating Buddha. Nobody moved for a time. 'We have lost the first of the ebb,' said the Director suddenly. I raised my head. The offing was barred by a black bank of clouds, and the tranquil waterway leading to the uttermost ends of the earth flowed sombre under an overcast sky – seemed to lead into the heart of an immense darkness.

Suppose Conrad had ended his story with a description of the sun rising on the group after Marlow had ended his tale – giving us, instead of that forbidding final sentence, one which emphasised the return of light: light strengthening in a blue sky, glinting off the water and the wheeling gulls, illuminating the bright sails of the passing boats. It would still be possible to take this very different ending as an ironic comment on matters that, as Marlow has made clear, are too dark to be spoken of, but many readers would see it as offering a consolatory vision of renewal. The final sentence as actually written by Conrad precludes consolation: the sentence confirms the darkness of Marlow's story. As readers, we may not all land in exactly the same place, but as writers we can, within certain parameters, direct our readers' landing by careful attention to our story's ending.

It's often the case that if you ask developing writers how their current story is going to end, they simply don't know. Some writers work on a story quite happily without knowing how things are going to turn out and this doesn't prevent them arriving at a satisfactory conclusion, but it's fair to say that you increase your chances of running into trouble if you have no sense at all of how your story is going to end. Once you have a destination in mind there's still a choice of routes but, speaking generally, it's helpful to have a strong sense of where you're going.

Again, however, it's a matter of balance. Of course it's helpful to know where we're going, but it can sometimes be profoundly *un*helpful to press onward to our planned destination with such single-minded determination that we close our minds to alternative possibilities. Perhaps in the process of writing you've learnt new things about your characters, or perhaps research has thrown up a new idea which better suits what you want to say. If, after interrogating your new idea, you're confident that it's preferable to your original idea, then you should change direction as necessary in order to accommodate it. Better to change an ending than to restrict the creative process.

A good ending is a fitting culmination of all that has gone before, usually gesturing back in some way to earlier events, and sometimes pointedly recalling the opening of the story. This is true, for example, of the ending of *Heart of Darkness*, where we return to the group on the boat and see, in the concluding reference to 'an immense darkness', an intensification of the 'mournful gloom' that hangs over London in the novel's opening scene. And in *My Home Is Far Away* a small incident, occurring just before the closing passage we looked at earlier, resonates with the first words of the novel. A boy selling fruit to the passengers recognises Marcia's poverty and slips her a pear and an apple without charging her. It doesn't particularly matter if the reader misses the reference back to the novel's opening ('This was the month of cherries and peaches, of green apples beyond the grape arbor ... '), but if we notice it we'll probably also notice that the opening scene shows Marcia and her sister about to embark on a journey that will change their lives ('We're moving, we're moving! We're moving to London Junction!'), while the final scene shows Marcia both chastened and strengthened by her experiences at London Junction, setting out on another significant journey. This structural patterning adds to the novel's sense of resolution: a cycle has been completed.

Tension and pace

Once we know how to open our story and how to close it, we're left with an obvious question: how do we keep the reader engaged between these two points?

Here's the opening of a story serialised in magazine form in 1912 and published as a novel two years later:

> I had this story from one who had no business to tell it to me, or to any other. I may credit the seductive influence of an old vintage upon the narrator for the beginning of it, and my own skeptical incredulity during the days that followed for the balance of the strange tale.
>
> When my convivial host discovered that he had told me so much, and that I was prone to doubtfulness, his foolish pride assumed the task the old vintage had commenced, and so he unearthed written evidence in the form of musty manuscript, and dry official records of the British Colonial Office to support many of the salient features of his remarkable narrative.
>
> I do not say the story is true, for I did not witness the happenings which it portrays, but the fact that in the telling of it to you I have taken fictitious names for the principal characters quite sufficiently evidences the sincerity of my own belief that it *may* be true.
>
> The yellow, mildewed pages of the diary of a man long dead, and the records of the Colonial Office dovetail perfectly with the narrative of my convivial host, and so I give you the story as I painstakingly pieced it out from these several various agencies.
>
> If you do not find it credible you will at least be as one with me in acknowledging that it is unique, remarkable, and interesting.

Rather than launch straight into the story, the narrator first has a little word with the reader. Our guide insists that, even if we don't believe what's coming, we'll be intrigued by it. Are we going to stop reading at this point and decide it's not worth our while? Probably not, because we have had a seed of curiosity planted in our minds: what is it about this story that raises these questions of authenticity? What is the story?

Tarzan of the Apes (1914) was the first of twenty-four Tarzan books by Edgar Rice Burroughs. No one has ever made a convincing claim for the literary merit of the Tarzan books, but Burroughs was a compelling storyteller and this preamble to the original Tarzan novel highlights his skill at creating an appetite in the reader. Edgar Rice Burroughs and Charles Dickens might seem to have little in common, but it's significant that they both wrote their novels initially for publication in serial form in magazines. The first readers of their novels were reading in advance of publication of the full story in book form; they had to wait for the next instalment, and the writers worked hard to make them want to buy it. Both Burroughs and Dickens made sure that when readers came to the end of an episode they would be eager to know what would happen next. By way of illustration of this culture of anxious expectation, it has been claimed that at one point in 1841, crowds gathered at New York harbour and, unable to await the unloading of the latest issue of *Master Humphrey's Clock*, in which *The Old Curiosity Shop* was being serialised, greeted incoming passengers from Britain with the cry: 'Is Little Nell dead?'

It is this appetite, created in the reader by the writer, and the implicit assurance of ultimate satisfaction, that makes a novel a 'page-turner' or 'unputdownable'. If (having secured their attention and interest with your brilliant opening) you want to keep readers on board, you have to make sure they feel a need to read on, and not just because they are enthralled by your luminous prose: there must be something they feel they need to know.

About halfway through Thomas Hardy's *A Pair of Blue Eyes* Elfride Swancourt and Henry Knight meet on a cliff path. Knight's hat is blown off by the wind. In retrieving it he slips over the edge of the cliff but manages to perch on a projecting rock. In attempting to help him Elfride slips too:

'Hold tightly to me,' he said.

She flung her arms round his neck with such a firm grasp that whilst he remained it was impossible for her to fall.

'Don't be flurried,' Knight continued. 'So long as we stay above this block we are perfectly safe. Wait a moment whilst I consider what we had better do.'

He turned his eyes to the dizzy depths beneath them, and surveyed the position of affairs.

Two glances told him a tale with ghastly distinctness. It was that, unless they performed their feat of getting up the slope with the precision of machines, they were over the edge and whirling in mid-air.

Do you want to know how they are going to extricate themselves from their perilous predicament? Of course you do, but Hardy ratchets up the suspense by pausing the action in order to give us a few statistics:

The crest of this terrible natural facade passed among the neighbouring inhabitants as being seven hundred feet above the water it overhung. It had been proved by actual measurement to be not a foot less than six hundred and fifty.

That is to say, it is nearly three times the height of Flamborough, half as high again as the South Foreland, a hundred feet higher than Beachy Head – the loftiest promontory on the east or south side of this island – twice the height of St. Aldhelm's, thrice as high as the Lizard, and just double the height of St. Bee's. One sea-bord point on the western coast is known to surpass it in altitude, but only by a few feet. This is Great Orme's Head, in Caernarvonshire.

And it must be remembered that the cliff exhibits an intensifying feature which some of those are without – sheer perpendicularity from the half-tide level.

Got how dangerous this is? Good. Now back to the action. Knight persuades Elfride to use him as a ladder as he clings to the cliff-face. She climbs back up and is able to get to a place of safety, but in using Knight for purchase she has pushed him down; he slips further, clutching at tufts of vegetation as he slides, and finally comes to rest in an even more perilous position:

> In spite of this dreadful tension of body and mind, Knight found time for a moment of thankfulness. Elfride was safe.
>
> She lay on her side above him – her fingers clasped. Seeing him again steady, she jumped upon her feet.
>
> 'Now, if I can only save you by running for help!' she cried. 'O, I would have died instead! Why did you try so hard to deliver me?' And she turned away wildly to run for assistance.
>
> 'Elfride, how long will it take you to run to Endelstow and back?'
>
> 'Three-quarters of an hour.'
>
> 'That won't do; my hands will not hold out ten minutes. And is there nobody nearer?'
>
> 'No; unless a chance passer may happen to be.'
>
> 'He would have nothing with him that could save me. Is there a pole or stick of any kind on the common?'
>
> She gazed around. The common was bare of everything but heather and grass.
>
> A minute – perhaps more time – was passed in mute thought by both. On a sudden the blank and helpless agony left her face. She vanished over the bank from his sight.
>
> Knight felt himself in the presence of a personalized loneliness.[106]

The novel's first readers couldn't turn the page to find out what happened next – they had to wait a whole month for the next edition of *Tinsley's Magazine*. (Only then would they learn that Elfride had not gone for help, but had instead ripped her voluminous underwear into strips, out of which she fashioned ropes, thus saving Knight.) It would be pleasing to believe that the term 'cliffhanger' was derived directly from Hardy's narrative. In fact the term is a later coinage, but Hardy understood the principle as clearly as the producers of television drama series do today.

We might well feel that the cliffhanger is the point at which the artificiality of the story is at its most obvious – the reader or viewer is clearly being manipulated by the storyteller, our appetites artfully stimulated – but that needn't significantly lessen our investment in the outcome. A cliffhanger doesn't, of course, have to be a matter of life or death but it does need to have significance for the character – and, by extension, the reader. The chapters of our novels won't all end on cliffhangers, but ideally the end of a chapter tips the reader forward: she should be aware there are things she doesn't yet know that she wants or needs to know. As readers we are hard-wired to want to satisfy our curiosity and resolve the story – as long as it has become sufficiently important to us. Creating, sustaining and developing that curiosity in the reader is the way a writer maintains tension in a narrative.

Writers can be ingenious in their strategies. Here's the narrator and protagonist of Laurence Sterne's *The Life and Opinions of Tristram Shandy* (1759–67) tempting us on to the next volume of his fictional autobiography (the novel was originally published in nine volumes) by suggesting that we can't possibly guess what happens next:

> ... I am of so nice and singular a humour, that if I thought you was able to form the least judgment or probable conjecture to yourself, of what was to come in the next page, – I would tear it out of my book.[107]

In *The Good Soldier*, Ford Madox Ford several times uses ellipsis (dot-dot-dot) as punctuation after the final word of a chapter – as here, where we're told how Leonora, Edward Ashburnham's wife, is cheated of her hopes by the narrator's wife, Florence:

> [Leonora] had the vague, passionate idea that, when Edward had exhausted a number of other types of women he must turn to her. Why should her type not have its turn in his heart? She imagined that, by now, she understood him better, that she understood better his vanities and that, by making him happier, she could arouse his love.
> Florence knocked all that on the head ...[108]

Ellipsis can be used to indicate a number of different things, but here it clearly suggests unfinishedness, confirming our sense that there's more to be said: at this pivotal point, between Parts III and

IV of the novel, Ford is subtly but deliberately piquing our curiosity, nudging us forward.

This kind of propulsive tension doesn't come into play solely at points of transition: the writer may feel a particular need to coax the reader across a chapter-break or the break between two instalments of a serial, but ideally every sentence of a narrative should make us want to read on to the next. This doesn't mean, of course, that every moment in a narrative should be a moment of high drama – as Jane Austen's tightly written narratives show, it's entirely possible to create forms of tension in a modest domestic setting – but there does need to be a sense of dynamic forward movement.

It's difficult to discuss narrative tension without also mentioning pace. Pace refers to the rate at which things seem to move along in your story. If we say that it's important to maintain a good pace in a narrative, we also need to make it clear that a good pace doesn't mean non-stop, high-octane action: it implies taut prose and a strong sense of direction.

Writers often talk about a 'baggy' or 'soggy' section, usually in the middle of a piece of writing, where the story seems to have lost direction and energy. If you find this happening in your own writing, stop and think about the reasons. You may be trying to show the passage of time by introducing scenes that occupy the relevant time-span but impede the flow of the narrative. In these cases you probably need to overleap the intervening time, succinctly summarising the 'not much' that happened in the interim. Or it may be that you've pursued a subplot which, having little or no relevance to the main plot, simply derails the story. Subplots need to bear an important relationship to the main story, and they need to have a structure of their own – otherwise they are not subplots at all; they are just more writing.

Writing can also feel baggy or lose pace where description outweighs the events of a narrative. We'll talk about the functions of description in Chapter 10, but it's worth noting here that all description should serve a purpose. Description that is merely decorative can sap a narrative's energy; it has to earn its keep. If you've stalled your story in order to write a descriptive passage – however beautifully – you are expecting the reader to indulge you as you have indulged yourself. If your descriptive passages are there because you like them rather than because the reader needs them, you might consider simply omitting them.

A good way to test a novel for tension and pace is to ask yourself two questions at the end of every chapter. The first is: *What has this chapter added to the story?* You might usefully think of those Victorian novels which have chapter headings summarising their content, as in Dickens's *Oliver Twist*, where the first five headings read:

I   – Treats of the place where Oliver Twist was born and of the circumstances attending his birth
II   – Treats of Oliver Twist's growth, education and board
III – Relates how Oliver Twist was very near getting a place which would not have been a sinecure
IV – Oliver, being offered another place, makes his first entry into public life
V   – Oliver mingles with new associates. Going to a funeral for the first time he forms an unfavourable notion of his master's business

If you were to provide a similar set of headings for your own work, would they be similarly substantial? Would the function and purpose of each chapter be clear?

The other way to interrogate your writing for pace and tension is to ask yourself: *What will the reader want to know at the end of this chapter?* The reader's curiosity about some matters will not be satisfied for a long time; her curiosity about others will be satisfied more quickly. Identify what new questions are in the reader's mind as a result of each of your chapters. Still using the example of *Oliver Twist*, we might imagine the following:

I – One big question, which is raised in this chapter but will not be answered until the end of the novel, is: who was Oliver's mother? Readers will also be wondering how Oliver will fare as a parish child. Questions in the reader's mind at the end of each of the next four chapters, might be:

II – Who will take the £5 reward to employ the troublesome boy as an apprentice?

III – Having narrowly escaped being apprenticed to a heartless chimney sweep, where will Oliver be sent now?

IV – How will Oliver fare in his new job at the undertaker's?

V – How will Oliver get on assisting at funerals as a mute, under jealous Noah's eye?

Each chapter not only has a clearly defined narrative function but also creates in the reader an appetite to find out what will happen next. Can the same be said of your own work?

We can help to maintain pace and tension by means of rigorous pruning. This matter will be discussed when we talk about editing but, in brief, you should aim to cut out anything that doesn't fully justify its existence. If it's not developing character or progressing plot you need to ask yourself why it's there at all. If it's simply because that paragraph took you a day to write, or because it's a paragraph you're particularly proud of, that's not a good enough reason to keep it. If you have the discipline to clear away the inert material, your narrative will flow more freely and with greater force.

− 10 −

Description

~

The purpose of description

Just about every example of writing we've looked at so far contains some element of description: simply to use an adjective or an adverb is to describe the object or action to which it's attached, and many of the examples go much further than that. In this chapter we're going to highlight the descriptive element in fiction, thinking carefully about its purpose.

Description allows us to enrich our narrative, providing colour, texture and atmosphere. The extent to which description plays a part in narrative is variable − contemporary writers tend to be more austere than their nineteenth-century forebears, and different kinds of narrative may require different levels of description − but it's hard to imagine a vibrant, engaging narrative which is not in some significant measure descriptive.

We've established that when we describe, we should keep firmly in mind the purpose of our description. Good description adds something to a story: if you feel you could omit a passage of description without detracting from your narrative, you might usefully ask yourself whether you can dispense with it.

It's important that descriptions don't overshadow the thing itself. A description can be so overwrought that it crosses the line between producing an effect and drawing attention to itself *as* an effect. And it can result in dense and indigestible prose which, rather than giving a vivid impression, impedes clear understanding. The writer has been distracted from his task of communication by the frisson he is getting from giving the reader a good beating with his thesaurus − a perverse pleasure indeed. Be on the lookout for this kind of excess, and work hard to counter it. You will best demonstrate your talents by learning to control them, by using your abilities (and the undoubted richness of the English language) in a measured way.

Preconceptions about style

Sarah Waters observes that 'Beginners, especially, seem to think that writing fiction needs a special kind of flowery prose, completely unlike any sort of language one might encounter in day-to-day life.'[109] It's certainly true that early-stage writers often seem to mistrust their own voice, perhaps imagining that there must be a voice more appropriate to literature: when they think of what they want to say they try and find some more elaborate way of saying it. But there's no reason to make something more complicated than it needs to be. A 'bloody rag' evokes a clear image; an 'ensanguined clout' takes us into potentially forbidding territory to say the same thing. 'He raced up the drive' is clear and immediate; 'he propelled himself up the drive at a rapid pace' takes us round the houses. In both cases the more difficult phrase isn't merely unnecessary; it actually reduces the impact of the sentence. If you're writing in a way that will send your readers on a detour before they get your meaning, or even prevent them getting your meaning at all, you need to consider the risk: that, having put the book down in bafflement, or to consult a dictionary, they may not return to it. For this most practical of reasons you should always aim to avoid unnecessarily difficult language.

Remember, though, that literary language isn't exactly – for most writers at least – everyday speech, but a sharpened and intensified version of it; it may also be *necessarily* difficult at times because what it has to convey is itself inherently difficult. The argument against over-ingenious writing isn't intended to imply that simplicity and directness are our only criteria, or that there's no need to work hard to avoid the obvious. As in all matters related to writing we're looking for balance, and we need to be as much on our guard against dull plain-speaking as against over-ingenuity.

Sometimes writers may simply be showing off. When Georges Simenon kept unsuccessfully submitting short stories to *Le Matin*, Colette, who was then its literary editor, finally told him: 'Look, it's too literary, always too literary.' According to Simenon what she meant was that he should cut out 'adjectives, adverbs, and every word which is there just to make an effect. Every sentence which is just there for the sentence. You know, you have a beautiful sentence – cut it.'[110] The great eighteenth-century critic Samuel Johnson had given much the same advice: 'Read over your compositions, and wherever you meet with a passage which you think is particularly fine, strike it out',[111] while in our own time Elmore Leonard has made a similar point in relation to his own practice: 'If it sounds like writing, I rewrite it.'[112] These observations come from particular places and suit particular purposes: Simenon and Leonard were both crime writers, while Johnson's massive literary output included only one work of fiction, *The History of Rasselas, Prince of Abissinia* (1759). However, all writers might take the observations as useful alerts; we'd do well to scrutinise our prose in the light of them, setting our own allowable limits. We should learn to recognise when we've written something that has no function in the text other than to show off what good or clever writers we think we are: we have at this point stopped communicating with the reader (which is our job) and started to indulge ourselves (which is a weakness).

Clichés

One has to respect clichés: they are sturdy so-and-sos. They endure because they are true and because they work; they are useful little devices that we all understand. Yet the term is derogatory, and no serious writer wishes to be accused of clichéd writing. We resist cliché where there's reason to expect something better than, or different from, the merely conventional. There's often something depressing about a cliché, precisely because it's not saying anything new. If we write about a breeze whispering through the trees we may be giving a very apt description of what the wind is doing but the phrase is so over-used that the reader no longer really hears the whispering. The difficulty is that we're not writing in a void: the world of the reader is already full of expressions worn thin by repeated usage and we can't afford to ignore that. Learning that the air is rent by an unearthly wail is more likely to provoke a sigh than a shiver, because the expression has lost its capacity to convey the horror it must originally have had. (The writer who writes this line would probably not use 'rent' in this sense in any other context; it has become glued into a clump of words which will do for this purpose.) Forms of words which are used over and over again simply lose their evocative power.

So we have to steer a careful path between the fancy formulations that obscure our meaning and the convenient expressions that render our meaning in ways too obvious and familiar to be interesting. We should know when our descriptions are tired and worn, and we should know when they're unhelpfully elaborate. If we don't, we need to develop what Hemingway called 'the writer's radar'. 'The most essential gift for a writer,' he maintained, 'is a built-in, shockproof shit detector.'[113]

Metaphors and similes

Since 1982, the Bulwer-Lytton Fiction Competition has challenged entrants to submit openings 'to the worst of all possible novels', and in 2001 the Lyttle Lytton Competition was launched, limiting entries to 200 characters in length. It's interesting to see how often these deliberately badly written openings rely for their comic effect on mangled metaphors and similes – as in these examples:

My lamestream friends told me to start dating again, but I knew the jet fuel of love couldn't melt the steel beams of my heart. (Klaus Virtanen)

They were ensnared, their limp limbs bound together like a bunch of Twizzlers that had melted in the sun. (Michelle Vongkaysone)

'Oh no,' Alex gasped when realization crashed over her like the ocean wave soon to be killing her. (Sarah Tizzard)

'I'm breaking up with you' – her words shot into my heart, like bullets from the gun that her mouth was like. (Jake Scott)

Here, writ amusingly large, are the common faults of failed similes and metaphors: the errors are not exactly the same in each case, but each example is absurd, clumsily missing the essential point of descriptive analogy. Similes and metaphors aim to illuminate one thing by sharply phrased reference to another. If they don't help the reader to see more clearly, then they're not doing their job.

The term 'mixed metaphor' is used to describe the effect of yoking together two or more dissonant images by way of illustration. Politicians, often speaking off the cuff, are great offenders – here's Simon Hughes MP:

Out of the hat on Monday night the Home Secretary produced the rabbit, the temporary provisions Bill, as her fig leaf to cover her major U-turn.[114]

Metaphors are, by definition, not to be taken literally, but they don't exist independently of the literal. It's important to keep in view the literal meaning of your metaphors, examining each detail in relation to the others and thinking carefully about the overall effect. In this instance, Hughes might have got away with *either* the rabbit produced from the conjuror's hat (here meaning something the Home Secretary has sprung on her audience) *or* the fig-leaf covering the private parts of an otherwise naked figure in an artwork (meaning something designed to conceal what she doesn't want her audience to see); but the minute we try to visualise the double image, we'll see what's wrong. When we add in the U-turn (also a metaphor, though it's so commonly used to mean a policy reversal that we may not immediately recognise it as one) the problem is compounded.

It's not simply that Hughes's metaphor is mixed; we might also notice that all three of its terms are clichés. Whenever a simile or a metaphor presents itself, stop and search it at the door. If it seems comfortable and familiar send it packing and look for something more interesting. Ideally, a metaphor or simile should be both apt and surprising, enhancing your reader's understanding of its primary subject by showing it in a new and interesting light; it should also be appropriate to the narrative in which it appears.

Frannie, the narrator of Sara Collins's *The Confessions of Frannie Langton*, makes extensive and inventive use of metaphor and simile. Taken out of the field where she has been working, Frannie is led into the house of her owner, Miss-bella. Like the ornately furnished room she sits in, Miss-bella is 'covered in silks and velvets, smooth and cool as lizards', while Frannie, confronting a mirror for the first time in her life, is brought up short by what she sees: 'It was the first time I'd seen myself properly – there I was, stamping towards myself like a wild creature, my own face darting about on the surface, like a fish I couldn't catch.'[115] All three of these similes draw on the outdoor world to illustrate what, for Frannie, is an alien indoor environment – she is looking for parallels with her own experience. The last of them – the representation of her own face as an elusive fish – is not merely arresting in itself, but strikingly apt, suggesting her inability to get a conceptual grip on what she's seeing.

Metaphors and similes can be particularly useful when you want to pin down and illuminate vague or abstract matters. In 'Araby', for example, James Joyce gathers up the young narrator's hazy and incompletely understood romantic yearnings in a telling concrete image:

Her name sprang to my lips at moments in strange prayers and praises which I myself did not understand. My eyes were often full of tears (I could not tell why) and at times a flood from my heart seemed to pour itself out into my bosom. I thought little of the future. I did not know whether I would ever speak to her or not or, if I spoke to her, how I could tell her of my confused adoration. But my body was like a harp and her words and gestures were like fingers running upon the wires.

The image of the harp allows us to retain something of the mystery and romance of the passage that leads up to it but it also adds an important physical dimension to the narrator's indeterminate longing. In likening his body to a musical instrument, he gestures obliquely towards the physical sexuality that he's unable to acknowledge directly: the simile, delicately suggesting – among other possibilities – the touch of the girl's fingers on his flesh, contributes importantly to the effect of the passage as a whole.

Modifiers

In recent years a good deal of advice to writers, both online and in writing manuals, has been to make war on modifiers – usually meaning adjectives and adverbs. The spare narratives of Ernest Hemingway and Raymond Carver are held up by campaigners as good examples in this respect (though neither writer rejects adjectives and adverbs entirely), while, as we've seen, Elmore Leonard is particularly and explicitly opposed to adverbs used in the attribution of dialogue. There is no 'right' way of addressing this matter, but it can be noted, by way of introduction to the discussion that follows, firstly that adjectives and adverbs exist for a good reason, and secondly that many writers have a tendency to overuse both.

Adjectives are invaluable when you want an economical way of evoking something in more particular terms than the noun alone allows. The car in your story may just be a car; or the reader may need to know, for reasons important to the story, that it's a red car, a vintage car, an expensive car, an unreliable car, or a car of a particular make. Here's Joseph Conrad describing the River Thames at the beginning of *Heart of Darkness*:

> The Nellie, a cruising yawl, swung to her anchor without a flutter of the sails, and was at rest. The flood had made, the wind was nearly calm, and being bound down the river, the only thing for it was to come to and wait for the turn of the tide.
>
> The sea-reach of the Thames stretched before us like the beginning of an interminable waterway. In the offing the sea and the sky were welded together without a joint, and in the luminous space the tanned sails of the barges drifting up with the tide seemed to stand still in red clusters of canvas sharply peaked, with gleams of varnished sprits. A haze rested on the low shores that ran out to sea in vanishing flatness. The air was dark above Gravesend, and farther back still seemed condensed into a mournful gloom, brooding motionless over the biggest, and the greatest, town on earth.

The passage is, by modern standards, rather adjective-heavy, but the point is that the adjectives serve an important purpose. Conrad's vivid depiction of space, light and colour depends on those adjectives – '*interminable* waterway', '*luminous* space', '*tanned* sails', '*red* clusters', '*varnished* sprits'; and then he introduces the shadows that will grow deeper as the narrative progresses – the dark air above Gravesend and the mournful gloom beyond hint at the horror of the story that is about to be told. Take out the adjectives and much of the force of this superb passage is lost.

So we'd be unwise to restrict our scope by dispensing with adjectives, but we do need to be certain that we're using them judiciously and with good reason. Some writers, especially inexperienced ones, can feel obliged to use adjectives at every opportunity: Sharon can't sit on a sofa drinking tea and flicking through her address book; she must sit on a bottle-green corduroy chesterfield, drinking peppermint and nettle tea out of a white bone china mug, flicking through her dog-eared ten-year-old Victoria and Albert Museum address book – even when none of these details might materially add to our understanding of who Sharon is or what she's doing. This style quickly wearies the reader, and when his attention is drawn to every detail he has no way of knowing which details might be significant. The advice of Mark Twain's character Pudd'nhead Wilson seems sound: 'As to the Adjective: when in doubt, strike it out.'[116] The 'when in doubt' clause is crucial: it implies that we shouldn't automatically regard every adjective as suspect, but it also tells us that we should trust our instincts when we feel uneasy about any particular example; that nagging doubt is often our literary conscience at work.

If we have to be sure about the use of a single adjective, surely only a madman or a genius might venture to use them in pairs. Henry James's story 'The Real Right Thing' (1899) concerns the experience of a young man, George Withermore, while writing the biography of a much more eminent writer, Ashton Doyne. Doyne's widow invites Withermore to use her late husband's study, the repository of all the personal papers he will need for the biography. Dazzled by the opportunity offered by the proposed book and excited by the thought of inhabiting the great man's private space, Withermore goes to the house at the first opportunity:

> He escaped from the black London November; he passed through the large hushed house and up the red-carpeted staircase where he only found in his path the whisk of a soundless trained maid or the reach, out of an open room, of Mrs Doyne's queenly weeds and approving tragic face; and then, by a mere touch of the well-made door that gave so sharp and pleasant a click, shut himself in for three or four warm hours with the spirit – as he had always distinctly declared it – of his master.

James achieves his effects partly through an unusual density and variety of adjectival patterns: in addition to the simple adjective/noun combination ('queenly weeds') we see the use of paired adjectives followed by a noun ('black London November', 'large, hushed house', 'soundless, trained maid', 'approving tragic face', four warm hours) and the use of double-barrelled adjectives followed by a noun ('red-carpeted staircase', 'well-made door').

There's something hypnotic about the rhythms set up by these patterns, and you may notice, too, the assonance of 'trained maid', 'queenly weeds' and 'four warm hours'. James creates an atmosphere not simply with the meaning of the words but with their music. Many modern readers find James's ornate prose too rich for their taste, but it's arguable that the densely packed adjectives are validated here by the complex uses to which James puts them.

Adverbs seem more controversial than adjectives, perhaps because there are occasions when you really need an adjective (try suggesting, without using one, that the door is red or the apple is unripe: it *can* be done, but probably shouldn't be) whereas a little thought can usually supply one verb to do the job of a verb and an adverb – and arguably do it better. Consider the verb/adverb combinations (italicised) in the passage below:

> The dog *ran quickly* along the beach, *pausing* only *occasionally* to *sniff curiously* at pieces of driftwood *lying haphazardly* on the sand. Jamie *followed* her *slowly*. He'd *behaved badly*, of course.
>
> 'I never wanted to come here anyway!' he had *shouted crossly* before *running angrily* up the stairs. He had *opened* the window *furiously* and *hungrily breathed in* the air. That was it. The house was airless. Their marriage was airless.
>
> It was better out here, *walking aimlessly* by the sea. Here everything seemed manageable. Perhaps it wasn't such a bad place, he *thought rationally*. Perhaps the problem was him. He had a short fuse, he knew that. He shouldn't have *spoken sharply* to her. He should apologise. He would apologise. He would turn round and go back to the house. As if sensing a change of direction, the dog *ran energetically* towards him.

This clunky example neatly illustrates Stephen King's claim that 'the road to hell is paved with adverbs'.[117] However, simply cutting the adverbs may remove a weakness without strengthening the phrase. See what happens when we replace most of the verb/adverb constructions with stronger verbs, verbs which do the job of both verb and adverb:

The dog *sped* along the beach, pausing only occasionally to *investigate* pieces of driftwood *scattered* on the sand. Jamie *trailed* behind her. He'd behaved badly, of course.

'I never wanted to come here anyway!' he had *bellowed* before *stomping* up the stairs. He had *flung* open the window and *sucked* in the air. That was it. The house was airless. Their marriage was airless.

It was better out here, *wandering* by the sea. Here everything seemed manageable. Perhaps it wasn't such a bad place, he *reasoned*. Perhaps the problem was him. He had a short fuse, he knew that. He shouldn't have *snapped* at her. He should apologise. He would apologise. He would turn round and go back to the house. As if sensing a change of direction, the dog *bounded* towards him.

We can see that replacing a verb and an adverb with a more muscular verb can be effective, but we should also consider the importance of variety. As in other contexts, it's wise to avoid imposing rules so stringent that they lead to monotony. Adverbs have a function and may, like any other part of speech, serve the needs of your narrative when appropriately used.

Describing place

Let's begin with a succinct statement of the obvious: in fiction, as in life, everything happens somewhere. The extent to which location is important differs from narrative to narrative, but it's seldom, if ever, irrelevant, and you're likely to find that descriptions of place will play a significant part in your own writing. And in order to describe your locations effectively, you'll need to consider their purpose and positioning in each particular narrative.

At the most basic level, your reader needs to be able to visualise the context of the events and actions that form the plot. Some of the necessary information may be implicit: if a character goes upstairs we understand that the house has at least two floors; if she runs at speed along a corridor the reader might reasonably conclude that the house is a large one. But these are clues of the most rudimentary kind, and any narrative is likely to require more detailed definition of its location than this.

There may be sound logistical reasons for detailing, let's say, the layout of a room or building, or the topography of the surrounding area. This might apply with particular force in detective fiction, where the omission of such details could make it impossible for the reader to solve the puzzle set up by the narrative; but if we think about it we'll realise that all narratives depend on the writer providing clues of one kind or another, clues that allow readers to build up pictures in their own minds. Establishing the location of the action is a crucial part of this process.

One of the most famous literary evocations of place can be found in Emily Brontë's *Wuthering Heights*. We're introduced early in the novel to the titular house and its bleak surroundings, as well as to its owner, Heathcliff:

> Wuthering Heights is the name of Mr Heathcliff's dwelling, 'Wuthering' being a significant provincial adjective, descriptive of the atmospheric tumult to which its station is exposed in stormy weather. Pure, bracing ventilation they must have up there, at all times, indeed: one may guess the power of the north wind, blowing over the edge, by the excessive slant of a few stunted firs at the end of the house; and by a range of gaunt thorns all stretching their limbs one way, as if craving alms of the sun. Happily, the architect had foresight to build it strong: the narrow windows are deeply set in the wall, and the corridors defended with large jutting stones.[118]

Although the narrator, Lockwood, observes in Heathcliff a gentlemanliness that seems at first sight to be at odds with his dismal surroundings, it should already be clear to the reader that the owner of Wuthering Heights – a man whose name hints at his relationship with the local topography – is very much a creature of the wild and desolate world he inhabits.

Character and location are often, in fact, intimately connected. Environment doesn't entirely define a character's personality but it will affect their expectations, their daily lives, the kinds of problem they might face. Equally, characters may deliberately choose, and to some extent define, their environment. Homes, in particular, are likely to reflect the character of their inhabitants. In 'A Bad Example' (1899), W. Somerset Maugham interweaves place and character to telling effect through a variety of well-chosen details:

> The Clintons lived in the fifth house down in the Adonis Road, and the house was distinguishable from its fellows by the yellow curtains with which Mrs Clinton had furnished all the windows. Mrs Clinton was a woman of taste. Before marriage, the happy pair, accompanied by Mrs Clinton's mother, had gone house-hunting, and fixed on the Adonis Road, which was cheap, respectable and near the station. Mrs Clinton would dearly have liked a house on the right-hand side of the road, which had nooks and angles and curiously-shaped windows. But Mr Clinton was firm in his refusal, and his mother-in-law backed him up.
>
> 'I dare say they're artistic,' he said, in answer to his wife's argument, 'but a man in my position don't want art – he wants substantiality. If the governor' – the governor was the senior partner of the firm – 'if the governor was going to take a 'ouse I'd 'ave nothing to say against it, but in my position art's not necessary.'
>
> 'Quite right, James,' said his mother-in-law; 'I 'old with what you say entirely.'
>
> Even in his early youth Mr Clinton had a fine sense of the responsibility of life, and a truly English feeling for the fitness of things.
>
> So the Clintons took one of the twenty-three similar houses on the left-hand side of the street, and there lived in peaceful happiness.

Through an artful combination of dialogue and description, Maugham suggests both the place itself and the aspirations of his protagonists; and if, in mocking Mr Clinton's mean-spirited conservatism and his wife's questionable taste, the author also betrays his own snobbery, this by no means robs the passage of its force.

As its title neatly suggests, the interplay of place and character is central to V. S. Naipaul's *A House for Mr Biswas* (1961). The setting is Trinidad, where Naipaul grew up, and the plot hinges on Mr

Biswas's quest for a place he can call his own, a house that will free him from dependence on his wife's bullying family. It's a testament to his dogged persistence that he ultimately finds himself 'in his own house, on his own half-lot of land, his own portion of the earth', but the detailed description of the house provided in the novel's prologue lets us know from the outset that his quest hasn't been entirely successful. Cheaply constructed by an unscrupulous solicitor's clerk, the house is a ramshackle affair:

> On the ground floor of Mr Biswas's two-storey house the solicitor's clerk had put a tiny kitchen in one corner; the remaining L-shaped space, unbroken, served as a drawingroom and diningroom. Between the kitchen and the diningroom there was a doorway but no door. Upstairs, just above the kitchen, the clerk had constructed a concrete room which contained a toilet bowl, a wash-basin and a shower; because of the shower this room was perpetually wet. The remaining L-shaped space was broken up into a bedroom, a verandah, a bedroom. Because the house faced west and had no protection from the sun, in the afternoon only two rooms were comfortably habitable: the kitchen downstairs and the wet bathroom-and-lavatory upstairs.
>
> In his original design the solicitor's clerk seemed to have forgotten the need for a staircase to link both floors, and what he had provided had the appearance of an afterthought. Doorways had been punched in the eastern wall and a rough wooden staircase – heavy planks on an uneven frame with one warped unpainted banister, the whole covered with a sloping roof of corrugated iron – hung precariously at the back of the house, in striking contrast with the white-pointed brickwork of the front, the white woodwork and the frosted glass of doors and windows.[119]

The emphasis on the building's structural flaws undercuts, for the reader, Mr Biswas's sense of triumph, but it doesn't simply negate it. The house represents an achievement of sorts by a man whose frustrations and failures are the novel's main story, but not its only story.

The importance of place in Sarah Hall's *Haweswater* (2002) is signalled on the title page. The Cumbrian lake of the novel's title was dammed in the 1930s to create a reservoir, and the consequent rise in the water level destroyed homes, farmsteads and rural livelihoods; Hall's fictional treatment of the episode skilfully balances detailed description of the landscape with an account of the human activity that takes place in it – both traditional farming and the activities of the men associated with the construction of the reservoir. In this passage the novel's protagonist, Janet, walks in childhood through the fields farmed by her father:

> It is early morning and a green dawn light covers the valley. There are flashes of dark green behind the night clouds, which she notices, looking up, as she walks next to her father. It is as if metal has found its way into the air and is burning. They walk on, down the rocky stone path, sightless, but aware of the distance of the walls on each side of the lane, their feet scuffing up loose pebbles. She takes three steps to his every long stride, a skip in the middle to keep pace. …
>
> A shower has passed. The rain, as if used up from its long, vertical descent, thins and finally holds off. Her father is ahead in the farmyard with the cows and she links the last gate closed behind him. The path on the way back up to Whelter is pitted and covered with miniature cairns of sheep droppings and its pebbles shine in the sudden light. As Janet approaches the farmhouse the track disintegrates into a flat, grass-tufted field. She deftly steps over the deep ruts of mud.[120]

Although obviously, and primarily, a description of place, the passage also highlights the presence of one of the place's inhabitants: Janet is a significant figure in this rural landscape, a young girl observing her environment with a child's intensity of vision, and literally finding her footing in it as her feet scuff the pebbles of the path or avoid the muddy ruts where the path gives out.

It's generally advisable to maintain a sense of human presence in our descriptions of place – Janet's actions and impressions help the reader to enter more fully into the imaginative space of Hall's narrative – but the opening chapter of Thomas Hardy's *The Return of the Native* (1878) comes close to excluding humanity altogether. None of the novel's characters appear in this chapter and, notwithstanding the brief illustrative reference to a generic furze-cutter, humanity itself seems to have been pushed so far into the background as to be almost invisible:

> A Saturday afternoon in November was approaching the time of twilight, and the vast tract of unenclosed wild known as Egdon Heath embrowned itself moment by moment. Overhead the hollow stretch of whitish cloud shutting out the sky was as a tent which had the whole heath for its floor.
>
> The heaven being spread with this pallid screen and the earth with the darkest vegetation, their meeting-line at the horizon was clearly marked. In such contrast the heath wore the appearance of an instalment of night which had taken up its place before its astronomical hour was come: darkness had to a great extent arrived hereon, while day stood distinct in the sky. Looking upwards, a furze-cutter would have been inclined to continue work; looking down, he would have decided to finish his faggot and go home. The distant rims of the world and of the firmament seemed to be a division in time no less than a division in matter. The face of the heath by its mere complexion added half an hour to evening; it could in like manner retard the dawn, sadden noon, anticipate the frowning of storms scarcely generated, and intensify the opacity of a moonless midnight to a cause of shaking and dread.
>
> In fact, precisely at this transitional point of its nightly roll into darkness the great and particular glory of the Egdon waste began, and nobody could be said to understand the heath who had not been there at such a time. It could best be felt when it could not clearly be seen, its complete effect and explanation lying in this and the succeeding hours before the next dawn; then, and only then, did it tell its true tale. The spot was, indeed, a near relation of night, and when night showed itself an apparent tendency to gravitate together could be perceived in its shades and the scene. The sombre stretch of rounds and hollows seemed to rise and meet the evening gloom in pure sympathy, the heath exhaling darkness as rapidly as the heavens precipitated it. And so the obscurity in the air and the obscurity in the land closed together in a black fraternization towards which each advanced halfway.

This is a powerful and justly famous passage, but it's a risky move to hold off for an entire chapter the moment at which – as Hardy himself puts it – 'humanity appears upon the scene'. Hardy's success in this particular instance shouldn't blind us to the danger of losing narrative pace and interest by focusing too narrowly and for too long on our descriptions of place. If we recognise these tendencies in our own writing it's worth reminding ourselves that, in good fiction, location isn't merely ornamental, but exists in dynamic relationship with the characters who occupy it and with their actions – actions which themselves drive the plot. Our fictional locations need their inhabitants as much as our characters need a place to stand.

This said, we might add that place has its own dynamic: a floorboard creaks, branches stir above a woodland path, rainclouds sweep in from the sea. Hardy's description of the heath registers the diurnal movement of the earth ('its nightly roll into darkness') and a similar energy is found in seasonal change, as registered in the opening paragraphs of Arundhati Roy's *The God of Small Things* (1997):

> May in Ayemenem is a hot, brooding month. The days are long and humid. The river shrinks and black crows gorge on bright mangoes in still, dustgreen trees. Red bananas ripen. Jackfruits burst. Dissolute bluebottles hum vacuously in the fruity air. Then they stun themselves against clear windowpanes and die, fatly baffled in the sun.
>
> The nights are clear but suffused with sloth and sullen expectation.
>
> But by early June the south-west monsoon breaks and there are three months of wind and water with short spells of sharp, glittering sunshine that thrilled children snatch to play with. The countryside turns an immodest green. Boundaries blur as tapioca fences take root and bloom. Brick walls turn mossgreen. Pepper vines snake up electric poles. Wild creepers burst through laterite banks and spill across the flooded roads.

Roy's description not only captures the swift seasonal transition, but does so in terms that emphasise the active life of the land, particularly after the breaking of the monsoon: plants root and bloom, vines snake, creepers burst and spill. These are not static snapshot images, but vibrant moving pictures.

In describing place it may be helpful to you to consider location as being itself a kind of character, an active presence in the narrative. Consider too, that the observer's position in relation to his environment needn't be fixed. Rudyard Kipling's short story, 'They' (1904), sets the scene in ways that emphasise the narrator's movement as he drives through a rich and varied landscape:

> One view called me to another; one hill top to its fellow, half across the county, and since I could answer at no more trouble than the snapping forward of a lever, I let the county flow under my wheels. The orchid-studded flats of the East gave way to the thyme, ilex and grey grass of the Downs; these again to the rich cornland and fig-trees of the lower coast, where you carry the beat of the tide on your left hand for fifteen level miles; and when at last I turned inland through a huddle of rounded hills and woods I had run myself clean out of my known marks. … I found hidden villages where bees, the only things awake, boomed in eighty-foot lindens that overhung grey Norman churches; miraculous brooks diving under stone bridges built for heavier traffic than would ever vex them again; tithe-barns larger than their churches, and an old smithy that cried out aloud how it had once been a hall of the Knights of the Temple.

Kipling was an early and enthusiastic motorist, and we feel in this description a lively delight in the speed and ease of the narrator's movement through the English countryside. We might also notice that his journey takes him through time as well as space: the Norman churches, the tithe-barns and the old smithy are vestiges of an older, less mechanised England. There's an irony here for the twenty-first-century reader – at the time Kipling wrote the story the character of this older, hidden England was about to be seriously compromised by a massive increase in road traffic – but this doesn't affect the essential point: the observer's movement in relation to his environment can impart valuable energy to a passage of description.

How much detail?

Let's suppose our first-person narrator has had an argument with her girlfriend in the canteen of the university library. She storms out in distress, looking for a quiet place where she can gather her thoughts. You may have imagined the setting in great detail (which is good) but if you try to incorporate every detail you've imagined, your narrative may look something like this:

> I pushed back the heavy oak door with its glossy black metal studs and walked along the red, green and white tiled floor of the brightly lit corridor, which was crowded with people moving between the catalogue-room and the bookstacks. I pushed through the throng of jostling bodies, letting the tears run down my face, until I arrived at the cool inner sanctum of the ornately decorated Victorian library: the awe-inspiring Rare Books Room.

You'll notice immediately that the passage is overloaded: the two sentences strain at the seams and the important action is swamped by the weight of descriptive detail. You may also realise that, in a first-person narrative such as this (and the same would apply to a tight third-person narrative), the details jar for a further reason: most of them would be unlikely to be noticed by the narrator at the moment in question. In privileging the decor of the library or noting that the Rare Books Room inspires awe, the narrative sets up a distance between the reader and the narrator: we're not convincingly in her mind and therefore don't fully participate in her distress.

A narrative may also be clogged with redundant actions. Consider the following passage, with an eye to how much of its meticulously recorded detail is actually necessary:

> I knocked on the door and Mr Tebbut called me in. I opened the door and went in, closing it behind me. Mr Tebbut indicated I should sit down so I took the seat in front of his desk.
>
> 'Well, Mrs Green,' he said. 'Have you found those sales figures?'
>
> I opened the box-file and took out the folder. I slid it across the desk to him. The phone rang and Mr Tebbut answered it.

'I'm rather busy,' he said. 'I'm with Mr Sanders. Can this wait?'

That was odd. Why had he said he was with Mr Sanders?

He shrugged his shoulders and indicated the phone, as if to say 'I'm sorry' and 'can we do this later?' I smiled and stood up, mouthing 'it's OK'. I went to the door and opened it. I went out into the corridor, closing the door behind me.

I didn't think any more about it, until much later.

We might reasonably suppose that the crucial information in this scene is that Mr Tebbut said he was with Mr Sanders when he wasn't. The business with chairs, doors, box-files and folders is largely unnecessary – you can't go into a room without going through a door and you can't sit down unless there's a seat there. Why have a character take a folder from a box-file when you might just as easily have had her bring in the folder alone?

This isn't to say that door and chair business – or its equivalent – can't ever be important. Whether the door is open or closed might be significant – if this is a conversation Mr Tebbut doesn't want overheard, or if the narrator is uncomfortable about being alone with Mr Tebbut. Whether the narrator breezes in and sits down at once or enters hesitantly and only sits when invited might also be significant, serving to define the relationship.

Consider this passage, from Katherine Mansfield's 'Life of Ma Parker' (1921). Ma Parker, grieving inarticulately for her dead grandchild, enters the apartment of the gentleman for whom she works as a cleaner:

> Ma Parker drew the two jetty spears out of her toque and hung it behind the door. She unhooked her worn jacket and hung that up too. Then she tied her apron and sat down to take off her boots. To take off her boots or to put them on was an agony to her, but it had been an agony for years. In fact, she was so accustomed to the pain that her face was drawn and screwed up ready for the twinge before she'd so much as untied the laces. That over, she sat back with a sigh and softly rubbed her knees …

If this description seems laborious, that's precisely the point. Actions that a younger or more light-hearted person might scarcely register are important to Ma Parker because of the difficulty she has in performing them. The catalogue of small actions slows the narrative, but it does so in order to reveal the state of Ma Parker's ailing body and sorrowful mind.

So the matter isn't clear-cut, but you should bear in mind that all details need to be tested for significance and value in the context in which they're found. In the end it's up to you to decide what is – or isn't – significant in the specific context of the story you are writing.

You may find it helpful in this context to consider 'Chekhov's gun'. The phrase refers to a piece of advice Anton Chekhov gave to several writers: if, in the first act of a play, or the early chapters of a novel, the writer has drawn attention to a gun hanging on the wall, then at some point in the narrative it has to go off. The gun stands, of course, for any detail to which attention is drawn: the detail implies a promise which the writer must keep. This is not to say, of course, that every detail you give must pay off in some important way, but be aware that everything you describe will be deemed by the attentive reader to be in some sense significant; if the detail is incongruous, or otherwise striking, the reader's expectations will be heightened.

As with all aspects of writing, the skill lies in finding a balance appropriate to the context. Give details *proportionate* attention: if you pay something a lot of attention, readers will have high expectations of its future significance. (Conversely, if you ignore something altogether and it later proves to be important, readers will feel they have been cheated.) Be aware, too, that details grow or shrink in importance depending on the scope of the story you are telling. The shorter a piece of fiction, the more significant any detail is. A cup of coffee that has been allowed to grow cold appears a weightier detail in a short story of 2,000 words than in a novel of 80,000 words.

So what we're looking for in description is what we might call the telling detail – the detail that informs and energises a narrative, bringing its meaning into sharp focus. An affecting example can be found in Daniel Defoe's *Robinson Crusoe* (1719). After suffering shipwreck Crusoe searches desperately for surviving shipmates, but 'I never saw them afterwards, or any sign of them, except three of their hats, one cap and two shoes that were not fellows.'[121] The poignancy of these details depends very much on context; the same items casually discovered on a municipal rubbish-tip wouldn't pack half the punch.

Detail can also give important clues: in crime fiction it's often small details that provide the key to the hidden story of what has happened – and not only in crime fiction. In Ford Madox Ford's *The Good Soldier* it's a tiny gesture of Florence's – 'And she laid one finger upon Captain Ashburnham's wrist' – that betrays, to the reader if not to the narrator, what is going on between her and Ashburnham.[122]

We've addressed character description in Chapter 3, but it's worth reminding ourselves here how effectively a few well-chosen details of appearance and behaviour may evoke personality. This is the opening of Dorothy Parker's short story 'Cousin Larry' (1934):

> The young woman in the crepe de Chine dress printed all over with little pagodas set amid giant cornflowers flung one knee atop the other and surveyed, with an enviable contentment, the tip of her scrolled green sandal. Then, in a like happy calm, she inspected her finger nails of so thick and glistening a red that it seemed as if she had but recently completed tearing an ox apart with her naked hands. Then she dropped her chin abruptly to her chest and busied herself among the man-made curls, sharp and dry as shavings, along the back of her neck; and again she appeared to be wrapped in cozy satisfaction. Then she lighted a fresh cigarette and seemed to find it, like all about her, good. Then she went right on with all she had been saying before.

Although we may find the first couple of lines rather too heavily loaded for the balance of the sentence, we can see that the passage gives us a great deal of significant information about the character.

The details that Parker has foregrounded lead us to expect – even before the young woman has opened her mouth – a selfish and superficial individual, and the self-serving monologue that follows this description quickly confirms our expectations. We might add that the way one of these details is presented is particularly significant: those fingernails, 'of so thick and glistening a red that it seemed as if she had but recently completed tearing an ox apart', foreshadow the disingenuous character-assassination that forms the substance of the young woman's monologue.

Showing through description

We've already mentioned, in our discussion of character, the value of *showing* as distinct from *telling*, and what applies to the rendering of character can be applied to all descriptive writing. By approaching a subject obliquely a writer can often work at a deeper level than through more obvious forms of description. Consider this passage:

> Beads of sweat stood out on the receptionist's forehead, despite the fan on her desk which, Rick noticed, was aimed squarely at her. Selfish, he thought. Through the open window, above the roar of traffic, he could hear kids playing football in the alley below. He couldn't imagine anyone wanting to run around in this weather. Still, he thought, as the high-pitched whine of the drill started up again in the next room, he'd rather be down there than up here. His tongue, for the hundredth time, explored the hole in his tooth. A sharp twinge shot through his jaw.
>
> The door opened. It was time.

The passage doesn't actually use the words 'dentist', 'waiting room', 'hot' or 'heat', nor does it describe the world outside the office, yet it gives us a sense of all these things. Approaching description indirectly in this way will oblige us, as writers, to participate more fully in a character's experience, and it follows that we are then more likely to engage the imaginations of our readers.

One further point arising from this: the human species is strongly visually orientated, and our descriptions tend to privilege what is *seen*. That's fine – we're writing for other humans, most of whom share our bias – but there's a danger that we may concentrate so single-mindedly on the visual that we forget about the other senses. It's not necessary to run through a checklist of the senses every time a character enters a new space or has a new experience, but it's worth cultivating a general awareness of the variety of ways in which we apprehend the world around us, and using that awareness to extend and enhance our powers of description.

– II –

Research

~

Barbara Taylor Bradford believes that a novel 'is a monumental lie that has to have the absolute ring of truth if it's going to succeed. The ring of truth is the underpinning of the book; it's very genuine, real-life research.'[123] For many kinds of novel good research is essential. Because there is so much ground to cover you will make life much easier for yourself if your subject is already familiar to you, or at least holds some fascination for you. If the prospect of researching the subject fills you with dread, it's probably wise to reconsider.

Then again, you might enjoy your research so much that you don't know when to stop. It's wise to define your parameters at a fairly early stage in the writing of any given novel or short story. To begin with you should have done enough background reading and basic fact-checking to know that your story will work: the things you want to happen in your book must be plausible in their context. Once you've cleared this hurdle you can begin to build your story. You can't know, when you start, exactly what research will prove necessary, but you can get a broad sense of the territory.

The writing of a work of fiction may involve research in a wide variety of fields. If, in what follows, the focus is on historical research, this is because the recreation of historical settings presents particular challenges, and if you can rise to these you can probably address any of the research issues normally associated with the writing of fiction.

The first sentence of L. P. Hartley's *The Go-Between* (1953) holds an important truth for writers of historical fiction: 'The past is a foreign country: they do things differently there.' Many details of everyday life in the past were different from the present-day equivalents and you need to be constantly alert to this fact. You'll need to know what mode of transport your character could or would use; what methods of communication are available to her; what she would eat and wear; how she might speak; what actions are open or closed to her due to factors such as gender, ethnicity, education, social standing, economic status and geographical location. Gradually you will flesh out the world your character inhabits, so that, as she sits in her room writing a letter, you will know not only what she's wearing and how the room is furnished but how that room is lit and heated, what she can see through the window, and what sounds, both outside and inside, might be background to her activity. It's inevitable that as you research the historical 'everyday' you will come across facts which will give you further ideas for your story. This is one of research's great incidental pleasures.

You should start writing your story as soon as you feel you comfortably can: since research of any significant subject might occupy an entire lifetime and still not be 'complete', you should dispense with the idea that you need to know everything about your subject before you start. So far your research has been broad, as you try to build up a sense of the particular 'foreign country' your characters inhabit. As you continue, your research will become more particular, answering specific questions. If your protagonist is going to the theatre in August 1923, what sort of play would he see? What show would be on the radio in his mother's kitchen in 1957? Could you get a taxi in 1928? How long would it take to get from London to Brighton in 1856? What would you eat at a rural wedding in 1780, or a picnic in 1948, or a cocktail party in 1968? The answers to routine searches can be surprising and can influence your story. (Mass-produced rubber condoms were available from the 1860s; in London in the late nineteenth century you could expect a letter to arrive within a couple of hours of being posted; before the nineteenth century women went about knickerless ....) This kind of research can be enthralling, and may prove relevant; equally, it may take you a long way from the needs of your story. It's very easy to fall in love with your findings and include them where they're not needed. Perhaps you've found a detail that you feel you just have to put in because it's so fascinating or extraordinary; but remember that the job of the fiction-writer is to tell the story and that the writer's research should always serve that imperative before any other. We shall return to this matter at the end of the chapter.

World events may figure in your narrative but you shouldn't let them overshadow the particular story you want to tell. For example, it would be odd if a story set in rural Cambridgeshire in 1916 made absolutely no reference to the war being fought in Europe, and the conflict might occasionally impinge on the characters and their actions; but it would probably be unhelpful to your narrative to keep updating the reader on the war's progress. As Bernard Cornwell explains it, historical novels tend to have a big story and a little story – the historical events and the events of the characters' lives:

> The big story in *Gone with the Wind* is: will the South win the Civil War? The little story is: can Scarlett save Tara? The trick is to flip them, so you put the big story in the background and the little story in the foreground.[124]

From the writer's point of view the big story exists to provide a context for the little story; if it becomes dominant the lives of our characters will be obscured.

As mentioned earlier, Henry James thought that the attempt to write historical fiction was doomed to failure: we can't, he says, adequately represent 'the old *consciousness* – the soul, the sense, the horizon, the vision of individuals in whose minds half the things that make ours, that make the modern world, were non-existent'.[125] It's true, of course, that we can't accurately *recreate* the outlook and mental processes of those who lived before us, but that fact doesn't invalidate all historical fiction. What we can do, having discovered and researched our 'foreign country', is to try to inhabit it as we write, so that we seem to show it from within, lightly, with the apparent familiarity of an insider. It's our role to bridge the gap in time, to explore, to interpret in such a way as to make the lives of our characters both accessible and plausible. We don't know everything about the psychology of our forebears (if it comes to that, we don't know everything about the psychology of our contemporaries) but this doesn't mean that we can't know anything about it. And we need always to bear in mind that across time, as across cultures, human experience is likely to reveal more similarities than differences. As long as we are writing about people, we are not on totally unfamiliar ground: at root, human fears and desires transcend their immediate historical context.

Keeping research unobtrusive

One of the challenges of historical fiction is providing sufficient detail to build a picture in the reader's mind while avoiding the clutter of unnecessary explanation. You'll see at once what's wrong with the following sentence:

> It was raining, so James hailed a brougham, one of the light four-wheeled carriages which had become popular in recent years, having the benefit of being enclosed and not open to the elements.

All we actually need is:

> It was raining, so James hailed a brougham.

We still speak of hailing a cab, so even without any further context the general picture is clear: no sensible reader is likely to imagine from this sentence that a brougham is an animal or an exotic dish. And since the sentence implies that the rain is to be avoided, many readers will guess that a brougham is enclosed. And suppose they don't? Maybe some will be content simply to understand, from this sentence and its wider context, that James is conveyed by a vehicle to his destination. If they've wrongly assumed that the brougham is an open vehicle, and if at a later stage in their reading of the narrative they find that James isn't (as they'd imagined) soaked through, they can be trusted to make the necessary adjustment to their understanding.

When we write an elaborately explanatory sentence we're often either showing off what we know or demonstrating our lack of confidence in the reader's ability to pick up the clues. We need to help our readers, but we also need to credit their intelligence.

However, you do have opportunities – and can create opportunities – to fill in a picture in detail when it is in some way new to the character, as Hilary Mantel makes clear:

> When your character is new to a place, or things alter around them, that's the point to step back and fill in the details of their world. People don't notice their everyday surroundings and daily routine, so when writers describe them it can sound as if they're trying too hard to instruct the reader.[126]

A character who has always lived in a Victorian slum would not perceive their surroundings with pitying eyes and might not even consciously notice them, but a more affluent visitor would. Similarly, the slum-dweller, entering a rich person's house, might be struck by every detail. That same character might then, when returning to their slum, see their own surroundings more critically, and notice details in new ways. Descriptions will often feel more natural to a reader when the material in question is new to, or seen anew by, a character.

Subjects

Your subjects for research are, of course, the subjects of your fiction; if, for example, you're writing a detective novel and need to find out how long a set of fingerprints might be expected to survive in an exposed environment, your research subject is obvious. But historical fiction makes particular demands on the writer, who needs a broad spectrum of knowledge in order to picture her fictional world and develop a sense of what living in it might be like. Here's a checklist that will be helpful to you if you choose, as many writers do, to set your fiction in the past:

Animals – Ours is a motorised society, but until the First World War horsepower was the most common way of moving people or goods; this affects the look and sound of the outside world. Other animals will be used in association with work in rural areas. Pets also go in and out of fashion. There have been periods when squirrels and native songbirds, for example, have been popular pets in British households.

Architecture – Houses haven't always had corridors and even in substantial houses you often had to go through rooms to get to other rooms – hence the curtained four-poster bed, which provided privacy as well as cutting out draughts. Knowing a bit about the layout, décor and furniture of the buildings of your period is very helpful when envisioning scenes. If your story depends on a detail it's worth checking it out: for example, before the Industrial Revolution it was rare for anyone to own a glass mirror much larger than about four inches square because the technology required to make mirrors was so expensive.

Communications – Would your characters be able to send a telegram or use the telephone? How long would their letters take from posting to arrival? How do they get their news?

Costume/dress/fashion – Before the Second World War most people wore some kind of headgear out of doors as a matter of course, so hats might be important. Wigs were *de rigueur* in certain circles at certain times and cosmetics have gone in and out of fashion. Women's dress is particularly important as it so often impeded free movement. Don't forget that knowing the fashion is not the same as knowing what people were wearing: then, as now, not everyone could afford to dress in the latest style, and some would have chosen not to do so.

Crime and punishment – Depending on the subject matter of your book you may need to be proficient in this area. Is this an age of capital punishment? Transportation? Branding? Flogging? What are the capital crimes? Is there a formally constituted police force?

Current affairs – As we've mentioned, while the news of the day need not obtrude in your story, it's helpful to be aware of the wider context of your characters' lives.

Education – It's always useful to have an overview of this for your period; the kind of education your characters have had will affect not only the skills available to them (literacy and numeracy levels vary widely over time) but also their view of the world.

Etiquette/conduct – When should a man stand up in the presence of (standing) women? In what circumstances was it socially acceptable for an unmarried woman to be alone with a man? Were domestic servants called by their first or surnames? Social niceties might be important: one of the reasons Quakers were regarded as subversive was that, believing all men equal and deferring only to God, they did not automatically remove their hats or bow to those who considered themselves their social superiors.

Health/treatment of disease – This is only necessary if it features in your story, but if so, it's important to be aware that treatments for various illnesses vary over time, as does the understanding of their causes.

Leisure pursuits – What games do children play in the street? What do people do for recreation at home? Where do people go when they have time and money to spare? What are the respectable and unrespectable places of resort?

Religion/rituals – Births, marriages and deaths are marked by different traditions and procedures at different times. Would your characters attend church regularly? How much would their beliefs influence their worldview and reactions?

Sex – The risks associated with sexual intercourse affect attitudes. The law, social norms and mores, the likelihood of sex resulting in pregnancy or venereal disease – all are historically variable.

Social stratification – Social class was more clearly defined in the past and you need to be clear about where your characters fit in. Do your characters use the front door or the servants' and tradesmen's entrance? Do they have their meals 'upstairs' or 'downstairs'? Are they privileged to speak first? Remember that there is not only a hierarchy within the upper- and middle-class household as a whole (the authority of masters over servants), but also within the family (the authority of parents over children and of men over women). This affects the way people relate to one another and also determines what actions are available to them.

Time – Do people have individual portable timepieces (a matter related to social class as well as historical period) or do they depend on the church clock? Do they negotiate the calendar by months or by saints' days, seasons or religious festivals?

Sources

Where do you go for your information? We're fortunate these days in having a great deal of material literally at our fingertips: a considerable amount of our research can now be carried out online, though you're still likely to need the support of libraries at times. And how do you begin? In general, it's a good idea to start wide and shallow (establishing a broad sense of the subject area or historical period) and later, as your needs define themselves more clearly, to go deep and narrow (digging down to find out specific details). Listed below are the broad categories of publication that you may need to go to for information.

Books – When starting research in any area where your knowledge is slender it's best to start with something general. If you want to know how people lived in a particular era, books of social history are more useful than books about national and international events (although you'll also need a broad understanding of these). Good introductions to a period or subject will usually have footnotes and a bibliography – these represent a bunch of keys which will unlock more specialised areas, and these specialist works will in turn provide more keys. If you have access to a library you can order pretty much any book you need to consult, though buying books online can be cheaper. Many out-of-copyright books can be consulted online without payment.

Specialist periodicals – Academic and professional journals are invaluable sources for deep and narrow research, offering a lot of detail about a specific area. A great deal is available online but you often have to pay for access. A copyright library is best, but university libraries also have specialist periodicals. If you are travelling some distance to visit a library you can use their online catalogue to narrow down what you want to look at before you go, so you're not wasting time when you're there. Many institutes, guilds, unions, professional associations and other interest groups have their own libraries, which you may be able to consult.

Contemporary newspapers and periodicals – These are absolutely invaluable for getting a feel of the everyday for historical fiction. The language gives you a vocabulary that you can be sure of. Reports of accidents provide you with information on the common hazards of the time. Reports of court proceedings expose the underbelly of this world. Advertisements tell you a lot about social norms, perceptions and aspirations. Many newspapers can be found online, though you'll usually have to pay for access.

Maps, paintings, illustrations and photographs – It's easy to overlook how much a landscape in the past can differ from how it appears today, and how differently the space is used by the people in it. Pictures (and moving pictures of course, if they exist for your period) bring a period alive, making its details concrete.

Music – Listening to music contemporary with your period and milieu can add a level of depth to your sense of a society, whether it's what the leisured classes might be listening to, or the songs sung in taverns or by ballad-sellers on street corners.

Travel writing – Contemporary writers writing about their own world don't particularly notice what is normal or everyday. However, visitors do. An account by a country visitor to, say, Victorian London, will contain detail which a contemporary Londoner would pass by. An Italian visitor to the English Restoration court will be struck by things that one of Charles II's courtiers would take for granted. If the past is a foreign country, 'foreigners' are useful witnesses because, like us, they are outsiders.

Diaries, letters and autobiographies – Diaries and letters often allow us to glimpse past lives in intimate detail. Whether or not they now exist in published form, they were usually conceived of by their authors as private or semi-private documents, and are likely to be less artfully constructed than works written with a view to publication. They tend to be more intimate in their focus, and to provide more everyday or domestic detail – which is often the kind of detail most useful to the fiction-writer. They are also likely to take you closer to the spoken language of their period – its vocabulary, syntax and idioms – than any other written source. Autobiography can provide useful material of a similar kind, though it's worth remembering that writing intended for publication may be more guarded than a diary or a letter, while its language is likely to be more polished, taking us a step further from the common speech of the age.

Serving your story

It's important to bear in mind that the essential purpose of your research is to serve your story. This usually means making the reader believe, if only for the duration of his reading, in the world you've created, and for most readers belief will depend on the narrative having a discernible relationship to the facts. But serving the story also requires flexibility in our treatment of the facts.

It's as desirable as it is inevitable that a writer of historical fiction will deviate, to a greater or lesser extent, from historical fact: it's often in the gaps between known facts that our imaginations work most freely and fruitfully. And occasionally a writer may depart radically from recorded history, as Colson Whitehead does in *The Underground Railroad* (2016).

Historically, the underground railroad was the secret network of travel routes and safe houses by which, with the help of sympathisers, people could escape from slavery in the southern United States to freedom in the north; the phrase 'underground railroad' was a useful shorthand, not to be taken literally. In detailing the events leading up to the escape of two such individuals, Cora and Caesar, Whitehead's story seems at first to be following the conventional lines of serious historical fiction: any detail may be an invented detail, but none runs counter to historical fact. Shortly after their escape, however, the narrative takes an unexpected turn as their helper opens a trapdoor in the floor of a barn to reveal an underground staircase:

> The stairwell was lined with stones and a sour smell emanated from below. It did not open into a cellar but continued down. Cora appreciated the labor that had gone into its construction. The steps were steep but the stones aligned in even planes and provided an easy descent. Then they reached the tunnel, and appreciation became too mealy a word to contain what lay before her.
>
> The stairs led onto a small platform. The black mouths of the gigantic tunnel opened at either end. It must have been twenty feet tall, walls lined with dark and light colored stones in an alternating pattern. The sheer industry that had made such a project possible. Cora and Caesar noticed the rails. Two steel rails ran the visible length of the tunnel, pinned into the dirt by wooden crossties. The steel ran south and north presumably, springing from some inconceivable source and shooting towards a miraculous terminus.[127]

'Inconceivable' and 'miraculous' may offer a clue that we've moved beyond the framework of history into another dimension (the marvel of engineering described here had no historical existence), but what is most remarkable about this transition is the smoothness with which it is accomplished. Up to this point the author has carried us with him on a journey that we knew to be fictional but were ready to take as reality; now he asks readers to give credence, for the duration of their reading, to a narrative that many will know cannot be factually true.

Few readers are likely to put aside this compelling novel on the grounds of its departure from historical fact. Both as researcher and novelist, Whitehead stamps his authority on its opening pages, and no careful reader is likely to mistake his audacious imaginative leap for an erroneous reading of the facts. Here the risk pays off, but we should note that writers of serious historical fiction, perhaps recognising the risks, tend generally to conform more closely to the contours of history.

Wherever you stand on this matter, you'll find it helpful to think of your narrative's likely effect on its reader. Since, by definition, all fictional narratives operate at some distance from the facts that form their basis, the most useful question is not 'Is it true?' but 'Does it carry conviction?' If you write in ignorance of the facts or with a wanton disregard for the historical record, you're unlikely to convince your reader; conversely, an over-rigid adherence to the facts may inhibit imaginative engagement on the part of the writer and therefore, inevitably, on the part of the reader. Success in this respect depends to a large extent on the writer setting up, and then honouring, an implicit compact with the reader concerning the story's relationship to the realities, past and present, of our own world. Provided you give your reader reason to believe your story, or (to borrow an idea from Coleridge) willingly to suspend her disbelief, you'll be free to move into imaginative territory that simultaneously reflects and transcends the factual material thrown up by your research.

– 12 –

Drawing it all together

~

Reading this book you'll have become increasingly aware that we're hardly ever able to discuss any one aspect of writing in isolation from other aspects of the craft. Whether consciously or unconsciously, we blend different skills and strategies to create the complex patterns characteristic of a good story. Let's have a look at a few passages in which the writer is seamlessly weaving together various literary elements in order to set his story on its feet. Here's the opening of Kazuo Ishiguro's *The Remains of the Day*:

> It seems increasingly likely that I really will undertake the expedition that has been preoccupying my imagination now for some days. An expedition, I should say, which I will undertake alone, in the comfort of Mr Farraday's Ford; an expedition which, as I foresee it, will take me through much of the finest countryside of England to the West Country, and may keep me away from Darlington Hall for as much as five or six days. The idea of such a journey came about, I should point out, from a most kind suggestion put to me by Mr Farraday himself one afternoon almost a fortnight ago, when I had been dusting portraits in the library. In fact, as I recall, I was up on the step-ladder dusting the portrait of Viscount Wetherby when my employer had entered carrying a few volumes which he presumably wished to return to the shelves. On seeing my person, he took the opportunity to inform me that he had just that moment finalized plans to return to the United States for a period of five weeks between August and September. Having made this announcement, my employer put his volumes down on a table, seated himself on the *chaise-longue*, and stretched out his legs. It was then, gazing up at me, that he said,
>
> 'You realize, Stevens, I don't expect you to be locked up here in this house all the time I'm away. Why don't you take the car and drive

off somewhere for a few days? You look like you could make good use of a break.'

This passage neatly illustrates the effective deployment of description, characterisation, narrative voice, dialogue and plot – aspects of writing which we have endeavoured to isolate in separate chapters in order to give them useful consideration, but which, both in the act of writing and the act of reading, would normally function as an organic whole.

Description tells us what kind of a house this is and what the characters' roles are. We're explicitly told that Mr Farraday is 'my employer', and this relationship is made concrete in the shape of Stevens up a step-ladder, dusting, while Farraday sits on a chaise-longue watching him work. And while we might guess from its name that Darlington Hall is an old house of impressive proportions, we're then offered several telling confirmatory details: a room designated as the library, with its 'volumes' (not plain 'books') and its portrait of a nobleman (only reachable on a step-ladder) – these, together with the chaise-longue (the term implying a certain grandeur in the furnishings), give us, with striking economy, an idea not simply of the room but of the wider domestic context. Ishiguro doesn't have his narrator pause in the story to describe the library but drops in the details most directly relevant to the action: the portrait is mentioned because Stevens is dusting it, the books because Mr Farraday is carrying them, the chaise-longue because Mr Farraday is sitting on it. Because it's Stevens who is narrating the scene (he's recalling something that happened a few days previously in the house that he has worked in for many years) Ishiguro gives us only those details that would impress themselves upon his narrator at this particular moment.

What do we learn about the characters? The only fact we're given about their relationship is that Mr Farraday is Stevens's employer. We are not necessarily conscious of the reasons for supposing that Stevens is the butler but the evidence is there: the fact that he's dusting an ancestral portrait suggests a level of responsibility and seniority which wouldn't have been suggested had Mr Farraday come in to find him mopping the floor. The way in which characters address each other is of course significant: it's 'Mr Farraday' and plain 'Stevens' of course, but Mr Farraday's manner to Stevens is more informal and intimate than it might be to a more menial member of staff. He lounges on the chaise as he addresses Stevens, and offering him the use of his car implies that Stevens is considered trustworthy and highly responsible – as well as suggesting that Mr Farraday might be concerned about his well-being. We quickly realise that Stevens is at the top of the servant class.

Perhaps the most telling suggestions of character are in the characters' voices and especially in the narrative voice. The story is told in the first person and yet as readers we may not immediately identify with Stevens; this is partly because of the very formal tone he takes with us. Right from the opening sentence, which might have been: 'I think I really will take the trip that's been on my mind recently' but is actually: 'It seems increasingly likely that I really will take the expedition that has been preoccupying my imagination now for some days', we understand we are in the presence of a particular sort of person. He speaks in a careful and formal way, unhurried and precise. As he goes on we might notice that he has a habit of adding little qualifying phrases ('I should say'; 'as I foresee it'; 'I should point out'; 'as I recall') which add to this impression of a desire to be exact. However, he doesn't evaluate anything he describes except in his rather formally phrased observation that Mr Farraday's suggestion is 'most kind'; this is the reticence of a discreet servant, but it's also a characteristic that will prove significant in the development of the narrative.

Mr Farraday's plain style of speech throws Stevens's narrative voice into sharp relief. Stevens's speech, here as throughout the novel, is elaborate in structure and makes considerable use of polysyllabic words; Farraday's speech is much more direct and consists largely of words of one syllable.

The opening of the novel also sets the plot in motion. Stevens is going on an expedition, and of course it's going to be more than just a road trip: we shall discover that it involves a journey through the past too, a revisiting and reconsideration of the events that brought him to the point at which the novel begins.

As you'll have seen from this analysis, many of the elements of writing we've been discussing are skilfully combined in an opening that provides a firm foundation for all that follows. Let's look now at the way Dickens sets up his narrative in the famous opening to *Great Expectations* (1861):

> My father's family name being Pirrip, and my Christian name Philip, my infant tongue could make of both names nothing longer or more explicit than Pip. So, I called myself Pip, and came to be called Pip.
>
> I give Pirrip as my father's family name, on the authority of his tombstone and my sister, – Mrs. Joe Gargery, who married the blacksmith. As I never saw my father or my mother, and never saw any likeness of either of them (for their days were long before the days of photographs), my first fancies regarding what they were like were unreasonably derived from their tombstones. The shape of the letters on my father's, gave me an odd idea that he was a square, stout, dark man, with curly black hair. From the character and turn of the inscription, 'Also Georgiana Wife of the Above,' I drew a childish conclusion that my mother was freckled and sickly. To five little stone lozenges, each about a foot and a half long, which were arranged in a neat row beside their grave, and were sacred to the memory of five little brothers of mine, – who gave up trying to get a living, exceedingly early in that universal struggle, – I am indebted for a belief I religiously entertained that they had all been born on their backs with their hands in their trousers-pockets, and had never taken them out in this state of existence.
>
> Ours was the marsh country, down by the river, within, as the river wound, twenty miles of the sea. My first most vivid and broad impression of the identity of things seems to me to have been gained on a memorable raw afternoon towards evening. At such a time I found out for certain that this bleak place overgrown with nettles was the churchyard; and that Philip Pirrip, late of this parish, and also

Georgiana wife of the above, were dead and buried; and that Alexander, Bartholomew, Abraham, Tobias, and Roger, infant children of the aforesaid, were also dead and buried; and that the dark flat wilderness beyond the churchyard, intersected with dikes and mounds and gates, with scattered cattle feeding on it, was the marshes; and that the low leaden line beyond was the river; and that the distant savage lair from which the wind was rushing was the sea; and that the small bundle of shivers growing afraid of it all and beginning to cry, was Pip.

'Hold your noise!' cried a terrible voice, as a man started up from among the graves at the side of the church porch. 'Keep still, you little devil, or I'll cut your throat!'

The first half of this extract invites us into the worldview of the child Pip once was. The way he has imaginatively embodied his parents, taking as his chief hint the style of the lettering on their gravestones, gives us a strong sense of the way a child makes sense of the world in the absence of more authoritative guidance, while at the same time usefully conveying the information that Pip is an orphan. Similarly, the little plain stones marking his brothers' graves and suggesting to Pip that 'they had all been born on their backs with their hands in their trouser-pockets', encourages us to picture the scene from Pip's point of view while offering further information concerning his family circumstances. So Dickens doesn't give us facts and characterisation separately but does both jobs at the same time. The economy with which this is done is important because Dickens is about to put Pip in peril and we must by that time be on his side and understand the way he makes sense, according to his own limited abilities, of what happens to him.

The third paragraph deals with the landscape but once more is not merely conveying hard facts: Dickens again places Pip at the physical and emotional heart of the picture and we see it through his eyes – or perhaps, rather, we feel its effect on him as he registers his own place in the world he inhabits. Dickens covers the realisation in a single long sentence ('At such a time … '), occupying three quarters of the paragraph, to better convey the sense of these ideas tumbling into place all at once. Then comes the terrible voice from the terrible man who emerges from among the gravestones, and with that burst of threatening dialogue the action begins.

Every writer has to find her own solution to packing a great deal – the elements of storytelling we've discussed – into a small space without appearing to be in any hurry to get all these jobs done. Let's look at how Alice Munro achieves this in the opening of her short story, 'The Beggar Maid' (1977):

> Patrick Blanchford was in love with Rose. This had become a fixed, even furious, idea with him. For her, a continual surprise. He wanted to marry her. He waited for her after classes, moved in and walked beside her, so that anybody she was talking to would have to reckon with his presence. He would not talk when these friends or classmates of hers were around, but he would try to catch her eye, so that he could indicate by a cold incredulous look what he thought of their conversation. Rose was flattered, but nervous. A girl named Nancy Falls, a friend of hers, mispronounced Metternich in front of him. He said to her later, 'How can you be friends with people like that?'
>
> Nancy and Rose had gone and sold their blood together, at Victoria Hospital. They each got fifteen dollars. They spent most of the money on evening shoes, tarty silver sandals. Then because they were sure the blood-letting had caused them to lose weight, they had hot fudge sundaes at Boomers. Why was Rose unable to defend Nancy to Patrick?

The story starts by *telling*: four short, unambiguous statements about the couple. Munro then *shows*, in unflattering terms, Patrick's strategies for winning Rose's attention. His attention is dominating, demanding exclusion of others; he encourages her to identify with his disdain of her friends. The one line of dialogue reveals his contempt, part genuine and part strategic. Then we are introduced to Nancy, and the details of the girls' activities are equally revealing; although they may not merit Patrick's contempt, their implied superficiality prevents the reader from coming down too neatly on their side.

This characterisation introduces the theme: the whole story will be about the ultimately irreconcilable needs of Rose and of Patrick. While nothing feels hurried or overtly plotty about this opening, Munro has economically and efficiently laid all the important foundation-stones for the story.

Analysis of this kind artificially separates the various elements of a piece of writing – elements that ultimately depend for their effect on working in combination – but it's an important part of learning to read well, and therefore of learning to write well. You'll find the insights it offers particularly useful when you come to edit your work.

An approach to editing

You've written the first draft of your book. Whether you think of this as a very rough draft or a fairly respectable one, you've reached a significant stage. Next you'll take that text and turn it into something that's worth the reader's while: this is editing. Editing is writing too – your work is largely shaped by the editing process – and can also be described as a drawing together: the drawing together of your story's elements into tighter – and therefore more potent – relationship with one another. Think about how a film is made: the director will shoot all the scenes knowing he's taking a lot more footage than he will actually use in the film. He then has to tell the story in, say, two hours' worth of images. What he chooses to keep and what he chooses to shed will define what that story is. Even the order in which he tells the story may change.

Editing – or rather the idea of editing – troubles many developing writers. They often seem to feel that this is a separate skill from that required for writing. But editing your own work means simply being your own critic and acting on your own judgements. If you have ever read a book or watched a film and been able to identify what you liked or didn't like about it, you have exercised your critical faculties. If you have ever written a letter, thrown it away and started again, or if you have ever redrafted an email, you have edited your own writing. Editing is simply invoking the right to change your mind – to give space to a better idea. Self-editing is simply a matter of approving decisions already taken or improving on them.

In a broad sense, we constantly edit in everyday life. You might choose with some care what you wear for a particular occasion – you select the clothes, put them on and then you check your image in the mirror. It's very likely you'll adjust something before you go out. Before you serve up a meal you've cooked you taste it – maybe it's fine or maybe it needs a little something. You adjust. We tend to cast a more or less critical eye over even the most mundane tasks in everyday life before we're satisfied with what we've done. We tweak things until they're good enough, if not perfect. It's all a form of editing.

Be aware, too, that you have already been editing as you write. When you are thinking of the right word or phrase, the best way to get into a scene, how this character would express that idea, you are running over possibilities, discarding and selecting in your mind as you go. Subsequent editing, after you've completed a first draft, is essentially a repeat of this process, but with a broader over-view of the work, and therefore with a clearer sense of its nature.

Many are capable of writing; fewer are willing to rewrite, but it's part and parcel of the serious writer's job. It may be helpful to some writers to think of the initial writing process as being largely *art* – inspiration, vision, imagination – and the editing process as being largely *craft* – examining, shaping, finishing – though the activities are not truly separable. However you frame it, the important point to bear in mind is that both are necessary.

Editing techniques

As you gain experience self-editing will become an increasingly natural activity, but it's usually less instinctive than that to start with. Perhaps you lack confidence in your ability to assess the value of what you've done and/or your ability to correct your own errors. If so, the most important thing is to be prepared to put yourself in a different place in relation to what you've written: in a certain sense, to let go.

Creating a distance between you the editor and you the original writer is the best way of achieving some level of objectivity. Ideally you'd be able to put yourself in the position of a reader who knew nothing about what she was reading, except as the story unfolded. But there's only one of you, and you're hampered by knowing what you *think* you have written. You have to try to forget what you think you've written, and read what you've actually written. So give your writer-self the day off and bring in your editor-self.

Time is your editor-self's best friend, because with each day that passes the relationship you have with what you have written weakens – the passing of time creates distance – so if you are able to put your writing away and revisit it some days later, you will approach it more objectively: editor-you can approach the text with all your literary sensibilities but without the emotional attachment of writer-you to the text. A distance of weeks and even months between writing and editing is ideal to allow you to read it, in Truman Capote's words, 'as coldly as possible'.[128] However, even one night's sleep between the completion of your first draft and the commencement of editing will make a difference to the level of dispassion you can bring to the text.

The advice that follows isn't going to suit everyone entirely and may be most helpful for writers who are looking for a way in. Take from it whatever seems to serve your needs.

- If your lines aren't already double-spaced or one-and-a-half-spaced, make it so, and then (preferably) print it up. Hard copy is useful at this stage. Set aside a block of time to complete your first reading so that you can read the whole thing in as narrow a window as possible – a whole day, or successive whole evenings, but definitely not short sessions with significant gaps between them. Approach your first reading of the complete draft by doing your best to pretend you have no idea how the story unfolds and know nothing about the characters except what you learn as you go along. Try to experience the text, in other words, as a new reader would. Apart from minor corrections which you can make quickly without interrupting the flow of your reading (for example, punctuation, tense slips, repetition) don't make any changes at this stage; just underline in the manuscript areas you perceive don't work as well as they should. It may be that you identify a problem that you know how to fix, in which case make a note in the text (for example, *Confusing. Need to attribute speech more clearly*). However, if a problem is apparent but its solution does not immediately occur to you, don't spend time puzzling over it: just underline the section and note the nature of the problem (for example, *Confusing*) – that's all you need for now.

– Next you can go back and fix the problems which you can immediately see how to fix. You're then left with the problems that you've identified but are not sure how to address. Make a separate list of these and consider that list. Are there problems which seem related? Problems may cluster around a particular storyline, for example, or a particular character. Identifying these may help you cure a number of problems with one remedy. Try to interrogate the problem. For example, if you've decided a plot step is unconvincing, work out what is unconvincing about it. Diagnosis is the essential first step towards a cure. There's always a way to burrow down to the root of the problem, and this will then allow you to consider a range of possible solutions.

– Allow more time to elapse before your next read-through. This should be a happier experience but don't be surprised if you find new problems, or if some of your solutions haven't worked as well as you'd hoped. If you're reasonably pleased (but not fully satisfied) with your work, it's time for a draft designed to tighten and sharpen the whole thing.

- Go through the manuscript again, concentrating this time only on taking out all the words, sentences and paragraphs that don't have to be there. Every word should be doing a job. Look critically upon anything that is not contributing usefully to the texture of the piece. Have you described things that don't need to be described? Have you clogged your prose with details? Have you taken ten words to say something you could describe in five? Don't be afraid to cut. If you've written 500 words and end up with 300 and a tighter, better read, then you are editing effectively. Quality trumps quantity every time. When you've finished doing this, take a break before reading this new, sleek, version.
- This should be your best draft so far. Read it aloud. This is the best way to discover errors which have escaped notice – the eye alone often passes over them. Other tricks are to print out your work in a font you don't usually use, or on colour-tinted paper – anything to make it feel less familiar.
- When you've addressed the issues arising from this read-through, think of this as your 'best' draft rather than your 'final' draft. You're likely to be asked to do more rewriting by an agent or an editor. The final draft will be the one that, if your novel or short story is published, goes to print.

It's important in editing to have confidence in your ability to improve your own work, to know that if you can identify a problem you can probably fix it. Trust your instincts and hold your nerve. If you think your narrative is slow, it probably is. If you feel your characters are unconvincing, they probably are. But you can fix these problems. Interrogate everything.

If this sounds simple, that's perhaps because identifying the problem isn't the hard part. The hard part is finding the courage, where necessary, to revise radically. You must be prepared to shed whole characters, whole subplots, if you see that they aren't working – they might not be working because they're not well done, but maybe they're not working because they have no business in the story. People often assume that the editing process is about cutting bad writing, but it's just as important to be prepared to cut good writing. The great editor Maxwell Perkins induced Thomas Wolfe to cut 90,000 words – a whole novel's worth – from *Look Homeward, Angel* (1929).[129] Wolfe later reflected:

> What I had to face, the very bitter lesson that everyone who wants to write has got to learn, was that a thing may in itself be the finest piece of writing one has ever done, and yet have absolutely no place in the manuscript one hopes to publish.[130]

You have to care more about getting the writing right than preserving a piece of prose you are particularly pleased with. Those beautiful sentences in the wrong place will strike the reader as self-indulgent – and if they are only there because you can't bear to cut them, they are. To return to the film-making analogy: whole scenes will end up on the cutting-room floor, not because they are not, in themselves, perfectly good scenes, but because they no longer serve the narrative.

It's worth remembering, though, that you have a huge advantage over the film editor. It is extremely expensive (and sometimes impossible) to reshoot scenes or shoot new ones once the film is at the editing stage – the film editor has to work with what he has, however inadequate. The fiction-writer, however, can alter and add material as she likes.

This stage of altering and adding material can feel difficult, because you're returning to your writer-self when, as editor, you've been out of the flow. Thornton Wilder commented:

> I forget which of the great sonneteers said: 'One line in the fourteen comes from the ceiling; the others have to be adjusted around it.' Well, likewise there are passages in every novel whose first writing is pretty much the last. But it's the joint and cement, between those spontaneous passages, that take a great deal of rewriting.[131]

When you're finding it hard, remind yourself that getting writing right – or as right as possible – is necessarily hard. None of the writers you admire produced their works without doing exactly what you're doing now: making difficult editorial decisions.

Getting value from a critical reader

You have now gone as far as you can on your own. However hard you try you can never read your own work with an entirely open mind because you're trying to measure the effect of something you've made yourself; as Margaret Atwood puts it: 'You've been backstage. You've seen how the rabbits were smuggled into the hat.'[132] You now need your work to be seen through fresh eyes, by someone who doesn't know what you know.

Only when you're happy that you've done the best you can for your story should you show it to someone else. You may well want to show it to your nearest and dearest, and that's fine, but in most cases you shouldn't look to their reading for any great benefit to your work. The most valuable feedback is likely to come from other sources: you should choose readers for their critical acumen, not their closeness to you. Fellow writers are ideal, but don't imagine that any writer will do. If you are part of a writers' circle or class, you'll know whose writing you admire, and if you've had feedback in the past you'll know whose opinions have been helpful – and whose have not. To ask someone to read a novel is an imposition on their time, so offer a reciprocal service.

If you don't have an appropriate fellow-writer to consult, remember that most of the readers of a published novel or short story won't be writers either, and that the opinion of a reader who isn't herself a writer may still be helpful. There's no point, however, in asking for help from someone whose taste in fiction differs radically from yours: your reader needs to share, or at least to have sympathy with, your literary values.

Don't alert your readers to areas of concern. Let them tell you what they think first. If they identify as problems the things you're worried about, that's helpful. If they don't, these may not be problems. But if you give them advance warning of the things you think might not work, they can't read as objectively as you need them to. Ask them to be honest, explaining that you need an impartial reader; and, if you feel you can, ask them to supply written notes. Otherwise, take notes when they talk to you about your book.

Editing in response to notes

Feedback is only helpful if you know what to do with it. This section is about extracting maximum value from notes you get from a reader, whether it's an interested friend or a literary professional (agent or editor). At this point we're talking generally about responding to feedback, but we shall return briefly to the matter in the next chapter, with more specific reference to the responses of literary professionals.

It's natural that we should want praise for our work, but the serious writer can't afford to dismiss adverse criticism out of hand. If you've chosen well, your reader will be someone who can set aside personal considerations in order to focus on the text; you, for your part, need to avoid taking textual criticism as a personal slight, understanding that a good reader's concern will be to highlight problems so that you can remedy them. If you're fortunate enough to have more than one good reader, pay attention to both/all, and pay particular attention to those points at which their comments coincide with one another.

What follows is a checklist, showing a number of common reader-responses indicating a need for improvement – either of particular passages or more generally – together with questions and suggestions aimed at helping you to take effective remedial action. You'll see that these encapsulate ideas covered in detail in the preceding chapters of this book, so if any of them apply to your work it would be worth revisiting the relevant sections. It's probably unnecessary to add that these questions and suggestions will be helpful to you at any stage in the process of composition: if you address them as part of that process your chosen readers will almost certainly have fewer notes to give you.

The plot is rambling/hard to follow/too complicated/unconvincing

— Is the story following the trajectory of the main character or is it wandering off unprofitably in other directions? Is your character driving the plot? Are the connections between events sufficiently complex? – meaning, in essence: is the plot proceeding on the lines of 'and then … and then … and then … ' or, more profitably, 'and then … but then … so then … '? Are you trying to cram in more twists and turns than your narrative can comfortably accommodate, or more than you have the power to control?

— Are you revealing the right amount to the reader, and at the right time? Go through your story and on a separate sheet write the plot developments as the reader experiences them. Isolating plot in this way should help show you where things are unnecessarily complex, where something happens for no reason or where a character acts without motivation. You should always know *why* a character has done something: if there's no reasonable explanation for an action or event, a reader quite reasonably won't believe it.

— Is the story's point of view insecure? Go through your story, checking that it's uniform if it's intended to be and, if it's intentionally varied, that you're not losing control of the variations or demanding too much of your reader in asking him to follow them.

— Are readers provided with a clear sense of time in your book? If you've chosen to present the passage of time in any form other than straightforward chronological sequence, you need to be sure you have a good reason to do so; even if you're satisfied on this score, you'll still need to ensure that you're not confusing your readers. In this connection, it's worth checking that the tenses used are always correct and consistent with your intention.

– Does your plot depend too much on coincidence? Of course, coincidences exist in real life, but it's unwise to rely on them in your fiction if you want readers to believe your story.

There are too many characters

– The question here isn't one of simple arithmetic: 'too many' means more than your particular text needs, or can accommodate. Don't start by considering who *you* can afford to lose, as you will probably be attached to a greater or lesser degree to all your characters; consider what characters *the story* can afford to lose. If you can cut a character without harming the story in any way, that character is clearly unnecessary: give him the chop. Where you have a number of characters, each of which exists only to perform one function in the text, consider how you might combine two or more of these functions in one character. This not only reduces the number of characters the reader has to remember, but also makes the multi-functioning characters more interesting than they were before. Think like a playwright: she knows that the fewer actors her play requires, the more attractive it is to a producer, as each actor costs the theatre more money. The playwright is therefore in the habit of thinking: what is the smallest number of characters I can tell this story with? You can translate this to your over-populated work of fiction: what is the smallest cast of characters required to deliver the story?

It's difficult to picture this character/this character is uninteresting

– It may be that, because *you* know this character, you assume you have communicated what you know to the reader. Would you believe in this character if you didn't already know her? Go through the text and on a separate sheet of paper note down all the evidence in the text for this character. You may find that you've given the reader much less to go on than you think.

- Is your treatment of the character lacking in dynamism? Maybe you've given a detailed description of her on page 3, on the assumption that the reader is going to remember every detail, and you haven't subsequently bothered to keep her real and individualised. Maybe you'll find that the character's later thoughts and actions are inconsistent with the description you originally gave, which itself suggests a failure to engage fully with the character.

- Have you merely described the character without showing her *being* that person – in other words, have you relied too heavily on telling and not enough on showing? Is she a victim of the over-planning discussed in Chapter 3 on character? Are there things you know about her, and which the reader doesn't – matters which inhibit the character's capacity for action in ways not made clear to the reader?

- Does the character represent an idea rather than coming off the page as a thinking, feeling individual? While we all write because we feel we have something to say, the fact that we have chosen fiction as our medium means we are writing primarily about people and relationships. A political or moral agenda may be served by a good story, but it can't be allowed to run the show. Whatever your own moral or political agenda, your readers need, first and foremost, to care about the characters. These have to seem to be real people, and not merely ciphers or puppets representing a particular standpoint. Think of novels such as Margaret Atwood's *The Handmaid's Tale*, John Steinbeck's *The Grapes of Wrath*, George Orwell's *Nineteen Eighty-Four* (1949) or Richard Wright's *Native Son* (1940), all of which carry a socio-political message but recruit our attention and sympathy through their characters.

It lacks interest/is too slow/is too long

- Are you taking risks? Are you doing anything you can't do easily? Does your writing ever surprise you? If you're just jogging comfortably along, it's unlikely that your writing will make your reader sit up and take notice.
- Does your story get going early enough in your text or is there unnecessary preamble? Have you carried on writing after the story is over?
- Is your narrative voice simply a vehicle for delivering the story or does it have personality? When you read it aloud does it sound like an individual or is it essentially neutral? Does the voice draw you into the narrative?
- Are your verbs working hard enough and are your adjectives adding the value you need or mean them to? Are there pages and pages with no dialogue? Could you replace any summary with scenes, or any narrative with dialogue? Are your descriptive passages adding enough to warrant the space they take up? When you reread the manuscript are there bits you want to skip? If there are, you can be fairly certain that your readers will also want to skip them, and perhaps put the book aside entirely.
- Does your dialogue sound sufficiently different from the narrative voice to convince the reader that the characters are speaking? Read it aloud to help you to hear whether people might really speak like this. Do the voices of your dialogue serve to differentiate one character from another? Is what they are saying worth reporting? Have you cluttered your dialogue with unnecessary attributions ('he said', 'she said') or burdened it with ingenious variations on 'said' ('he admonished', 'she expostulated')?
- Are there enough ups and downs in the plot? Try plotting your protagonist's journey on Kurt Vonnegut's axes of time and fortune. If the events are almost exclusively above the line, or almost exclusively below it, this is worth examining. Is your

character in real danger of not getting what he wants or needs? Where is the jeopardy? You may be making life too comfortable for him, giving the reader no reason to feel concerned for him – and therefore no interest in following his story.

- Is there insufficient momentum in the narrative? If so, try the chapter function test. Go through the text summarising in a few bullet-points or in one sentence the narrative function of each chapter, and noting at the end of each chapter what the reader might want to know but doesn't yet know. If the chapter (or any part of it) has no real function in propelling the story forward, developing character, or making the reader want to find out more, you might reasonably ask why it's there at all. Can its work be done more economically by a couple of sentences somewhere else? Any writing that fulfils no necessary function acts as a drag on your narrative and is an imposition on the reader, who expends time and energy for little or no return.
- Do you keep pausing the story in order to share with the reader interesting information you found out in the course of your research? You need to ask yourself whether your story can do without the details in question. If it can, then however fascinating they are, and however much they add to the reader's store of factual knowledge, they should be jettisoned.

This checklist isn't, of course, exhaustive, but it will help you to address most of the general criticisms your readers are likely to make. As you develop as a writer you'll find that its queries and suggestions become an increasingly natural part of your thinking, but they will remain a useful touchstone throughout your writing life.

Accepting imperfection

'Writing,' said Hemingway, 'is something you can never do as well as it can be done.'[133] Writers rarely – if ever – experience the sense that every page of the thing they've written is exactly as they want it to be. On the day that *Under Milk Wood* was first performed at the Kaufmann Concert Hall in New York, Dylan Thomas was still tinkering with the text; indeed some of the actors' new lines were handed to them as they went on stage. When published writers are reading from their work at literary festivals it is not unknown for them to make running improvements to the printed text. So you may need to accept that you'll never be entirely satisfied with what you've written. There should, however, come a point when it feels complete – when it's as finished as you can make it and you are generally pleased with it. You should relish that moment: you've accomplished a task which, in all probability, seemed hugely daunting at the outset. You may feel liberated, even elated; you may want to celebrate. Go ahead – you deserve it.

And then, unless you're a very unusual writer indeed, you'll want to see whether you can find a wider readership.

− 13 −
Publication and the writing life

~

Publishing short stories

It's probably pointless for an unknown writer to pitch a collection of unpublished short stories to either an agent or a publisher. You need to build the profiles of your stories individually. There are three principal routes: writing websites, print periodicals and competitions.

Writing websites

Internet publications vary vastly in their quality. Some sites will publish pretty much anything and it won't do your career any favours to be associated with them. Others are more discriminating and for present purposes we'll treat them as print periodicals.

Periodicals

Good periodicals receive a high number of submissions and consequently can devote little time and attention to each one. It's part of their business to eliminate the vast majority from serious consideration, so you need to minimise the risk of immediate rejection. A few tips:

– The most receptive home for your writing is a magazine – or online equivalent – that is already publishing work of a similar nature. So research the preferences of any magazine before submitting your work to it. There's obviously no point in sending

a slice-of-life story about a dysfunctional marriage to a period-ical that specialises in science fiction.
– Read submission guidelines and follow them. There's no point sending 10,000 words when the guidelines specify a maximum of 3,000.
– Your covering note should ideally be very brief – essentially a request for the editor to consider your story.
– If editors come back to you and want to publish your work, don't surrender your copyright unless you think this is justified by the fee offered or the prestige of the publication.

Competitions

You don't have to win a competition to get value out of having entered: a commendation or runner-up placing shows that you're heading in the right direction, and it's a way to get your work noticed, and sometimes published.

– If possible, read material which has been highly placed in this competition in previous years. It will give you a sense of the kind of thing which is appreciated (though this is no guarantee, and new judges may have new criteria).
– Follow the rules to the letter.
– Never surrender copyright to a competition. (Most competi-tions want the right to publish the winning entries, and that's reasonable, provided copyright remains with the writer.)

As soon as you get any recognition at all, whether an honour-able mention in a competition or a higher placing, or publication of any kind, you can start building a portfolio of published stories. Even if a number of your stories have done well you may still, as an early-stage author, find it difficult to get a collection pub-lished; but you at least have something to show, and could con-sider approaching an agent with these stories as your calling card.

Agents and editors

Representation by an agent is almost essential. It's true that some direct approaches to publishers by first-time writers do eventually result in publication, and also true that not all established writers have agents, but such cases are rare. Most established writers consider it worth having someone to negotiate on their behalf and to ensure that contracts serve them well. For new writers an agent is a huge asset. With an agent your work has a champion. When an agent takes on a new writer it's usually because she admires his work and because she thinks she stands a chance of selling it. If this happens to you it's a huge boost to your confidence, and it dramatically increases your chances of publication.

When an editor commissions a novel from a new writer he's taking a step in the dark because he's committing his publishing house to considerable expense with no guarantee that readers are going to buy the book. By contrast, established writers may have a following of loyal readers; in addition there will be a body of book-buyers who have at least heard of them. Even having heard of a writer gives a reader some confidence that the book is likely to be worth the money. And confidence is a vital commodity at every level of publishing. It's transferable, being often underpinned by the fact that someone else rates your writing. If you've been placed first, second or third in a significant writing competition, this means that someone else – usually a panel of judges – believes your story was better than hundreds of others. If you have a story published, this means that someone else considers your work to be of publishable standard. If you gain some kind of academic qualification in creative writing, this shows not only that you've invested serious time and effort into developing your writing skills, but that others endorse your work. If you have the interest and support of an established writer, this also counts towards your credibility as a serious proposition. Any or all of these factors help an editor feel that the chance they are taking has some kind of foundation beyond their own assessment of your talent.

So while none of these achievements will help you if an editor isn't interested in your work, they will give him added confidence in you if he is, because each of these is a selection process – a kind of filter through which the more talented writers pass. And the most reliable filter of all is the literary agent. Apart from the quality of the writing itself, having an agent is the single factor which will most strongly influence your chances of publication.

Publishers who don't accept unsolicited manuscripts are relying on agents to do the filtering for them (unsolicited, in this context, means sent directly to the publisher rather than arriving via an agent). After quality comes content: it's in an agent's interest not to waste an editor's time, as she wants to be able to approach him in the future, so she will carefully match her submission to the editors most likely to be receptive – again she is acting as a filter.

Editors trust agents because they are in the same family. It is not at all uncommon for editors to become agents and vice versa: the two professions are very closely related. They move in the same circles, of course, but they also share the same understanding of the business. So if you are represented by an agent you have the best endorsement possible as far as an editor is concerned, because an agent is essentially one of their own. And because agents and editors are looking (broadly speaking) for the same thing, your approach to either is essentially the same.

Targeting and pitching

Start by thinking about where your novel would be in a bookshop. What section is it in? Within that section identify the writers whose work you feel is nearest to what you do. The publishers of those books are likely to be a good fit for your work; the agents of those writers (you can usually find out online who a writer's agent is) are similarly likely to be a good fit for you, as they will already have a network of contacts and other specialist knowledge in that field. This said, an agent is unlikely to offer to represent someone whose work is in clear and direct competition with a writer they already represent. So you're looking for an agent who will be sympathetic to your work but will not see it as problematically similar to that of any of his authors.

Literary agencies usually have submission guidelines on their websites: follow these to the letter. These guidelines will usually ask you to email a covering letter, a one to two-page synopsis and the first three chapters – or something similar. Keep your covering note brief and to the point. They don't want your life story, but it might be helpful to explain why *you* are the person to write this novel, so include any relevant credentials. Also state who the novel is about, where and when it is set, the broad movement of the plot and the theme – one or two sentences serve best. (Look at the blurb on the back of novels – they usually have the relevant information in this form.) Your format should be a clear, unpretentious and widely used font, 12 point, with one-and-a-half or double spacing. Oddities such as coloured text or unusual fonts don't make you look interesting; they make you look weird, and not in a good way.

Never send anything out with a copyright symbol on it (©). To anyone in the business it is a wearying sign of amateurism. Anyone who publishes your work without your permission or without compensating you is infringing your copyright, whether you have put a little symbol on it or not. Apart from the fact that it's actually very unlikely that anyone *will* steal your work (and in a computer age it's very easy to prove that it *is* your work) you don't want your overture to an agent or publisher to be clouded by the implication that you don't trust them.

Remember how busy agents and editors are and how many submissions they have to read: anything that makes it easy for them to say 'no' saves them time, so avoid anything that might turn them off.

Understanding rejection

You're going to have to come to an understanding with rejection as it's likely to happen a lot. Rejection – in one form or another – is a normal part of being a writer and there is no moment in even the most successful writer's career when he can be sure he has had his final rejection. You need to accept it, and also to expect it.

It helps if you set out on this journey understanding what rejection, in a literary context, really means. It can feel as though you, as a person, are being judged and found wanting in some way. You've poured your hopes, dreams, experience, ideas, talent, time and energy into your work; the rejection of the thing you've made at such a cost can feel like an insult, a slap in the face, a cruel mockery of your efforts. But in fact this is nothing to do with your relationship with the thing you have made, but the relationship between a complete stranger and the thing you have made. As a person, you don't feature at all in this.

Agents and editors spend most of their time looking after the writers they are already contracted to work with. The reading of unsolicited submissions comes very low down on their 'to-do' list and is done under immense time pressure. They may well be approaching their full inbox thinking not so much: 'I hope some fantastic new writer has sent me something wonderful' as 'I need to get through this lot as efficiently as possible.'

They will reject the vast majority of what they read. They may go months without reading anything they want to take any further, because they are approaching this process much as you might approach making a major financial investment. That's what it amounts to. If an agency or a publishing house takes on your writing it is committing to a significant expenditure of time and money: time spent working with you on your manuscript, on phone calls, emails, meetings and contracts; then time on preparing for publication, publicity and promotion. For publishers there is also the expense of designing, typesetting, proofing, printing, marketing and distributing your book, not to mention your advance.

An editor accepting your manuscript is in a position similar to that of a man buying a new car. The car he chooses to buy doesn't represent an indictment of all the cars he didn't buy. The cars he didn't buy were not all bad cars. And there's a limit to how many cars he can have and how often he can buy one. Viewed in this light we can see how very unlikely it is that we'll find securing an agent or an editor easy, however good our writing is. They are much more likely not to bite than to bite, and their response will have much more to do with what they are looking for than what you have written. You will save yourself a lot of heartache if you resolve not to take it personally.

Interpreting rejection

You can extract significant value from rejections. Here are some basic types:

Thanks, but no thanks or it's not for me

No explanation for the rejection is the least helpful response as it may mean any of the following: they think your writing is bad; they think your writing is good but they don't like it; your submission is inappropriate for their list; their list is already full; or they don't have the time or will to read it. You just have to take it on the chin and try somewhere else.

I like it/it's good, but my list is full

This is likely to be true. They could just say their list is full and that would be a good enough reason. So this is encouraging, and useful too if they tell you any of their thoughts on what you have written. It might be worth approaching this person again when you think you have exhausted all other possibilities. Their list may no longer be full by then and you can remind them that they liked your work.

I like it but nobody else here does

This could just be a kind way of saying no, but it probably isn't. If they've shown it around, that's good. And if they outline what they liked and what objections their colleagues made to it, this is all useful to you. In this case, too, it might be worth making a second approach at a later date if other lines of enquiry fail. Remember that both personnel and criteria can change over time.

Any opinion of your work and why they're not taking it further

The easiest thing in the world for an agent or an editor is to write a 'thanks, but no thanks' rejection. So if they've taken the time and trouble to write anything else it is an implicit acknowledgement that it is at least worth their time. And what they have to say – however negative – is valuable to you. It's very easy to see only the rejection and miss the value in such responses. The longer a rejection message is, the better it is for you. It's all helpful, because even if you don't agree with the assessment, the fact that someone has bothered to come back to you with her thoughts means some-one is taking your writing seriously. And, once you've got over any disappointment, you may well see some validity in what she has said. And if, deep down, you come to recognise that the comments are fair, then you can work on what you've written and resubmit it to that person (reminding her of her remarks/advice) with a much stronger chance of a positive reaction from her.

So there are positives to be gained from rejections if they include any feedback. And if you get two or three agents or editors saying broadly the same thing, this is even more useful, as consensus, if broadly positive, is a strong indication that you should persist and, if negative, may provide you with the means of improving your work. If you get serious feedback of this kind, you'll almost certainly find corresponding notes in the checklist of questions and suggestions provided in the previous chapter. This would be a good time to return to those notes with a sharpened sense of what's needed.

Finally there's a form of rejection which might more appropriately be understood as a provisional acceptance. An agent may suggest that, with certain changes, your manuscript might become marketable, and therefore worth her while. In such cases your surest route to publication is to go straight back to the manuscript and make the changes as requested. If you find those changes unacceptable for artistic reasons, that's a legitimate position (we'll touch on this in a moment) but you have to be prepared to accept the consequences of your decision, one of which will almost certainly be that the agent in question will no longer be interested in representing you.

It's just an opinion

William Goldman, screenwriter of such classics as *Butch Cassidy and the Sundance Kid*, *The Right Stuff* and *The Stepford Wives*, asserted in his appraisal of the film industry, *Adventures in the Screen Trade* (1983): 'Nobody knows anything. Not one person in the entire motion picture field *knows* for a certainty what's going to work. Every time out it's a guess – and, if you're lucky, an educated one.'[134] This is also true of publishing: it has to be, as no one can predict what people will want to read. Agents and editors are fallible. They may put a lot of money and effort behind books that don't sell and pass up on books that turn out to be best-sellers or award-winners. Nobody can be certain in advance of a book's success and caution guides any process when someone is investing his own reputation and the company's funds, so agents and editors may be reluctant to champion or commission books different from the books which are selling well at that time. Yet pretty much every standout work in any field of writing – poetry, writing for performance, non-fiction and fiction – has been a game-changer, significantly different from anything that immediately preceded it.

Between 1905 and 1914, James Joyce's ground-breaking collection of short stories, *Dubliners*, was submitted eighteen times to fifteen publishers. On its publication, Joyce was hailed as a writer of extraordinary talent; he went on to become one of the most influential writers of the twentieth century. William Golding's *Lord of the Flies* was rejected by twenty-one publishers, and was almost rejected by Faber, who eventually published it. It went on to become a best-seller, translated into over thirty languages; Golding was later awarded the Nobel Prize in Literature. *Dune* (1965) by Frank Herbert had been published as a magazine serial but twenty-three publishers passed on it in book form. It subsequently won awards, became a best-seller and is widely considered one of the best science fiction novels ever written. One of the most successful writers of our time, Stephen King, had not found a publisher for his first three novels when his fourth, *Carrie*, was finally accepted – having been rejected thirty times.

It's well known that the first Harry Potter novel was rejected twelve times, and that only one of the fifteen approaches Stephenie Meyer made to agents about the first *Twilight* novel got a positive response. More recently, sixty agents rejected Kathryn Stockett's *The Help* (2009), which has now sold millions of copies and been made into a highly successful film (this in turn, of course, boosting book sales). As Stockett later said of her sixty rejections: 'What if I had given up at 15? Or 40? Or even 60?'[135] Agent no. 61 took her on and in three weeks had secured a publication deal. But the gold medal for perseverance must go to Robert M. Pirsig, whose cult novel *Zen and the Art of Motorcycle Maintenance* (1974) also went on to sell in millions, but not before his manuscript had been rejected more than 120 times.

Goldman was right: nobody knows anything. Something different breaks through and becomes a hit, confounding received wisdom concerning what will and won't sell. The new thing then becomes the thing (editors and agents believe) that readers want, so a lot of that thing follows and it's harder to get other kinds of book published. Then there's another surprise success and everything changes again. The speed with which this wheel turns is also unpredictable, so there may be no point in trying to write the thing that seems to be selling at the moment, especially if it's not what you want to write.

Just keep on doing your best work and at some point it may cross the path of someone who believes in it as much as you do, just as the wheel is turning to your advantage.

Hold your nerve

Until you have an agent or an editor on board you have to be your work's champion and just keep banging on doors. You may also have your integrity tested. When someone does finally show an interest in your work, you have to be very strong indeed to resist making changes that run counter to your strongest beliefs about it. Daniel Keyes steadfastly refused to change the ending of *Flowers for Algernon* to a 'happy' one, losing his first publisher over it, and returning the advance he had from his second. He stuck to his guns while a further five publishers rejected the book in its original form. When the book was finally published (with its ending intact) it won the Nebula Award and has since gone on to be widely read, taught in schools around the world and adapted for film, television and radio. And it's the slowly dawning tragedy of its ending, doggedly defended and preserved by Keyes, which gives the story its deep and enduring appeal, leading Simon Spanton to observe: 'In its pitilessly tight focus and tragic story arc, delivered in a first-person narrative whose very nature cuts to the core of what is gained and then lost, it is for me the most heartbreaking book in the genre.'[136]

The path to publication is rarely easy and there's no way of guaranteeing success. You will best serve yourself by working methodically (including keeping a record of approaches made and outcomes), by carefully considering all feedback and by accepting that rejection comes with the territory.

The writing life

Regardless of whether publication is your ultimate goal, if you have decided to make writing a part of your life you have to make room for it.

A place to work

It's helpful to avoid having to pack your work away when you've finished a session: the thought of getting it out again can be enough to put you off beginning what is always a demanding occupation – you need to be able to get straight down to work. Make a place devoted entirely to writing if you can, even if it's a fold-up table in your bedroom; that means that if you have an idea, or if it's your time to write, your notes and materials are immediately accessible. If domestic distractions make working at home impossible, don't give up; work somewhere else. A library, a coffee shop, a kind friend's house. Somewhere. The shed at the bottom of the garden is not to be despised – garden sheds worked for both Roald Dahl and Philip Pullman. You don't need to be comfortable as much as you need to be writing.

A time to work

If you have every reason to believe that you can realistically set aside two hours a day to write, that's fantastic. But you probably can't: you may well be snatching odd hours or moments here and there. The problem with this is that almost everything else will be clamouring for your attention more noisily than your writing does, and the writing will repeatedly get pushed to the end of the queue. So you have to prioritise your writing time: allot specific hours and then be prepared to defend that time. Here are some ways to make it easier to reserve and preserve your writing times.

Allocate regular days and times for writing – for example, 6 pm to 8 pm on Mondays, Wednesdays and Fridays. Or maybe you can reserve one day in the week exclusively for writing (many published writers who have other jobs manage their time this way). Or it could be that you get up early and write for an hour before the other demands of the day assail you. But put it in your diary, like a real appointment. If you have to postpone, then do postpone, but treat it as you'd treat a real appointment with the doctor or the dentist: don't cancel it without rescheduling it.

If you live with other people and are writing at home, make sure they are aware that this time is exclusively yours. You can't be called to deal with minor domestic issues. You're working and this is sacred time. It should be as if you're not in the house. (You'd be wise to choose times when the house is naturally quiet. And, before you start, log out of email, social media or anything else that might prove a distraction.)

Never sit waiting for inspiration to strike. Just write; ideas will follow. Writing at your desk, you're in the right place for inspiration to find you. This doesn't mean, though, that you can't make good use of time when you're away from your desk. Use all available downtime to think about your current project – in the bath, during lunch hour, on the bus, waiting for the kids to come out of school. The habit of keeping a notebook with you is important here.

Little and often can be more efficient than extended blocks of writing time interspersed with long periods of time away from writing. This is because when you've been away from your writing for a while it takes time to reconnect with it. However, sustained periods of writing are extremely helpful, particularly in the early stages when you're still getting to grips with the material. It may be that you can batten down the hatches at home, or go on a writing retreat, or somewhere else where there are no distractions. The opportunity to immerse yourself fully in your novel or short story and make significant progress may allow you to get it to a point where it's robust enough to withstand a less than ideal routine.

If you *are* able to write most days, start your writing session by reading only what you wrote yesterday; do any edits which seem obviously necessary, but don't get bogged down in them – try to maintain the flow of the writing. If you try to read the whole thing from the beginning every time you settle down to write, there will come a point when you'll be spending most of your writing time reading. You also risk becoming too familiar with your story and may even start to find it boring when it actually isn't.

Keep a notebook

This is your portable study and you'll be wise always to have it with you. Include it in whatever your leaving-the-house checklist is: phone, keys, wallet, notebook and pen. As Ted Hughes advised: 'record moments, fleeting impressions, overheard dialogue, your own sadnesses and bewilderments and joys'.[137] You never know when an idea will strike and it's best to get it down straight away. You will forget that fascinating bit of dialogue you heard on the bus. You will forget that idea you had just as you were about to fall asleep. You will forget that thing you noticed that you don't even know you have a use for yet.

Find other writers

Taking a course or joining a class can be a good way of making connection with a wider writing community. Apart from anything else, rightly or wrongly, people are more likely to leave you alone and let you get on with it if your writing is carried out as part of a course of study. The advantage of a formal class is that a professional tutor is particularly likely to be knowledgeable about her subject and skilled at establishing a classroom culture conducive to fruitful discussion and good writing. If you don't have room in your schedule for a regular class, writing retreats and short courses (day schools and weekends) may help you to refresh or re-engage with your writing practice and provide you with excellent opportunities to meet other writers.

Alternatively, you might find a good writers' circle – a group of like-minded individuals who will support each other and be constructively critical. However, you need to remember that an informal writers' group is only as good as the writers in it; you need to make sure that the feedback from the group is going to be helpful, and that it will be responsibly mediated. If this isn't the case, you risk receiving ill-informed or tactless criticism which may knock you back rather than helping you forward; or it may be that time is wasted in managing members of the group who are quick to take – or give – offence. You need to find (or assemble) a group that will work for you, where you are comfortable and where the work is more important than the personalities.

Writer's block

This is the name given to the condition of finding it extremely hard to come up with anything worth saying, although there's nothing unique to writing about this state; many endeavours, creative and otherwise, can hit sticky areas where practitioners can't see the way forward and feel a kind of despair. Perhaps writers have claimed it as their own because the nature of their work means they don't have anyone to share this feeling with: it's a private anguish and that makes it feel worse. Yet writer's block isn't out there somewhere, waiting to pounce; it comes from within us, which means we stand a good chance of preventing it raising its ugly head in the first place. So here are some tips (not rules), one or more of which might work for you:

- Don't write yourself out. Quit while you're ahead. If you're flagging, and it's all getting a bit hard, stop. But in any case make a note of what you think is going to come next. Hemingway would leave his work mid-sentence, believing that this made it easier to get back into the flow of his writing when he returned to it. Think kindly on your tomorrow-self when you put down your pen or close your laptop. Leave yourself something that will be easy to take up and run with the next day. If you write and write and think and think and work yourself into a corner, that's a very hard place to start from next time. Give your tomorrow-self a break. Conversely, if it's going brilliantly and you've done your allotted hours but you just want to keep going, and have the opportunity to do so, then of course you should continue.
- Use your notebook. Assuming you've taken the advice to keep one handy at all times, you own a rich assemblage of observations, quotes and notes that can prove invaluable when you're finding it hard to write – even if all they do is remind you that you *can* write.
- Don't be a slave to the sequence of your plot. Whether you're writing fiction or non-fiction, prose, drama or poetry, you don't have to work relentlessly from A to Z. If something's giving you a problem and you know what happens next, don't assume you have to fix that particular problem before you can continue. Sidestep the obstacle and move on. Highlight the fact that there's a problem and return to it later. A later step of the story will often suggest the solution to the earlier problem.
- If you feel yourself getting bogged down, and you absolutely can't skip over this moment and return to it later, you can sometimes jolt things out of a rut by making something unexpected happen, or bringing forward some action planned for

later. Raymond Chandler once said: 'When in doubt have a man come through the door with a gun in his hand.' You don't have to take this literally – Chandler was referring to his time writing for pulp fiction magazines in the 1920s and 1930s when 'the demand was for constant action' – but you may be able to find an equivalent intrusion of appropriate kind and scale, just to move the story beyond an apparent impasse.[138]

- You may simply be tired. Do you need a nap? Or a walk? Do it. When we are writing we often, both literally and figuratively, have the windows shut. Sometimes we need to open them and see what floats in. Close focus is good; isolation is good, to a point. But you need to remember that the world exists. Sometimes a walk can distract you enough to bring you back to where you need to be. Go and have a cup of tea somewhere. Dig the garden, plant seeds – fresh air is always good. Give your brain the time off it needs to restore itself. But it's best to decide what time you're going to return to your work before you take your break, and to stick to your plan.

It helps if you accept that the writer's task is, by its nature, a difficult one. 'You just have to *go on* when it is worst and most helpless,' Hemingway advised F. Scott Fitzgerald. When you hit a bump you're simply experiencing what all serious writers at some point go through, and sometimes you need simply to concentrate, as Hemingway recommends, on writing as well as you can and finishing what you start.[139]

A level of dissatisfaction with what you've achieved is actually healthy. Faulkner believed the writer

> must never be satisfied with what he does. It never is as good as it can be done. Always dream and shoot higher than you know you can do. Don't bother just to be better than your contemporaries or predecessors. Try to be better than yourself.[140]

If we ever felt that we'd said everything we wanted to say, in precisely the way we wanted to say it, that would suggest that we might as well give up writing. Everything we write is an adventure, an attempt at mastering the unmasterable. You've finished when you know you've done your best to make it as true and good as it can be.

Set achievable goals

As E. B. White said, a writer 'must sit down and get words on paper, and against great odds'.[141] Whatever you write on, or with, and wherever you do it, setting out to write a novel is a daunting prospect and has been compared with trying to eat an elephant. The only way to manage either task is simply to do it a bit at a time. Novels vary in length of course, but if you estimate your novel's eventual length at somewhere around 90,000 words you at least have a ball-park sense of what you need to achieve.

It's extremely helpful to have a deadline in mind for completion of your first full draft. Either decide how much time a week you can devote to writing and work out your estimated completion date from that, or boldly set a deadline and work backwards. For example, if you want to get the job done in 9 months, you need to produce 10,000 words a month, and can break that down to 2,500 words each weekend or 500 words a day, working Monday to Friday. Beware, however, of interpreting a failure to meet your own deadlines as a failure in your writing: deadlines may act as useful spurs to continued action but they mustn't be allowed to govern our thinking about our work.

Stick at it

Expect setbacks; learn to embrace them as part of the process. Expect to have to rewrite, even when you think you're done. Accept that your writing, even if published, may never get the recognition it deserves, or may not be recognised for years. You have to want to do the work for its own sake and not be discouraged if your writing doesn't meet with universal approval. And remember that for some the journey to publication was a long one. Writers as diverse as Anna Sewell, Raymond Chandler, Richard Adams and Annie Proulx published their first novels when they already had half a century of life under their belts.[142] Mary Wesley (1912–2002) herself said that her chief claim to fame was 'arrested development – getting my first novel published at the age of seventy'.[143] Over the next fourteen years she published a further nine best-selling novels (sales exceeding three million copies), making her one of Britain's most successful writers.

Feed the compost heap

Keep in mind Tolkien's image of the compost heap, and the way stories grow, as he put it, 'out of the leaf-mould of the mind: out of all that has been seen or thought or read'. One of the pieces of advice most commonly and sensibly given by established writers to developing writers is simply to read books. Read widely and regularly. If you think you don't have time for reading, make time. See the time spent reading books as a necessary part of your training as a writer.

Andrew Miller likens writing to painting, observing that a painter who wants to paint a tree 'needs to do two things: look at trees and look at paintings of trees. The first task shows what trees are like, the second shows the possibilities of the medium.'[144] We need to observe life and to observe how others have written about life. Ray Bradbury suggests that a writer's reading should be wide and various: it pays the writer, he says, to 'play the dilettante'.[145]

The pleasures of writing

Writing to a friend in January 1956, with the first draft of a short story recently completed, Sylvia Plath spoke of the happiness she was finding in her work:

I am writing at least a few hours a day ... you have no idea how happy it makes me, to get it out on paper, where I can work on it, even though the actual story never lives up to the dream. When I say I *must* write, I don't mean I *must* publish. There is a great difference. ... I am dependent on the process of writing, not on the acceptance.[146]

What Plath is describing here is the immediate pleasure found in the act of writing, the artist's delight in her own creative energies at a propitious moment in her writing life. In her celebration of the act itself, as distinct from the fact or prospect of publication, she affirms a truth we'll do well to bear in mind: that the process of writing may be a pleasure regardless of any actual or imagined goal. Gustave Flaubert describes the pleasures of writing in rather different terms, but still with an emphasis on the essentially private nature of the writer's enjoyment:

No matter whether good or bad, it is a delectable thing, writing! not having to be yourself, being able to circulate in amongst the whole creation that you are describing. Today for instance, as a man and as a woman, as lover and mistress both, I have been out riding in a forest on an autumn afternoon, and I was the horses, the leaves, the wind, the words that they spoke to each other and the red sunlight that made them half-close their eyes, eyes that were brimming with love.[147]

To escape from oneself, becoming a character or object – any character or object – in a world of one's own creation: this is Flaubert's particular pleasure, and it's one that many writers will understand. But the pleasures of writing are found not only in the writer's private world, but in fruitful contact with other minds. Whatever Plath may have felt at the time she wrote her letter, she understood the importance of writing as communication, the importance of reaching out to a readership. It's not simple vanity that makes writers seek publication; it's the belief that they have something to say to others. And when a reader tells a writer that his book has illuminated some aspect of her life, or comforted her, or entertained her, the pleasure the writer feels is unlikely to be merely narcissistic.

The novelist Anne Tyler, writing from the reader's viewpoint, presents a mirror image of Flaubert's comments on the pleasures of writing: 'I read,' she says, 'so I can live more than one life in more than one place.'[148] And it seems absolutely appropriate to end this book on a note celebrating the twin pleasures of reading and writing. As writers we come to see that the pleasures of writing are often discovered through a protracted personal struggle with words and ideas, but they are pleasures nonetheless; indeed, they may be all the keener for having been arrived at through hard work. And writers write, among other reasons, because of the pleasure they have taken in reading, and the pleasure they hope to give to other readers through their own writing. If we want to write well we must take both our writing and our reading seriously, but our seriousness should go hand in hand with a keen sense of enjoyment – the enjoyment we experience ourselves and the enjoyment we offer our readers.

NOTES

The notes mainly direct to non-fiction sources, and to novels where the location of a quoted passage is not broadly indicated in the text. Short stories referred to in the text are not referenced in the notes but are listed in the bibliography along with the author's name and the collection in which they appear.

– 1 – Getting started

1 'Maureen Duffy talking to Dulan Barber', *Transatlantic Review*, 45 (Spring 1973), p. 10.

2 'James Baldwin interviewed by John Hall', *Transatlantic Review*, 37/38 (Autumn/Winter 1970–71), p. 10.

3 Margaret Atwood, 'What's the difference between Science Fiction and Fantasy?', *Guardian*, 13 October 2011.

4 Samuel Beckett, *Company/ Ill Seen Ill Said/ Worstward Ho/ Stirrings Still* (Faber and Faber, 2009), p. 81.

5 Samuel Beckett and Georges Duthuit, 'Three Dialogues', *Transition*, 5 (1949).

6 John O'Mahony, 'The write stuff', *Guardian*, 11 October 2003.

7 Ernest Hemingway to F. Scott Fitzgerald, 28 May 1934, in *Ernest Hemingway: Selected Letters, 1917–1961*, ed. Carlos Baker (Simon and Schuster, 2003), p. 408.

8 'Write Drunk, Revise Sober', *Quote Investigator*, 21 September 2016 https://quoteinvestigator.com/2016/09/21/write-drunk/ [accessed 28 October 2019].

9 Frank O'Connor interviewed by Anthony Whittier, in 'The Art of Fiction No. 19', *Paris Review*, 17 (Autumn/Winter 1957).

10 James Thurber interviewed by George Plimpton and Max Steele, in 'The Art of Fiction No. 10', *Paris Review*, 10 (Fall 1955).

11 Ray Bradbury, *Zen in the Art of Writing* (Harper Voyager, 2015), pp. 4–5.

12 Virginia Woolf, *Orlando*, ed. Brenda Lyons (Penguin, 2019), pp. 57–58.

13 *Conversations with E. L. Doctorow*, ed. Christopher D. Morris (University Press of Mississippi, 1999), p. ix.

– 2 – *Memory and imagination*

14 Letter from Henry James to Sarah Orme Jewett, cited in Rachel Cohen, *A Chance Meeting* (Random House, 2005), p. 88.

15 Geraldine Brooks, 'Timeless tact helps sustain a literary time traveler', *New York Times*, 2 July 2001.

16 *By-Line: Ernest Hemingway; Selected Articles and Dispatches of Four Decades*, ed. William White (Simon and Schuster, 2002), p. 219.

17 'Maureen Duffy talking to Dulan Barber', *Transatlantic Review*, 45 (Spring 1973), p. 5.

18 Cited in Stephanie Hale, *How to Sell One Million Books: Tips from Famous Authors Who Were Once Unknown* (Oxford Literary Consultancy, 2015), p. 152.

19 Carol Shields, 'Opting for invention over the injury of invasion', *New York Times*, 10 April 2000.

20 William Faulkner interviewed by Jean Stein, in 'The Art of Fiction No. 12', *Paris Review*, 12 (Spring 1956).

21 Ray Bradbury, *Zen in the Art of Writing* (Harper Voyager, 2015), p. 27.

22 Ibid., p. 25.

23 Cited in Thomas F. Gossett, *Uncle Tom's Cabin and American Culture* (Southern Methodist University Press, 1985), p. 97.

24 Ernest Hemingway to F. Scott Fitzgerald, 28 May 1934, in *Ernest Hemingway: Selected Letters, 1917–1961*, ed. Carlos Baker (Simon and Schuster, 2003), p. 408.

25 Cited in Humphrey Carpenter, *J. R. R. Tolkien: A Biography* (Houghton Mifflin Harcourt, 2014), p. 131.

26 'Kate Hamer on her 21st-century fairytale, *The Girl in the Red Coat*', *The Irish Times*, 11 March 2015.

27 Toni Morrison, foreword to *Beloved* (Vintage, 2007), pp. xi–xii.

– 3 – Character

28 Charles Dickens, *Oliver Twist*, ed. Philip Horne (Penguin, 2003), p. 60.

29 Thomas Hardy, *A Pair of Blue Eyes*, ed. Alan Manford (Oxford University Press, 2009), p. 7.

30 Eudora Welty, Preface to *The Collected Stories* (Houghton Mifflin Harcourt, 2019), p. xvii.

31 'Sara Collins sets out to rewrite the characters who have traditionally been invisible in Gothic fiction', https://dev-www-65.penguin .co.uk/articles/2018/oct/sara-collins-on-frannie-langton.html [accessed 18 October 2021].

32 Sara Collins, *The Confessions of Frannie Langton* (Penguin, 2019), p. 70.

33 'Sara Collins sets out to rewrite the characters.'

34 Sarah Waters, 'Rules for writers', *Guardian*, 23 February 2010.

35 L. Frank Baum, *The Wizard of Oz* (Puffin, 2008), p. 2.

36 Zora Neale Hurston, *Their Eyes Were Watching God* (Virago, 1986), p. 259.

37 'William Trevor interviewed by Mark Ralph-Bowman', *Transatlantic Review*, 53/54 (Autumn/Winter 1975–76), p. 6.

– 4 – Plot and structure I

38 Geoffrey Chaucer, 'The Pardoner's Tale', in *The Canterbury Tales*, trans. Nevill Coghill (Penguin, 1951).

39 Chris Power, 'A brief history of the short story, part 49: Guy de Maupassant', *Guardian*, 24 May 2013.

40 L. Frank Baum, *The Wizard of Oz* (Puffin, 2008), p. 133.

41 Julie Myerson, 'Jamaica Inn: No place for a girl', *Guardian*, 19 April 2014.

42 William Boyd, 'A short history of the short story', *Prospect*, 10 July 2006.

43 Chris Power, 'Darkness in literature: James Joyce's "Araby"', *Guardian*, 20 December 2012.

– 5 – Plot and structure II

44 Christopher Booker, *The Seven Basic Plots* (Continuum, 2004) pp. 1–2.

45 *Boswell's Life of Johnson*, ed. George Birkbeck Hill (Oxford University Press, 1934), vol. 4, p. 236.

46 Gustav Freytag, *Technique of the Drama: An Exposition of Dramatic Composition and Art*, trans. Elias J. MacEwan (S. C. Griggs and Co., 1895), pp. 114–40.

47 Joseph Campbell, *The Hero with a Thousand Faces* (Pantheon, 1949).

48 Tzvetan Todorov, 'Structural Analysis of Narrative', *Novel*, 3, no. 1 (Autumn 1969), p. 75.

49 Ray Bradbury, *Zen in the Art of Writing* (Harper Voyager, 2015), p. 114.

50 See Kenn Adams, 'Back to the Story Spine', *Aerogramme Writers' Studio*, 5 June 2013, www.aerogrammestudio.com/2013/06/05/back-to-the-story-spine/ [accessed 27 October 2019].

51 Kurt Vonnegut's 'Shapes of Stories' lecture, 4 February 2004, www.youtube.com/watch?v=GOGru_4z1Vc [accessed 27 October 2019].

52 Quoted in Stephanie Hale, *How to Sell One Million Books: Tips from Famous Authors Who Were Once Unknown* (Oxford Literary Consultancy, 2015), p. 117.

53 Ibid., pp. 126–27.

54 Cited in Martha Schulman, 'How the story comes together: Anthony Doerr', *Publishers Weekly*, 11 April 2014.

55 William Faulkner, *The Sound and the Fury* (Vintage, 1995), p. 6.

– 6 – *Form and length*

56 'Alan Sillitoe interviewed by Brendan Hennessy', *Transatlantic Review*, 41 (Winter/Spring 1972), p. 111.

57 Frank O'Connor interviewed by Anthony Whittier, in 'The Art of Fiction No. 19', *Paris Review*, 17 (Autumn/Winter 1957).

58 Truman Capote interviewed by Pati Hill, in 'The Art of Fiction No. 17', *Paris Review*, 16 (Spring/Summer 1957).

59 Erskine Caldwell interviewed by Elizabeth Pell Broadwell and Ronald Wesley Hoag, in 'The Art of Fiction No. 62', *Paris Review*, 86 (Winter 1982).

60 William Boyd, 'A short history of the short story', *Prospect*, 10 July 2006.

61 Joanna H. Wós, 'The One Sitting There' (1989); Michael Oppen-
    heimer, 'The Paring Knife' (1982); Julia Alvarez, 'Snow' (1991);
    Lydia Davis, 'The Bone' (1986).

62 Cited in Robert Shapard and James Thomas, ed., *Sudden Fiction*
    (Gibbs M. Smith Inc., 1986), p. 246.

63 Spencer Holst, 'Brilliant Silence' (1983); Bruce Holland Rogers,
    'Aglaglagl' (2010); Luigi Malerba, 'Consuming the View' (2005).

64 Charles Baxter, introduction to *Sudden Fiction International*, ed.
    Robert Shapard and James Thomas (Norton, 1989), p. 23.

– 7 – *Dialogue*

65 Elmore Leonard, *Elmore Leonard's Ten Rules of Writing* (William
    Morrow, 2007), pp. 63–65.

66 Hilary Mantel, *Wolf Hall* (Fourth Estate, 2010), pp. 136–37.

67 Charles Dickens, *The Pickwick Papers*, ed. Mark Wormald (Pen-
    guin, 2000), p. 103.

68 William Faulkner, *The Sound and the Fury* (Vintage, 1995),
    pp. 10–11.

69 Elmore Leonard, *Elmore Leonard's Ten Rules of Writing*, pp. 21–23.

70 Ibid., pp. 27–29.

71 Ibid., p. 3.

72 Niall Griffiths, *Runt* (Vintage, 2008), p. 56.

73 Maya Angelou, *I Know Why the Caged Bird Sings* (Virago, 2007),
    p. 97.

74 Sam Selvon, *The Lonely Londoners* (Penguin, 2006), p. 23.

75 William Golding, *The Inheritors* (Faber and Faber, 2015), p. 49.

76 Henry Mayhew, *London Labour and the London Poor* (Wordsworth,
    2008), p. 255.

77 'Wolf Hall: author Hilary Mantel talks Tudors, historical accuracy
    and winning the Man Booker Prize', *History Extra*, www.history
    extra.com/period/medieval/wolf-hall-author-hilary-mantel-talks-
    tudors-historical-accuracy-and-winning-the-man-booker-prize/
    [accessed 12 February 2021].

78 Thomas Hardy, *Jude the Obscure*, ed. Dennis Taylor (Penguin,
    2003), p. 18.

79 Virginia Woolf, *To the Lighthouse*, ed. Margaret Drabble (Oxford University Press, 2000), pp. 75–76.

80 James Joyce, *Ulysses*, ed. Jeri Johnson (Oxford University Press, 2008), p. 690.

– 8 – Narrative viewpoint and narrative voice

81 Anne Enright, 'Ten rules for writing fiction', *Guardian*, 20 February 2010.

82 Jane Austen, *Emma*, ed. Fiona Stafford (Penguin, 2015), p. 170.

83 Marlon James, *A Brief History of Seven Killings* (Oneworld, 2015), p. 52.

84 Ibid., p. 56.

85 Virginia Woolf, *Jacob's Room*, ed. Kate Flint (Oxford University Press, 2008), pp. 56–57.

86 Chris Power, 'A brief survey of the short story, part 32: James Joyce', *Guardian*, 9 March 2011.

87 John Updike, 'Both rough and tender', *The New Yorker*, 22 January 2001.

88 M. John Harrison, 'Here be monsters', *Guardian*, 24 February 2007.

89 Ford Madox Ford, *The Good Soldier*, ed. David Bradshaw (Penguin, 2002), pp. 16 and 75.

90 Kazuo Ishiguro, *The Remains of the Day* (Faber and Faber, 2015), pp. 109–10.

91 Ibid., pp. 251–52.

92 Ibid., p. 252.

93 Jeffrey Eugenides, *The Virgin Suicides* (Fourth Estate, 2013), p. 114.

94 Ibid., p. 243.

95 'A Clockwork Orange', *The International Anthony Burgess Foundation*, www.anthonyburgess.org/a-clockwork-orange/ [accessed 29 November 2019].

96 'A Clockwork Orange and Nadsat', *The International Anthony Burgess Foundation*, www.anthonyburgess.org/a-clockwork-orange/a-clockwork-orange-and-nadsat/ [accessed 29 November 2019].

97 Anthony Burgess, *A Clockwork Orange*, ed. Andrew Biswell (Penguin, 2013), p. 7.

98 'Afterword', Russell Hoban, *Riddley Walker* (Bloomsbury, 2012), p. 225.

99 'A note on language', Paul Kingsnorth, *The Wake* (Unbound, 2015), p. 355.

100 Kingsnorth, *The Wake*, p. 3.

101 'Glossary', Russell Hoban, *Riddley Walker* (Bloomsbury, 2012), p. 233.

102 Kingsnorth, 'A note on language', p. 356.

– 9 – *Beginnings and endings; tension and pace*

103 'Material' (1973); 'The Ottowa Valley' (1974); 'Wild Swans' (1978); 'Miles City, Montana' (1985).

104 'Marriage à la Mode' (1921); 'Honeymoon' (1923); 'The Singing Lesson' (1920).

105 Vladimir Nabokov, 'Good Readers and Good Writers', in *Lectures on Literature* (Harvest, 1980), p. 5.

106 Thomas Hardy, *A Pair of Blue Eyes*, ed. Alan Manford (Oxford University Press, 2009), pp. 195, 197–98.

107 Laurence Sterne, *The Life and Opinions of Tristram Shandy*, ed. Melvin New and Joan New (Penguin, 2003), pp. 69–70.

108 Ford Madox Ford, *The Good Soldier*, ed. David Bradshaw (Penguin, 2002), p. 144.

– 10 – *Description*

109 Sarah Waters, 'Rules for writers', *Guardian*, 23 February 2010.

110 Georges Simenon interviewed by Carvell Collins, in 'The Art of Fiction No. 9', *Paris Review*, 9 (Summer 1955).

111 *Boswell's Life of Johnson*, ed. George Birkbeck Hill (Oxford University Press, 1934), vol. 2, p. 237.

112 Elmore Leonard, *Elmore Leonard's Ten Rules of Writing* (William Morrow, 2007), p. 71.

113 Ernest Hemingway interviewed by George Plimpton, in 'The Art of Fiction No. 21', *Paris Review*, 18 (Spring 1958).

114 John Rentoul, 'The top ten: mixed metaphors', *Independent*, 16 March 2014, www.independent.co.uk/arts-entertainment/books/ features/top-ten-mixed-metaphors-9191302.html [accessed 28 February 2021].

115 Sara Collins, *The Confessions of Frannie Langton* (Penguin, 2019), p. 13.

116 Mark Twain, *The Tragedy of Pudd'nhead Wilson* (American Publishing Co., 1894), epigraph to chapter 9.

117 Stephen King, *On Writing: A Memoir of the Craft* (Hodder, 2012), p. 139.

118 Emily Brontë, *Wuthering Heights*, ed. Ian Jack (Oxford University Press, 2020), p. 2.

119 V. S. Naipaul, *A House for Mr Biswas* (Picador, 2016), pp. 3–4.

120 Sarah Hall, *Haweswater* (Faber and Faber, 2016), pp. 10–12.

121 Daniel Defoe, *Robinson Crusoe*, ed. Thomas Keymer (Oxford University Press, 2008), p. 41.

122 Ford Madox Ford, *The Good Soldier*, ed. David Bradshaw (Penguin, 2002), p. 42.

– 11 – Research

123 Cited in Stephanie Hale, *How to Sell One Million Books: Tips from Famous Authors Who Were Once Unknown* (Oxford Literary Consultancy, 2015), p. 61.

124 Cited in ibid., p. 119.

125 Letter from Henry James to Sarah Orme Jewett, cited in Rachel Cohen, *A Chance Meeting* (Random House, 2005), p. 88.

126 Hilary Mantel, 'Rules for writers', *Guardian*, 22 February 2010.

127 Colson Whitehead, *The Underground Railroad* (Fleet, 2016), p. 80.

– 12 – Drawing it all together

128 Truman Capote interviewed by Pati Hill, in 'The Art of Fiction No. 17', *Paris Review*, 16 (Spring/Summer 1957).

129 A. Scott Berg, *Max Perkins: Editor of Genius* (Pan, 1999), p. 134.

130 Clarence Hugh Holman, *The World of Thomas Wolfe* (Scribner, 1962), p. 29.

131 Thornton Wilder interviewed by Richard H. Goldstone, in 'The Art of Fiction No. 16', *Paris Review*, 15 (Winter 1956).

132 Margaret Atwood, 'Rules for writers', *Guardian*, 22 February 2010.

133 Ernest Hemingway to Ivan Kashkin, 19 August 1925, in *Ernest Hemingway: Selected Letters, 1917–1961*, ed. Carlos Baker (Simon and Schuster, 2003), p. 419.

– 13 – *Publication and the writing life*

134 William Goldman, *Adventures in the Screen Trade* (Abacus, 1996), p. 39.

135 Kathryn Stockett, 'Don't Give Up, Just Lie', in *The Best Advice I Ever Got*, ed. Katie Couric (Random House, 2011).

136 Cited in Alison Flood, 'Flowers for Algernon's sad, sweet genius', *Guardian*, 18 June 2014.

137 Recalled by Michael Morpurgo in 'Rules for writers', *Guardian*, 23 February 2010.

138 'When in doubt have a man come through a door with a gun in his hand', *Quote Investigator*, 31 March 2014, https://quoteinvestigator. com/2014/03/31/gun-hand/ [accessed 27 October 2019].

139 Ernest Hemingway to F. Scott Fitzgerald, 13 September 1929, in *Ernest Hemingway: Selected Letters, 1917–1961*, ed. Carlos Baker (Simon and Schuster, 2003), p. 306.

140 William Faulkner interviewed by Jean Stein, in 'The Art of Fiction No. 12', *Paris Review*, 12 (Spring 1956).

141 E. B. White interviewed by George Plimpton and Frank H. Crowther, in 'The Art of the Essay No. 1', *Paris Review*, 48 (Fall 1969).

142 Anna Sewell (57), *Black Beauty* (1877); Raymond Chandler (51), *The Big Sleep* (1939); Richard Adams (52), *Watership Down* (1972); Annie Proulx (57), *Postcards* (1992).

143 Cited by Wolfgang Saxon, 'Mary Wesley, wry novelist of British mores, dies at 90', *The New York Times*, 1 January 2003.

144 Andrew Miller, 'How to write fiction', *Guardian*, 16 October 2011.

145 Ray Bradbury, *Zen in the Art of Writing* (Harper Voyager, 2015), pp. 26–27.

146 Sylvia Plath to Gordon Lameyer, 21 January 1956, in *The Letters of Sylvia Plath*, ed. Peter K. Steinberg and Karen V. Kukil (Harper, 2017), vol. 1.

147 Cited by Adam Foulds, 'How to write fiction', *Guardian*, 20 October 2011.

148 Anne Tyler, 'Because I want more than one life', *Washington Post*, 15 August 1976.

SELECT BIBLIOGRAPHY

Most of the works of fiction referred to in the text are listed below. The choice of editions is informed by considerations of reliability, availability and affordability.

Angelou, Maya, *I Know Why the Caged Bird Sings* (Virago, 2007)

Armitage, Simon, *Seeing Stars* (Faber and Faber, 2011). ('I'll Be There to Love and Comfort You')

Atwood, Margaret, *Alias Grace* (Virago, 2019)

    The Handmaid's Tale (Vintage, 2017)

Austen, Jane, *Emma*, ed. Fiona Stafford (Penguin, 2015)

    Pride and Prejudice, ed. Vivien Jones (Penguin, 2003)

    Sense and Sensibility, ed. Ros Ballaster (Penguin, 2003)

Baum, L. Frank, *The Wizard of Oz* (Puffin, 2008)

Brontë, Anne, *Agnes Grey*, ed. Robert Inglesfield and Hilda Marsden (Oxford University Press, 2010)

    The Tenant of Wildfell Hall, ed. Stevie Davies (Penguin, 1996)

Brontë, Charlotte, *Jane Eyre*, ed. Stevie Davies (Penguin, 2006)

    Shirley, ed. Jessica Cox (Penguin, 2006)

    Villette, ed. Margaret Smith (Oxford University Press, 2008)

Brontë, Emily, *Wuthering Heights*, ed. Ian Jack (Oxford University Press, 2020)

Brooks, Geraldine, *Year of Wonders* (Harper, 2002)

Burgess, Anthony, *A Clockwork Orange*, ed. Andrew Biswell (Penguin, 2013)

    Nothing Like the Sun (Norton, 1975)

Burroughs, Edgar Rice, *Tarzan of the Apes* (Canterbury, 2015)

Burt, Simon, *Floral Street* (Faber and Faber, 1986). ('Wh'appen?')

Caldwell, Erskine, *The Stories of Erskine Caldwell* (University of Georgia Press, 1996). ('Daughter')

Calvino, Italo, *If on a winter's night a traveller*, trans. William Weaver (Vintage, 1992)

Carey, Peter, *True History of the Kelly Gang* (Faber and Faber, 2011)

Chaucer, Geoffrey, *The Canterbury Tales*, trans. Nevill Coghill (Penguin, 1951)

Chekhov, Anton, *Selected Stories* (Wordsworth, 1996). ('The Malefactor', trans. Marian Fell)

Collins, Sara, *The Confessions of Frannie Langton* (Penguin, 2019)

Collins, Wilkie, *The Moonstone*, ed. Francis O'Gorman (Oxford University Press, 2019)

   The Woman in White, ed. John Sutherland (Oxford University Press, 2008)

Conrad, Joseph, *Heart of Darkness*, ed. Owen Knowles (Penguin, 2007)

   Lord Jim, ed. Allan H. Simmons (Penguin, 2007)

de Maupassant, Guy, *A Parisian Affair and Other Stories*, trans. Siân Miles (Penguin, 2004). ('The Necklace')

Defoe, Daniel, *Moll Flanders*, ed. G. A. Starr and Linda Bree (Oxford University Press, 2011)

   Robinson Crusoe, ed. Thomas Keymer (Oxford University Press, 2008)

   Roxana, ed. John Mullan (Oxford University Press, 2008)

Dickens, Charles, *Bleak House*, ed. Stephen Gill (Oxford University Press, 2008)

   Great Expectations, ed. Charlotte Mitchell (Penguin, 2004)

   The Old Curiosity Shop, ed. Norman Page (Penguin, 2001)

   Oliver Twist, ed. Philip Horne (Penguin, 2003)

   Our Mutual Friend, ed. Adrian Poole (Penguin, 1997)

   The Pickwick Papers, ed. Mark Wormald (Penguin, 2003)

Doerr, Anthony, *All the Light We Cannot See* (Fourth Estate, 2015)

du Maurier, Daphne, *Jamaica Inn* (Virago, 2003)

Edgell, Zee, *Beka Lamb* (Hodder, 2007)

Eugenides, Jeffrey, *The Virgin Suicides* (Fourth Estate, 2013)

Faulkner, William, *The Sound and the Fury* (Vintage, 1995)

Ferris, Joshua, *Then We Came to the End* (Penguin, 2008)

Fielding, Henry, *Tom Jones*, ed. John Bender and Simon Stern (Oxford University Press, 2008)

Ford, Ford Madox, *The Good Soldier*, ed. David Bradshaw (Penguin, 2002)

Forster, E. M., *Howards End*, ed. David Lodge (Penguin, 2000)

Gaskell, Elizabeth, *Cranford*, ed. Patricia Ingham (Penguin, 2005)

Golding, William, *The Inheritors* (Faber and Faber, 2015)

   Lord of the Flies (Faber and Faber, 1997)

Grass, Günter, *The Tin Drum*, trans. Breon Mitchell (Vintage, 2010)

Graves, Robert, *I, Claudius* (Penguin, 2006)

Griffiths, Niall, *Runt* (Vintage, 2008)

Hall, Sarah, *Haweswater* (Faber and Faber, 2016)

Hamid, Mohsin, *The Reluctant Fundamentalist* (Penguin, 2017)

Hardy, Thomas, *Jude the Obscure*, ed. Dennis Taylor (Penguin, 2003)

    A Pair of Blue Eyes, ed. Alan Manford (Oxford University Press, 2009)

    The Return of the Native, ed. Simon Gatrell, Nancy Barrineau and Margaret R. Higonnet (Oxford University Press, 2008)

Hartley, L. P., *The Go-Between* (Penguin, 2004)

Hemingway, Ernest, *The Short Stories of Ernest Hemingway*, ed. Seán Hemingway (Scribner, 2018). ('Hills Like White Elephants')

Henry, O., *100 Selected Stories* (Wordsworth, 2012). ('The Furnished Room'; 'The Gift of the Magi')

Herbert, Frank, *Dune* (Hodder, 2015)

Hoban, Russell, *Riddley Walker* (Bloomsbury, 2012)

Hurston, Zora Neale, *Their Eyes Were Watching God* (Virago, 1986)

Ishiguro, Kazuo, *The Remains of the Day* (Faber and Faber, 2015)

Jackson, Shirley, *The Lottery and Other Stories* (Penguin, 2009). ('Charles')

James, Henry, *Ghost Stories* (Wordsworth, 2008). ('The Real Right Thing')

James, Marlon, *A Brief History of Seven Killings* (Oneworld, 2015)

Johnson, Samuel, *The History of Rasselas, Prince of Abissinia*, ed. Thomas Keymer (Oxford University Press, 2009)

Joyce, James, *Dubliners*, ed. Terence Brown (Penguin, 2000). ('Araby'; 'Eveline')

    A Portrait of the Artist as a Young Man, ed. Seamus Deane (Penguin, 2006)

    Ulysses, ed. Jeri Johnson (Oxford University Press, 2008)

Keyes, Daniel, *Flowers for Algernon* (Gateway, 2002)

King, Stephen, *Carrie* (Hodder, 2011)

Kingsnorth, Paul, *The Wake* (Unbound, 2015)

Kingsolver, Barbara, *The Poisonwood Bible* (Faber and Faber, 2017)

Kipling, Rudyard, *The Man Who Would Be King: Selected Stories of Rudyard Kipling*, ed. Jan Montefiore (London: Penguin, 2011). ('Mary Postgate'; 'They')

Lawrence, D. H., *The Rainbow*, ed. Anne Fernihough and James Wood (Penguin, 2007)

Selected Stories, ed. Sue Wilson (Penguin, 2007). ('Odour of Chrysanthemums')

Sons and Lovers, ed. Carl Baron and Helen Baron (Penguin, 2006)

Women in Love, ed. David Farmer and Lindeth Vasey (Penguin, 2007)

Mann, Mary E., *The Complete Tales of Dulditch* (Larks Press, 2008). ('Little Brother')

Mansfield, Katherine, *The Collected Stories of Katherine Mansfield* (Wordsworth, 2006). ('A Dill Pickle'; 'An Ideal Family'; 'Honeymoon'; 'Life of Ma Parker'; 'Marriage à la Mode'; 'The Daughters of the Late Colonel'; 'The Garden Party'; 'The Singing Lesson')

Mantel, Hilary, *Wolf Hall* (Fourth Estate, 2010)

Morrison, Toni, *Beloved* (Vintage, 2007)

Munro, Alice, *Selected Stories* (Vintage, 2010). ('Material'; 'Miles City, Montana'; 'Royal Beatings'; 'The Beggar Maid'; 'The Ottowa Valley'; 'The Turkey Season'; 'Wild Swans')

Nabokov, Vladimir, *Lolita* (Penguin, 2000)

Naipaul, V. S., *A House for Mr Biswas* (Picador, 2016)

O'Connor, Flannery, *A Good Man Is Hard to Find* (Faber and Faber, 2016). ('A Circle in the Fire')

Oates, Joyce Carol, *We Were the Mulvaneys* (Fourth Estate, 2020)

Orwell, George, *Animal Farm* (Penguin, 2000)

Nineteen Eighty-Four (Penguin, 2000)

Parker, Dorothy, *The Collected Dorothy Parker* (Penguin, 2001). ('A Telephone Call'; 'Cousin Larry'; 'Here We Are')

Pirsig, Robert M., *Zen and the Art of Motorcycle Maintenance* (Vintage, 1991)

Poe, Edgar Allan, *The Portable Edgar Allan Poe*, ed. J. Gerald Kennedy (Penguin, 2006). ('The Tell-Tale Heart')

Powell, Dawn, *My Home Is Far Away* (Steerforth, 2000)

Richardson, Samuel, *Clarissa*, ed. Angus Ross (Penguin, 1985)

Pamela, ed. Thomas Keymer and Alice Wakely (Oxford University Press, 2008)

Roy, Arundhati, *The God of Small Things* (Harper, 2004)

Salinger, J. D., *The Catcher in the Rye* (Penguin, 2010)

Selvon, Sam, *The Lonely Londoners* (Penguin, 2006)

Smith, Ali, *The Accidental* (Penguin, 2006)

Smith, Zadie, *White Teeth* (Penguin, 2001)

Spark, Muriel, *The Collected Stories* (Penguin, 1994). ('You Should Have Seen the Mess')

Steinbeck, John, *The Grapes of Wrath* (Penguin, 2014)

Sterne, Laurence, *The Life and Opinions of Tristram Shandy*, ed. Melvin New and Joan New (Penguin, 2003)

Stockett, Kathryn, *The Help* (Penguin, 2010)

Swift, Jonathan, *Gulliver's Travels*, ed. Robert DeMaria, Jr. (Penguin, 2003)

Trevor, William, *The Collected Stories* (Penguin, 2003). ('The General's Day')

Twain, Mark, *The Adventures of Huckleberry Finn*, ed. R. Kent Rasmussen (Penguin, 2014)

The Adventures of Tom Sawyer, ed. R. Kent Rasmussen (Penguin, 2014)

Whitehead, Colson, *The Underground Railroad* (Fleet, 2016)

Wolfe, Thomas, *Look Homeward, Angel* (Penguin, 2016)

Woolf, Virginia, *Jacob's Room*, ed. Kate Flint (Oxford University Press, 2008)

Mrs Dalloway, ed. David Bradshaw (Oxford University Press, 2008)

Orlando, ed. Brenda Lyons (Penguin, 2019)

To the Lighthouse, ed. Margaret Drabble (Oxford University Press, 2000)

The Years, ed. Jeri Johnson (Penguin, 2019)

Wright, Richard, *Native Son* (Vintage, 2000)

INDEX

Printed in the United States
by Baker & Taylor Publisher Services